Robert R. Young,
the Populist
of Wall Street

TIME

THE WEEKLY NEWSMAGAZINE

ALLEGHANY CORP.'S ROBERT YOUNG
Coast to coast for pigs and kings.
(Business)

Time cover, February 3, 1947.

Robert R. Young, the Populist of Wall Street

BY JOSEPH BORKIN

HARPER & ROW, PUBLISHERS

NEW YORK, EVANSTON, AND LONDON

1817

Time cover by Ernest Hamlin Baker; copyright Time Inc. 1947. Printed by permission of Time Inc.

Newsweek cover, copyright 1954, printed by permission of Newsweek, Inc.

"Richard Cory," from *Children of the Night,* by Edwin Arlington Robinson (Charles Scribner's Sons, New York, 1897).

Interview with Robert R. Young and William White, courtesy Associated Press.

FIRST EDITION

LIBRARY OF CONGRESS CATALOG CARD NUMBER: 69-15300

69707172738765432 1

Contents

Contents

Illustrations

Acknowledgments

My gratitude to Meg Leary, the indispensable, for supervising all aspects of this work and without whom it could not have been completed; to Irene Gordon for undertaking much of the research so brilliantly; to Anne Greigg, who organized the files and made the various libraries in the Washington area working partners in this project; to Pat Carter for her diligence and accuracy in the typing of the manuscript; and to Tina Dropkin, who ably assisted in all phases. My gratitude also to my family and to the army of colleagues, friends, and erstwhile opponents who jogged my memory, provided precious information, and were so generous with their time.

J. B.

Washington, D.C.
December 11, 1968

Robert R. Young,
the Populist
of Wall Street

1

The Populist of Wall Street

ROBERT R. YOUNG was an original. A private businessman, he was driven by a public mission: capitalism must be saved from the Capitalists.

From the moment he took control of the Alleghany Corporation in 1937 until the day he died in 1958, he kept Wall Street in a state of turmoil. In command of a multibillion-dollar railroad and financial empire, he waged unrelenting war on the major investment banks, insurance companies, and law firms. His corporate bouts raged in every available forum, in courts and commissions, in board rooms and at stockholders' meetings, in committee rooms and on the floor of Congress, and even in the White House itself. Convinced that his opponents, the custodians of the established order, controlled conventional legal processes, Young confounded them by enlarging the field of conflict to include extralegal arenas. Relying on the element of surprise, he sought constantly to keep the initiative. Armed with the legal advice that truth is an absolute defense against libel, he deliberately created tumult by peppering his charges with sensational detail. In all these confrontations, Young, the "little man," enlisted public opinion as an ally. "David against Goliath" became the theme of his career and controversy the essence of his public personality.

Young never retreated from the conviction that his financial opponents were arrogating to themselves the powers of government. These "private governments" had to be curbed, he believed, before they became so powerful that they corrupted the free market and destroyed democracy itself. In his view, even the courts and legis-

How Can Slave Railroads Serve the Public?

About one-fifth of the country's railroad mileage is held in bondage to "voting trusts" or will soon be delivered to them. The stockholders of these roads will have no voice in their management. Let's urge Congress to act!

IT is time America went on another trust-busting party!

A number of important railroads in our country are now held in complete vassalage to certain groups known as "voting trusts."

Back in the thirties the banker-insurance ring thought up that expedient ostensibly to protect the creditors of the roads, but actually to keep themselves in power. They warned solemnly that our railroads were overbuilt and had too much equipment. (Look at it now!) They argued that many roads should be "put through the wringer," that thousands of security holders should be "washed out" and that representatives of the ring should be set up as "voting trustees."

And eventually they had their way—*though it meant wiping out billions of dollars' worth of securities!*

What's Free About This Enterprise?

As a result, the true owners of these railroads, their thousands of stockholders all over the country, find themselves disenfranchised with no voice whatever in the management of their properties. They must accept whatever decisions the trusts hand down.

And what has the record been to date? Many pleas for progress in the last five years have been received by the trusts with pessimistic head-shaking about the dismal future of American railroads. *As though we could entrust any business to men who don't believe in it!* And proposed reforms have found an iron curtain dropped in their path—by disciples of the *status quo.*

Was it the voting trusts who campaigned for competitive bidding on railroad securities? They and the powers behind them fought it to the last. Was it the trusts who promoted through coast-to-coast passenger service or who broke the Black Market in sleeping car tickets? They sat on their hands while others campaigned for these reforms until the trusts were overwhelmed by public opinion.

What can the public expect until these carriers are freed from involuntary servitude?

Where would Ford or Du Pont or Chrysler be if they were run by outside "trusts"—with their real owners having no voice in their affairs? Is this in the American tradition?

Why We Are Short of Box Cars

Thousands of businessmen are sweating today to get freight cars and coal cars to move the goods of industry. Why? Because back in the thirties the banker-insurance groups preached the fallacy that our railroads were overexpanded.

As a solution to the problem posed by this mournful viewpoint they recommended that whole properties be turned over to the voting trusts to run. And that is what was done! Is it any wonder that, on these and other railroads, we are asked to ride in creaking old sleeping cars, and that goods are backing up on factory sidings all over the country?

What You Can Do About It

If you are one of those who believe that progress is overdue in our railroads if you believe that our best assurance of public service is in free business, freely run by thousands of Americans who have invested their money in the enterprise, write to your congressman. Ask him why so many of our railroads must be led in chains by banker-controlled trusts. Ask him to insist that Congress pass legislation that will sever these chains by dissolving the trusts. Tell him that involuntary servitude went out of this country in 1865.

The voting trusts are only one of many practices that are keeping our railroads from advancement. If you would like to join in an effort to remove these evils, and promote progressive ideas in railroading, write the Federation For Railway Progress. We will send you information on all the aims of this new organization, and how to become a member.

Federation For Railway Progress

Terminal Tower, Cleveland 1, Ohio

Robert R. Young, Chairman

Advisory Committee: Edward R. Stettinius, Jr., Chairman; Hon. Charles Edison, Albert S. Goss, Adm. William F. Halsey, Philip LaFollette, Hon. Clare Booth Luce, M. Lincoln Schus

Young advertisement depicting a "dambanker"

latures were not free from the morbid influence of these sovereign monopolists.

Young did not use academic or abstract terms. Yet some of the ideas he expressed are recognizable in the concepts of such scholars as Thorstein Veblen, Walton Hamilton, Adolph Berle, and Gardiner Means. Such phrases as "pecuniary sabotage," "the conscientious withdrawal of efficiency," "the conflict of ownership and control," "the separation of risk and management," found pragmatic meaning in Young's performance. He also had a talent for reducing these concepts to terms which were meaningful to stockholders and would gain him their support. Those with a sense of history sometimes called Young "the Populist of Wall Street," and that expression was more than a clever paradox. As John Chamberlain pointed out in early 1947, in *Life* magazine, "A Texan, Young says 'dambanker' or 'goddambanker' the way other Texans say 'damyankee.'" And in references by Texas populists to the eastern financial establishment, the terms damyankee and dambanker were interchangeable.

A distillate of Young's attitude is to be seen in a cartoon of "voting trusts" he advertised in the major newspapers and financial journals. It depicts an overstuffed, silk-hatted banker on whose paunch is a dollar sign for a watch fob. The only element distinguishing it from a classic portrayal in the left-wing press is that, instead of representing oppressed people in chains, it shows a collection of "slave railroads."

Still, Young did not regard himself as a muckraking reformer. Instead, he preferred to call himself a "true capitalist." If he was a reformer at all, he maintained, it was because of his belief that capitalists ought to be made to live and let others live according to the canons of a free market economy. He was determined to lead a capitalist revolution.

Young's view of capitalism was simplistic, unencumbered by philosophical systems and dialectical reasoning. For him, the essentials of capitalism were uncomplicated propositions. His outlook stemmed from a devotion to the sanctity of private property and to the sanctity of freedom of contract. Profit was the reward for risk. To guarantee a profit either through government supports or by a rigged and monopolized market was immoral and, worse, it was uneconomic. Private monopoly was as much a threat to capitalism as was a "big brother" government and its welfare philosophy. Non-owning managers and bankers wearing the outer garb of capitalists were, in fact, among the more dangerous subversives.

These beliefs resulted in some public confusion, and the term "radical" was sometimes applied to him. Young objected to this description, for he considered himself a conservative, both politically and economically. Broadly speaking an "isolationist" in foreign affairs, he believed in the principles of "America First." Yet he originally supported Roosevelt because of F.D.R.'s economic policies, particularly those curbing the power of Wall Street. Later he supported Senator Burton K. Wheeler for the presidency.

The Towers, Young's home at Palm Beach, Florida . . .

(Courtesy of C & O Railroad)

. . . and Fairholme, at Newport, Rhode Island

(Courtesy of C & O Railroad)

The companies Young dominated were financial giants listed on the New York Stock Exchange. He owned a great deal of their stock. He was personally very rich and had even richer associates. Among experts he was recognized as a financial genius with an extraordinary capacity to analyze and grasp quickly the controlling elements of the most complicated corporate statements. Coupled with this ability was the gift of knowing when to buy and when to sell.

He had palatial homes in Newport and Palm Beach and a luxurious apartment at the Waldorf Towers in New York. One had only to read the newspapers to know that Mr. and Mrs. Young were members of the inner circles of the social elite. The Youngs were gracious hosts, and leaders of industry and finance, of royalty, and of high society were their constant visitors. He was a skilled hunter (a crack shot since childhood, and his devotion to guns never abated), a very low handicap golfer (the winner of at least one publicized tournament), and a billiard expert (Willie Hoppe confirmed his competence). Even in play, Young had an unquenchable need to be best.

Only in the world of business did Young depart from tradition. As an innovator, he had an extraordinary talent to excite the public's interest. In fact, his name first came to the public's attention through his skillful use of newspaper advertising. He was among a small number of big businessmen who considered enforcement of the Sherman Act and antitrust laws generally as necessary to protect the free market and as an essential instrument of the capitalist system.

Young was the only railway executive who openly opposed passage of the Reed-Bulwinkle bill, designed to provide the railroads with an exemption from the antitrust laws in collective rate-making. He was the only major railroad figure who supported the

Young greeting the Duke and Duchess of Windsor, April, 1948 . . .
(Courtesy of C & O Railroad)

Department of Justice's antitrust suit against the Association of American Railroads; the Western Association of Railway Executives; J. P. Morgan & Company; Kuhn, Loeb & Company; and a variety of western railroads and railroad executives. The defendants, a Who's Who of the railroad industry, were charged with engaging in a conspiracy in restraint of trade in violation of the Sherman Act, "collusive rate fixing and agreements to limit services and suppress technological improvements." In an extraordinary communiqué, U.S. Attorney General Francis Biddle and Robert Young jointly announced Young's support of the government's case.

In the government's antitrust suit against the so-called "money trust," in which the seventeen largest investment bankers were defendants, Young was the prosecution's chief witness. Particularly important to the case were Young's efforts to bring about

. . . and C & O locomotive shop workers in West Virginia

(Courtesy of C & O Railroad)

compulsory competitive bidding in railroad securities over the opposition of the defendants. In his testimony, as in his daily conduct, he left no doubt that he was an important opponent of the "Wall Street bankers."

He was devoted to the principle of "truth in securities" as embodied in the Securities Act of 1933 and believed that the government should develop a parallel policy of "truth in politics" by which all public servants, including congressmen, senators, and judges, should be required to reveal their income, assets, and other economic ties. He was specific in his identifications, and Young's immediate self-interest proved no deterrent to the uninhibited character of his charges. He identified his targets, whether judges, commissioners, or congressmen. Sometimes his lawyers as well as his business associates who had to face these public servants in the courts, in commission proceedings, and in congressional hearings, shuddered at the directness with which Young expressed his views.

However, there was an essential consistency to Young's views which many of his liberal followers either had to suffer or ignore. His devotion to private property and free enterprise made him a vehement opponent of all things smacking of Communism and Socialism. He hated and feared the governments of the Soviet Union, China, Yugoslavia, and their bloc. England he regarded as the captive of the socialist principles under the Labor party. He suspected that the United States government was infiltrated with subversives, and in this posture was an unashamed supporter of Senator Joseph McCarthy, giving money, collecting signatures, and joining organizations pledged to the anti-Communist crusade.

He regarded the political and economic power of labor unions as far too great, although organized labor frequently supported him. He was a vocal advocate of the more serious curbs on labor, as provided, for example, by certain sections of the Taft-Hartley Act. This didn't stop him from mounting a vigorous attack on Senator Robert Taft, whose law firm Young charged with serving the investment banker "cabal," although he felt it a pity that McCarthy did not have the intelligence or the manners of Taft.

He abhorred government planning and welfare services, often

inveighing against government waste, spending, and high taxes. Franklin D. Roosevelt's fiscal policies in time became an abomination: soaking the rich was, after all, a discriminatory attack on the Horatio Alger principle, while deficit spending was Marxism in Keynesian clothing. All were threats to the free market and the free-enterprise system. He further came to detest the so-called Roosevelt revolution as a front behind which favored investment bankers operated, and he was explicit in his accusations of complicity. It was no accident, in his view, that W. Averell Harriman[1] (chairman of the board of the Union Pacific Railroad as well as senior partner of Brown Brothers, Harriman and Company) and James Forrestal (president of Dillon, Read & Company) occupied favored positions in the New Deal Administration.

Young became more and more aware that his main body of public support came from New Dealers, Fair Dealers, liberals, Populists, crusading journalists, senators like Harry S. Truman and Estes Kefauver, and representatives like Wright Patman. At first this puzzled him, but in time he came to understand the rationale of their position and to have a greater appreciation of their support. On the other side of the political coin, such conservatives as Admiral William F. (Bull) Halsey, former Governor Charles Edison of New Jersey, and Clare Boothe Luce were among his advisers in the Federation for Railway Progress. Yet also serving as Federation advisers were such moderates as M. Lincoln Schuster of Simon & Schuster; Edward R. Stettinius, Jr., former Secretary of State under President Roosevelt; and Philip La Follette, former governor of Wisconsin and a member of the great family of political liberals. Classification was not so easy when measuring his business associates. Some members of his immediate staff fell into the liberal tradition, as did his most trusted investment banker, Cyrus Eaton. Yet most of the principal officers of his companies and certainly the board members were like their

---

[1] Young has often been compared with E. H. Harriman, Averell's father, because of their early careers on Wall Street, their enormous drive, and particularly their jousts with the J. P. Morgan interests. It is mainly a surface similarity.

prototypes in American corporate life, generally quite conservative. Each side felt the other exerted an unhealthy influence on Young.

Few people were neutral about him. His detractors charged him with being a Texas "wheeler-dealer" and a demagogue preying on unsuspecting investors. His admirers credited him with enlightened self-interest, refreshing candor, and being a progressive twentieth-century capitalist. Lasting feuds resulted; even hatred developed among those who felt the sting of his shafts during moments of corporate strife.

Nowhere was Young's public personality more revealed than in his struggle for control of the New York Central Railroad. His whole career seemed pointed toward this event.

Young's battle for this prize spanned seven years and culminated in a bitterly fought proxy contest that dwarfed other such battles both in its ramifications and its impact. It involved almost 6,500,000 shares of stock, more than 44,000 shareholders, more than 100,000 Central employees, more than 10,500 miles of track, more than $2,500,000,000 worth of assets. The campaign for the stockholders' votes rivaled a national election in scope, intensity, and public interest.

As Young saw the proxy contest, it was simply a question of "whether the owners of the New York Central property shall run it or whether a handful of bankers shall run it. Those bankers have conflicts with the owners. It's purely a matter of principle, and I am fighting for the principle which is in the interest of the public, and they're fighting for the principle which is in the interest of themselves." As such it was a historic encounter between economic democracy and financial oligarchy. When he repeatedly used the phrase "Morgan-Vanderbilt board," he meant a board of investment bankers and entrenched management owning little stock but usurping the rights of the common shareholders. In testimony before a Senate committee looking into the New York Central proxy contest, he warned,

. . . You need only look here to find the devices by which a small group of men have assumed control of many of our great corporations, . . . and through their interlockings with each other to dominate the corporate, if not the political, life of the Nation. Some way must be found to diffuse this power before it becomes absolute. . . .[2]

Robert Young determined to find that way. He would do so by making the power of the Vanderbilts, the Morgans, and their corporate associates his prime target.

[2] Hearings before the Subcommittee on Securities, Committee on Banking and Currency, U.S. Senate, on S. 879, "Stock Market Study (Corporate Proxy Contests)," June 9, 1955, p. 1457.

2

Vanderbilt to Van Sweringen

FOR ALMOST a century the New York Central Railroad was known as the "Vanderbilt Line." When Commodore Cornelius Vanderbilt took over control of the company just after the Civil War, he began the most famous dynasty in American railroading. From that time on, at least one Vanderbilt was expected to be on the board of the Central. So great was the Vanderbilts' influence, so magic their name, that it was inconceivable that their dominant position in the Central could ever be challenged.

A commodore heading a railroad was symbolic of the changes taking place in transportation technology a century ago. The earliest railroads had been mere links between the major waterways. The sixteen-mile Mohawk & Hudson Railroad, the first stretch of what was eventually to become the New York Central, was in fact built in 1831 for the sole purpose of joining the Hudson River and the Erie Canal. The new mode of travel proved itself almost immediately, and in little more than a decade ten short roads, separately owned, running end to end, connected Albany with Buffalo. The logic of consolidation soon exerted itself, and in 1853 these were merged into a corporate entity, the New York Central Railroad.

By the end of the Civil War, the roles of the waterways and the railroads were reversed. Commodore Vanderbilt, already sixty-eight years old, abandoned ships for trains. He began putting together what was to become the giant Vanderbilt trunk line with the purchase in 1864 of the Hudson River Railroad, running between New York City and Albany. He pushed the Vanderbilt line from Albany to Buffalo when he purchased control of the original New York Central Railroad in 1867.[1] A little later he extended his line from Buffalo to Chicago, bringing within his orbit the Lake Shore & Michigan Southern Railroad. The basic outline of the present New York Central was then established.

When the Commodore died in 1877, he was reputed to be the richest man in America, with a net worth of approximately $100,-000,000. Determined to leave his empire intact, he willed almost his entire estate, including 87 percent of the stock of the Central, to his oldest son, William Henry.[2]

During the 1870s railroad mileage had increased by 50 percent, but overexpansion led to cutthroat rate wars and, occasionally, to piracy and manipulation in railroad finance. The railroads came under mounting attack, not only by shippers and farmers but also by the press and politicians. During the brief reign of the younger Vanderbilt, the epithet "robber baron" was first introduced by Kansas farmers in one of their antimonopoly pamphlets. William Vanderbilt, often the target of the attacks, was cast as the prototype of the robber baron.

Despite this reputation, he was in fact a victim of one of the more dramatic forms of robber baron morality. The New York, Chicago & St. Louis Railroad Company, better known as the Nickel Plate,[3] was built parallel to Vanderbilt's Lake Shore for no other purpose than to blackmail him into buying it. Confronted by the threat of cutthroat competition, he submitted and bought the Nickel Plate. For the rest of his life he was bitter about it.

Vanderbilt had other reasons to be resentful. One of his offhand remarks was to go down in history—"The public be damned." Reformers for generations were to use it as a rallying cry. And yet, as Matthew Josephson indicates in his classic study, *The Robber Barons,*

---

[1] When he consolidated these two roads in 1869, they became known as the New York Central & Hudson River Railroad Company. The road continued to be known by this name until 1914, when it became the New York Central Railroad Company again.

[2] The Commodore's eight daughters and his other son, the epileptic Cornelius Jeremiah, received relatively minor bequests.

[3] A nickname which probably came from the initials N.Y., C. & (St.) L. and the high regard then held for the newly developed nickel-plating process.

the actual circumstances of Vanderbilt's unfortunate remark may have been misunderstood.

Billy Vanderbilt, a man of much softer mold than his father, has been represented as the paragon of capitalist despotism. In reality he had simply been explaining [to two newspaper reporters] why the fast extra-fare mail train between New York and Chicago was being eliminated. It wasn't paying, he asserted. But the public found it both useful and convenient; should he not accommodate them? "The public be damned. I am working for my stockholders," he had answered his interlocutor. "If the public want the train, why don't they pay for it?"[4]

William Vanderbilt owes his place in history as much as anything to this unfortunate remark (and sometimes even it has been credited to his father, the Commodore). Actually he deserves better. It was he as much as his father who was responsible for putting together the New York Central trunk line. He made another contribution which was truly significant in American railroad history: he introduced J. P. Morgan to the Central.

By 1879, only two years after his father's death, Vanderbilt was no longer able to suffer the unremitting attacks by reformers. "We get kicked and cuffed by Congressional committees, legislatures, and the public, and I feel inclined to have others take some of it, instead of taking it all myself." He decided to sell over half of his Central holdings and thereby, hopefully, remove himself as a prime target.

The immediate problem was to avoid depressing the price of Central stock by the sale of such a large block. He approached J. Pierpont Morgan, then a moderately successful but imaginative investment banker who, with his father, Junius, had built up a strong clientele in England. Morgan agreed to undertake the project, but with qualifications which would protect his investors: the Central must guarantee to pay the current dividend of $8 for five years and a Morgan representative must have a place on the Central board of directors.

The sale was no light undertaking. Since 1873, European investors

[4] Matthew Josephson, *The Robber Barons* (New York: Harcourt, Brace & World, Inc., Harvest Book, 1962), p. 187.

had lost more than $500,000,000 in railroad securities through bankruptcies and frauds. In 1879 alone, when the Vanderbilt shares were being sold, sixty-five railroads were foreclosed.

Nevertheless, Morgan took the offering to his British customers. Despite the enormous amount of stock to be sold—up to that time the largest single block of securities ever offered—he succeeded beyond Vanderbilt's dreams. On November 26, Morgan called the press to his office at 23 Wall Street ("the Corner") and announced that he had sold 250,000 of Vanderbilt's 400,000 shares of New York Central stock. The House of Morgan, in an extraordinary feat of salesmanship, had moved with such precision and discretion that the price of the shares had never dipped. Vanderbilt received an excellent return and Morgan a fee of $3,000,000. Both were delighted.

The event resulted in much more than mere individual profit. The dispersion of ownership among a very large number of small stockholders and the consequent separation of control from ownership brought with it a change in the character of financial and industrial life. Muckrakers and scholars would write about it for generations. Henceforth the investment banker, as he brought in new owners through underwriting, would use this leverage to take a directing hand in management as well as financing. Solitary ownership of a majority of the stock of a large corporation had become an anachronism. With the change came a potential arena for struggles for corporate control.

A Morgan rival, Jacob M. Schiff of Kuhn, Loeb & Company, also became involved in railroad financing at this time. While Morgan entered the field through Vanderbilt and the New York Central in 1879, Schiff came in by way of the Chicago & North Western in 1877 (though with a relatively modest fee of only $500,000). Kuhn, Loeb grew with the industry and achieved a standing only slightly less than that of the House of Morgan. However, in the protocol of this banking royalty, it was always Jacob Schiff who walked down the street to call on J. Pierpont Morgan.

It was not long after Morgan's successful performance in the Vanderbilt sale that his powerful position in the railroad business became apparent. In 1885 he was able to settle a nearly disastrous rate war between the Central and the Pennsylvania Railroad. A few years earlier the West Shore[5] had been built deliberately to parallel the Central tracks all the way from New York City to Buffalo. William Vanderbilt was apoplectic. "The West Shore was built as a blackmailing scheme," he told a New York *Tribune* reporter, "just as the Nickel Plate was." One of the original backers was George M. Pullman, who was spurred by a monumental hatred toward Vanderbilt for having replaced Pullman sleeping cars with those of the Wagner Palace Car Company. That Wagner was controlled by the Vanderbilts added to Pullman's rage. Pullman mounted his attack on Vanderbilt by joining Jay Gould and others to build the West Shore. The new road, emotionally conceived and uneconomically constructed, lost money from the start in a rate war with the Central and went bankrupt only to be taken over by another Vanderbilt enemy, the Pennsylvania Railroad.

Vanderbilt couldn't be dissuaded from thinking that the Pennsylvania was really the prime mover behind the West Shore from the beginning. In retaliation, he invaded Pennsylvania territory and started to build the South Pennsylvania Railroad directly paralleling the Pennsylvania's main line between Pittsburgh and Harrisburg.

In the meantime, the rate war between the Central and the West Shore flared with a white heat. The bonds of the West Shore dropped from 65 to 28, and Central stock was traded below its par value for the first time in the company's existence. When the Central was forced to halve its dividends, Morgan, impelled by the interests of his customer stockholders, stepped into the situation. After notifying Vanderbilt (who had retired because of ill health), Morgan summoned Central's new president, Chauncey Depew,[6] and Pennsylvania's president, George B. Roberts, to a conference on his

[5] Its full name was the New York, West Shore & Buffalo Railroad.

[6] Depew was with the Central sixty-two years—as lawyer, general counsel, president, and, finally, during his last thirty years, until 1928, as chairman of the board. Even his election and service as a distinguished United States senator from New York did not interfere with his chairmanship of the Central.

yacht, the *Corsair*. He made it clear to the two railroad presidents that the West Shore–South Pennsylvania conflict must be settled, and he gave instructions to his captain that the *Corsair* was not to dock until the warring parties had found a way out of their ruinous feud. His tactics worked. In the terms of peace that followed, the Pennsylvania agreed to buy the South Pennsylvania Railroad—which it didn't want and never completed.[7] The Central unhappily agreed to lease the West Shore for 475 years, until 2360 A.D., with an option to renew the lease for another 500 years, or until 2860 A.D.[8] William Vanderbilt barely survived the signing of the compromise. Within three days, he died of a stroke.

Nevertheless Morgan could not suppress all the rate wars that broke out during the nineteenth century. These resulted in various forms of discrimination that aroused the ire of shippers and the public, such as "long and short haul" abuses, rebates, free passes, and underbilling. Moreover, cases of unscrupulous financial manipulation were given widespread publicity.

Many of the railroad leaders, faced with continued rate wars, overexpanded facilities, the prospects of bankruptcy,[9] and oppressive and conflicting regulation in some of the states, concluded that a federal regulatory commission was the only possible alternative to chaos in the industry. Rarely have regulatees been so anxious for federal regulation.

Actually Congress had been considering the possibility of railroad regulation since shortly after the Civil War. Between 1868 and 1886 more than 150 bills and resolutions had been introduced involving some sort of regulation. Finally, in January 1887, Congress

[7] Fifty-five years later, the roadbed of the South Pennsylvania, with its nine tunnels, reappeared as the Pennsylvania Turnpike, a symbolic ghost to haunt the Pennsylvania Railroad.

[8] Seventy years after settlement of hostilities, passenger service on the West Shore became utterly uneconomic, its termination written in the New York Central's West Shore Discontinuance Case before the I.C.C. in 1957. To dramatize the economic folly of passenger service of this line, Central's President Alfred E. Perlman pointed out that it would be cheaper to supply each commuter with a Cadillac every year than to continue service.

[9] Most of the railroads went into bankruptcy at some point before the end of the century.

passed the Act to Regulate Commerce,[10] which established the first regulatory commission, the Interstate Commerce Commission.

Despite the great pressure which brought forth this Act, in its early years the Commission found itself with relatively little power. The law was vaguely worded, and the Supreme Court regularly overruled the Commission's orders. As a result, there was little abatement of the rate wars. Morgan found it necessary to exert his influence to maintain rates and establish economic stability.

In the meantime, public outrage at the excesses of powerful economic interests, particularly in the creation of the "trust" device, led to the passage of the Sherman Antitrust Act in 1890. For several years, however, there was some question as to the extent of the Sherman Act's applicability to railroads. In January 1896, Morgan, convinced that the Sherman Act was not applicable to railroads, set up a Joint Traffic Association to fix rates. When the Supreme Court ruled that the Sherman Act did apply,[11] the always resourceful Morgan then turned to the "community of interest" plan as an alternative. Under this plan, large railroads purchased a controlling interest in independent "rogue" railroads that showed signs of refusing to observe the jointly established rates.[12]

The "community of interest" plan, while relatively short-lived, had an explosive history. When it was utilized to resolve a competitive war with Morgan's archenemy, E. H. Harriman, it backfired in a landmark Supreme Court decision extending even further the application of the Sherman Act to railroads.[13]

The small, intense Harriman had come into conflict with Morgan soon after he shifted from the brokerage business to railroading in the 1880s.[14] His first challenge to Morgan occurred in 1887 in a con-

[10] Renamed in 1920 the Interstate Commerce Act.

[11] *United States* v. *Trans-Missouri Freight Association,* 166 U.S. 290 (1897); *United States* v. *Joint Traffic Association,* 171 U.S. 505 (1898).

[12] In 1900 and 1901, following this practice, the Central and Pennsylvania jointly acquired control of the Chesapeake & Ohio Railway Company. They purchased over 46 percent of its stock, agreeing to hold it for ten years and to give the copurchaser the right of first refusal should either decide to sell.

[13] *Northern Securities Co.* v. *United States,* 193 U.S. 197 (1904).

[14] Harriman devoted his early life to learning every facet of Wall Street. During the Civil War he began work as an office boy, and by the time he

test to control a minor railroad, the Dubuque and Sioux City. Even though Harriman won, Morgan developed a strong contempt for him. He frequently referred to Harriman as "that two-dollar broker." Harriman's next tussle with Morgan took place in the Erie reorganization in 1894. So effective was Harriman's interference, legal and financial, that Morgan had to change the plan. A year later, when Morgan had abandoned the reorganization of the bankrupt Union Pacific as a hopeless project, Harriman undertook it with brilliant success and enormous profit to himself. Now Morgan's contempt matured into hatred.

Harriman's activities seemed destined to annoy Morgan. The most dramatic contest between the two began in 1901. At that time James J. Hill, with the backing of J. P. Morgan & Company, dominated railroading in the Northwest through control of the Great Northern Railway Company and the Northern Pacific Railway Company. Harriman, supported by Kuhn, Loeb & Company and the Rockefeller interests, exercised similar suzerainty in the Southwest and Midwest through control of the Southern Pacific Railroad and the Union Pacific Railroad. In the spring of 1901, both the Harriman–Kuhn, Loeb, and Hill–Morgan factions began to eye the Chicago, Burlington & Quincy Railroad, an eight-thousand-mile road extending through the Midwest. Hill coveted the Burlington because it would give him an entrance into Chicago and the vital Mississippi ports and make possible an invasion of Middle West territory. Harriman wanted the Burlington not only because he was aware of Hill's intentions but also because he knew that the Burlington, by pushing on to the West Coast, could emerge as a fearsome competitor to his Union Pacific. A head-on crash was indicated.

---

was twenty-two he owned a seat on the New York Stock Exchange. As his fortune grew, so did his position with the "society set" in New York. The proper clubs as well as the fashionable Seventh Regiment became part of his social life. He was a crack marksman, an unusually fine billiards player and an "exceptional boxer," upon occasion even demonstrating his skill in "exhibitions" with the former lightweight champion, Billy Edwards.

Harriman's first big money came from accurately divining the depths of the panic of 1873 and speculating with every cent he could gather. With the profits, he made his first move in railroads, buying into the Illinois Central. By 1883 he was sufficiently involved to resign from his brokerage business and make railroading his main interest.

Hill and Morgan had moved swiftly and silently, using the Northern Pacific and Great Northern to purchase the Burlington stock. Before Harriman and his investment banker associate, Schiff, could realize what was happening, Hill and Morgan had bought up 96 percent of the Burlington.

Harriman was furious when he learned of the Hill coup. Schiff, determined to gain even a minimum advantage, called on Morgan and appealed to his pride by suggesting a "community of interest" arrangement which would make a place for Harriman. According to Schiff's suggestion, Harriman should be permitted to buy a third of the Burlington and go on the board together with William Rockefeller, a Harriman backer. Morgan turned Schiff down flatly. Schiff then called on Hill, with even less success.

On the surface, the first round in the Battle of the Burlington was a decisive win for Hill and Morgan. So confident was Morgan that he departed for Aix-les-Bains, France, on his annual vacation. With 96 percent of the stock, he could not contemplate anyone's trying another challenge. Even Schiff thought Morgan's victory was final. The resourceful Harriman, however, had a better idea.

Since Hill had bought the Burlington mainly through the Great Northern Railroad and the Northern Pacific Railroad, Harriman devised a strategy both brilliant and simple. He would bypass the Burlington and mount an attack on one of Hill's basic fortresses— *he would buy control of the Northern Pacific, and then the Burlington would fall.*

To undertake the "raid" on the Northern Pacific, Harriman needed $78,000,000. Schiff, while realizing the risk to Kuhn, Loeb, knew that such a coup would make him every bit the equal of Morgan. After a sleepless night, he agreed to go along with Harriman. With the added help of the Rockefeller forces, a sufficient war chest was accumulated.

Now it was Schiff's turn to perform. He moved to the attack with such precision that it was some time before Morgan and Hill even knew the Battle of the Northern Pacific was under way. Morga Company even sold $14,000,000 worth of Northern Pacific st the belief that the sudden demand was the result of an

public's appetite for "glamour" stocks. Actually the real purchaser was Kuhn, Loeb & Company. Schiff had carefully spread the rumor that the unusual demand came from the public's realization that the acquisition of the Burlington had made the Northern Pacific a fine buy.

Before long, Hill divined what was happening. According to legend, he was supposed to have had a vision from a dark angel who revealed the peril awaiting him. J. P. Morgan, aroused from his vacation in France, cabled Hill a pledge of support. With both sides girded for battle, the struggle for the Northern Pacific could not be averted.

On Monday, May 6, 1901, a fully equipped army of Morgan's aides moved into the New York Stock Exchange and laid down a barrage of orders. The stock rose from 110 to 131. By Tuesday, it reached 150. The excitement of battle was too much for the speculators to resist. Not only did they join in the feverish buying, but the "shorts" entered the market, selling large amounts of stock which they didn't have with the expectation of buying enough to cover the sales when the "inevitable" bust arrived. As a result of the activities of these uninvited participants, the stock moved madly from $300 to $500 and then to the absurd figure of $1000. Between Harriman and Hill a corner of Northern Pacific was taking shape. The shorts, now realizing the nature of the war they had joined as greedy camp followers, became desperate. In their rush to cover, they drove the money market up to a rate of 40 and even 60 percent. As the sources of money dried up, the shorts were forced to unload everything they owned. Panic followed. The entire market crashed.

Morgan's vacation in Aix-les-Bains was spoiled. Not only reformers, muckrakers, and politicians but Wall Street speculators and gamblers, victims of their own greed, pointed accusingly at him as an evil influence whose power must be extirpated before he ruined the country. In this kind of an atmosphere, Morgan showed up at the office of his affiliate in Paris. From all sides he was besieged for help, advice, and directions. The press added to the tumult by demanding interviews and explanations. To one particularly annoying newspaperman who insisted that the public was due a statement, Morgan blurted out the infamous "I owe the public nothing." These words echoing their way across the Atlantic did nothing to dampen the widespread outrage at the damage caused by the baronial war. Both the Hill-Morgan and the Harriman–Kuhn, Loeb forces became alarmed by the possible consequences—even during a McKinley Administration. Since neither side could claim a victory, both were eager for peace. To shore up the disaster, they helped arrange a pool of $20,000,000 to relax the money squeeze, and they also agreed to delay pressure on the shorts for Northern Pacific stock, pegging the price for covering at $150 per share.

With the aggrieved part of the Wall Street community as well as the public now somewhat mollified, Morgan was ready to prepare a new "community of interest" plan. A holding company would be formed called the Northern Securities Company. The erstwhile "enemies" would exchange their Northern Pacific and Great Northern stock for Northern Securities stock. Hill was allocated ten of the fifteen directors with Hill as chairman, and Harriman was given five places. This solution was welcomed by all the participants. Morgan's failure to achieve a decisive victory over Harriman spelled enormous benefit to Kuhn, Loeb. In railroad finance Kuhn, Loeb was now regarded as an equal with J. P. Morgan & Company. As one historian has written, Harriman, supported by Kuhn, Loeb, had removed "Morgan from his lone pedestal as sole monarch of money. Never again would the will of a single man be supreme."[15]

On November 13, 1901, the Northern Securities Company became a reality. The parties looked forward to a burst of prosperity for the new enterprise, a resumption of the boom triggered off by the McKinley election in 1896 and temporarily set back by the Northern Pacific panic. There was no reason to suspect the assassination of President McKinley two months earlier would have any meaning to the Northern Securities Company plan. But President Theodore Roosevelt, hardly two months in office and with the Northern Pacific panic still fresh in his memory, instructed his Attorney General to move for dissolution of the Northern Securities Company under the Sherman Antitrust Act.

Hoping to find an amicable solution, Morgan headed for Washing-

[15] John K. Winkler, *Morgan the Magnificent* (New York: Garden City Publishing Co., Inc., 1930), p. 185.

ton to see what could be worked out with the new President. At their meeting Morgan suggested to Roosevelt that "if we have done anything wrong, send your man to my man and they can fix it up." Roosevelt, however, did not regard Morgan as either an equal or a sovereign power. He made it very clear that there was no room for a "gentleman's agreement." The case would have to be settled publicly, in court. Morgan left in the kind of rage for which he was noted. He drafted an angry letter to Roosevelt, but after several hours of persuasion by his nervous associates, he agreed to tear it up.

In 1904 Roosevelt prevailed; the Supreme Court, by the narrow margin of five to four,[16] ordered the dissolution of the Northern Securities Company.[17]

The "community of interest" concept continued to run into difficulty. In March 1906 the I.C.C. was directed by Congress "to make an examination into the subject of railroad discriminations and monopolies in coal and oil." The hearings did nothing to enhance the standing of the railroad industry with the public. In June 1906, the Hepburn Act, which was directed primarily at separating the railroad business from its mining interests, was passed. Finally, in November 1906, an investigation of all of Harriman's activities was undertaken by the I.C.C. Harriman's arrogant frankness did not improve the railroad industry's image. Soon after, the "community of interest" principle was abandoned. Under these pressures, for example, the Pennsylvania and the Central gave up their joint control in the C & O.[18]

[16] Although Roosevelt rejoiced at this legal victory he was upset by the dissenting opinion of Justice Oliver Wendell Holmes, who had been his first appointment to the court.

[17] The unscrambling of the Northern Securities Company had Morgan and Harriman back at each other's throats. Harriman complained that he was being unfairly treated under Morgan's plan of redistribution. Morgan insisted that he would not be dictated to by a despicable "two-dollar broker." Harriman thereupon took Morgan to court but lost and was compelled to accept Morgan's plan. A year later, a stock-market boom pushed Harriman's share of the dissolved Northern Securities Company to the point where it netted him a profit of over $58,000,000. As more than one observer remarked, even in defeat the knack of making money did not desert Harriman.

[18] Of incidental interest is the fact that the New York Central tried at this time to buy Pennsylvania's C & O holdings and thereby assume control of the C & O, but Central's offer was not high enough.

The antitrust movement received further support with the election of Woodrow Wilson. In 1914 the Clayton Act, designed to supplement and reinforce the Sherman Antitrust Act, was passed. Under its provisions, railroads would have to divest themselves of competing lines within two years. For the Central the Nickel Plate would once again become a problem. The Central would have to divest itself of it, but unloading a railroad, if for no other reason than the very size of the project, is not easy. The Department of Justice began to exert pressure for some action by the Central. By 1916, with the deadline approaching, divestiture of the Nickel Plate had become an immediate problem. The solution not only had the profoundest long-term implications for the Central but also introduced a set of extraordinary personalities into the railroad business.

Two moonfaced bachelor brothers, Oris Paxton Van Sweringen and Mantis James Van Sweringen, were prototypes in the Horatio Alger tradition. Born into a very poor family in Wooster, Ohio, they were educationally and economically deprived. They were, however, bright, energetic, and ambitious. Real-estate opportunities requiring small capital beckoned to them. In time they pyramided these into a sizable real-estate empire in Cleveland.

The development of Shaker Heights became one of their more ambitious real-estate ventures. In 1913, desiring to expand this operation, they sought an adjoining farm owned by A. H. Smith, then senior vice president of the New York Central. Apparently a singular empathy arose between Smith and the brothers, and the deal was closed in less than three minutes.

In 1916 the Van Sweringens were assembling land for a new railroad terminal in downtown Cleveland and found that much of the land they wanted was owned by the Central's Nickel Plate. They called upon Smith, who was by then president of the Central. Out of that meeting came the suggestion that the Van Sweringens buy the entire Nickel Plate. Smith, mindful of his previous comfortable experiences with the brothers, was delighted at this solution of the Central's divestiture problem and promised generous terms. The Van Sweringens knew from their real-estate dealings the "leverage" opportunities of "easy" financing. Smith introduced the Van Sweringens

O. P. Van Sweringen
(Courtesy of the Cleveland Press)

M. J. Van Sweringen
(Courtesy of the Cleveland Press)

to Thomas W. Lamont, a partner of J. P. Morgan & Company. Testifying before a Senate committee in 1937, Lamont recalled that Smith brought the Van Sweringens into his office one day in 1916 and said,

I have concluded arrangements to sell to them the Nickel Plate Railroad; and I have done it on very easy terms, because I think it will be to our advantage—well, the New York Central is obliged anyway to divest itself of the property, and we believe it would be to our advantage and to the advantage of the property to have these gentlemen in charge. We believe they will live up to their obligations, and we have no hesitation in telling you we have taken their obligations in payment, to a large extent, and that the down payment is comparatively small.[19]

[19] Hearings before Committee on Interstate Commerce, U.S. Senate, on S. Res. 71, "Investigation of Railroads, Holding Companies and Affiliated Companies," Part VI, p. 1996, March 3, 1937.

With Lamont's help, Smith then arranged the financing through the Guaranty Trust Company of New York, with terms so attractive that the Van Sweringens shifted their major interest from real estate to railroads. Smith also arranged for the extraordinarily able operating man J. J. Bernet, a Central vice president, to become president of the Nickel Plate. A Senate committee years later noted that "the hand of President Smith was present at almost every turn of Van Sweringen affairs during that period" and further noted that the credit extended to the Van Sweringens by the Central and its financial allies was "the foundation stone of the whole structure."[20] From this start with the Nickel Plate, the Van Sweringens in time would put together a huge railroad empire, almost as large and important as the Central itself.

America's entry into World War I propelled the nation's railroads into a new phase. The U.S. Railroad Administration assumed control and operation of all railroads,[21] but wartime government control proved no elixir. While the other major industries of the United States were sharing in wartime prosperity, the railroads deteriorated. Their physical plant fell apart; their income dwindled until bankruptcy was a real threat to many of the roads.

Whether the cause was federal operation of the railroads or the afflictions of excess capacity, wasteful duplication, inequitable rates, and the strain of wartime demands, the roads came out of the war faced with a financial crisis of such catastrophic and immediate dimensions that Congress was compelled to act.

In the Transportation Act of 1920, in which operation of the nation's railroads was returned to their owners, Congress undertook to rearrange the railroads into a limited number of systems according to a national transportation plan. Combination and consolidation were now looked upon with favor. For the railroads, at least, the

---

[20] Report No. 1182, "Investigation of Railroads, Holding Companies and Affiliated Companies," Committee on Interstate Commerce, U.S. Senate, 1940, Pt. II, p. 625.

[21] A. H. Smith of the New York Central served as Administrator in the Eastern Region.

national policy of antitrust was to be modified; roads consolidating in accordance with the plan would be partially relieved from the operation of the Sherman and Clayton Antitrust Acts. Rarely has government policy undergone so dramatic a reversal.

The Interstate Commerce Commission was instructed by Congress to prepare a plan for the consolidation of the railroads of the United States into a series of systems into which it was hoped the railroads would voluntarily merge.[22] However, the consolidation provisions of the Transportation Act of 1920 had weaknesses which were to prove fatal. The Act provided no sanction by which the I.C.C. could compel railroads to consolidate in accordance with a national plan; therefore the cooperation of the powerful roads became an absolute requirement. Moreover, the Commission lacked legal power to prevent the railroads from proceeding with their own consolidations through methods outside I.C.C. jurisdiction—purchase of less than a majority of stock of another road, purchase agreements worded as options, purchase through holding companies, and others. Also, there was the problem of the inclusion of unprofitable "orphan" railroads in the big systems—none of the big roads wanted them. Not to be underestimated was "Willard's law," enunciated by Daniel Willard of the B & O: no railroad executive will voluntarily merge himself out of a job! An equivalent railway labor law was also operating: no union leader will support a merger if jobs are threatened.

These difficulties soon became obvious to the I.C.C., which delayed any final decision on a consolidation plan all during the twenties, regularly pleading with Congress to relieve it of this unwelcome responsibility. In the meantime the big eastern railroads—the Pennsylvania, New York Central, C & O, and B & O and even the Wabash —were engaged in a frantic race to accomplish their own combinations before the I.C.C. plan could be imposed on them. This was

---

[22] To create a plan of regional systems, the I.C.C. employed Professor William Zebina Ripley of Harvard, the leading authority of the time on the economics of railroads. Ripley was an extraordinary scholar. Many years before he became a transportation authority, he was world-renowned as an anthropologist.

later described by Otto Kahn of Kuhn, Loeb & Company as "a scramble [by the railroads] to put themselves in a position where possession was nine points of the law."[23]

Of those engaged in the scramble, the Van Sweringens must be regarded as the most aggressive. To them could very well be assigned the title of "chief spoilers."[24] Not only were their acquisitions in total disregard of the public transportation policy but their equally reckless borrowing violated almost every rule of sound financing. The day of reckoning for both borrower and lender would not be long in coming.

At the height of this wild buying campaign, in early 1929, the Van Sweringens formed their super holding company, the Alleghany Corporation.[25] The securities in this new company were sold to the public through a banking syndicate headed by J. P. Morgan & Company.

Morgan usually dealt in the more conservative field of bonds, but in 1929 it offered common stock in a few new companies, including Alleghany, to a select list which became known as the "Morgan Preferred List"—"people that we know intimately and that we be-

[23] The Pennsylvania acquired control of the Wabash, the Lehigh Valley, the Pittsburgh & West Virginia, and the Detroit, Toledo & Ironton; tightened its control of the Norfolk & Western; and bought stock in the New Haven and the Boston & Maine. The Baltimore & Ohio acquired control of the Western Maryland, the Alton Railroad, the Buffalo & Susquehanna, the Buffalo, Rochester & Pittsburgh, and the Cincinnati, Indianapolis & Western and tightened its control of the Reading. The New York Central, which consistently followed a more conservative policy than the other large eastern systems during these years, bought only a "piece" of the Lackawanna and the Reading. As Commissioner Joseph B. Eastman later observed, "The New York Central has a practically clean record of nonaggression. . . ."

[24] The Van Sweringens acquired control of the Lake Erie & Western and the Toledo, St. Louis & Western (and merged them into the Nickel Plate), the Chesapeake & Ohio, the Erie, the Pere Marquette, the Wheeling & Lake Erie, the Chicago & Eastern Illinois, and the Missouri Pacific.

[25] According to what may be an apocryphal story, the adventurous but poorly educated Van Sweringens had intended to name their new holding company after the Allegheny Mountains but could only approximate the spelling. After all the legalities were completed and the certificates printed, a horrified clerk in J. P. Morgan & Company discovered the misspelling—but too late.

lieve have enough knowledge of business and general conditions to know exactly what they are buying."[26] The privileged few on the Alleghany "Preferred List," about 225, were offered Alleghany common stock approximately at cost, $20 a share. Alleghany's official opening price was $24, but the stock was in such demand that two weeks before the corporation even went into operation, it was being sold on a when-issued basis at $35 to $37 a share. In today's Wall Street jargon, it would be called a "hot issue." Among those accepting Morgan's largesse were Charles Francis Adams, who was soon to become Secretary of the Navy under Hoover; William Gibbs McAdoo, who had been Director General of the wartime U.S. Railroad Administration, had served as Secretary of the Treasury, and was soon to become a United States senator from California; William H. Woodin, who was to become Secretary of the Treasury under Franklin D. Roosevelt; Owen D. Young, chairman of the board of General Electric Company; John J. Raskob, a General Motors director and chairman of the Democratic National Committee; General John J. Pershing; Charles A. Lindbergh; members of the Morgan firm, including Thomas W. Lamont; W. C. Potter of Guaranty Trust; and other members of the Wall Street community, including lawyers who had represented the Morgan firm. At the time there was no reason for any of the recipients to think that they would regret the investment opportunity Morgan was conferring on them.

The very prominence of these names, however, was later to provide headlines at a very inopportune time for Morgan. When the "Preferred List" was made public in 1933 during the Senate investigation

[26] Testimony of George Whitney, partner in the firm of J. P. Morgan & Co., May 25, 1933. Hearings before the Committee on Banking and Currency, U.S. Senate, on S. Res. 84 (72d Congress) and S. Res. 56 (73d Congress), "Stock Exchange Practices," 1933, Pt. I, p. 165. Whitney added, "We have never [sold common stock] for very many reasons. The chief, perhaps, is that our reputation in connection with the security business has been on sound investments. We do not think common stock ought to be sold publicly, or by us, at least, for the reason that we think they get into the hands of people who do not know what they are buying. We think, secondly, that if you have an offering of common stock, or perhaps if we did, that that might carry with it some implication of speculations which we would not want to be a party to. Now, I am afraid I have talked a little more than I meant to. . . ."

of the Wall Street banking community (popularly known as the Pecora investigation, after its chief counsel, Ferdinand Pecora), it became a front-page story that scandalized the country. Disclosures such as these led to the passage of the Securities Act of 1933, and the Securities Exchange Act of 1934 (which created the Securities and Exchange Commission).

In early 1929 there was great optimism about the future of Alleghany. The prime reason for its formation was to secure new funds for further expansion, particularly the purchase of the twelve-thousand-mile southwestern Missouri Pacific lines[27]—an undertaking which was a complete departure from any of the proposed national consolidation plans. Undeterred even by the October 1929 crash, the Van Sweringens continued buying until the spring of 1930, when they had accumulated a majority interest in Missouri Pacific. The total cost was $100,000,000. On May 13, 1930, control of the Missouri Pacific passed from Kuhn, Loeb & Company to Alleghany— or as some claimed who viewed such matters more cynically, from Kuhn, Loeb & Company to J. P. Morgan & Company.

Yet, the Van Sweringens could not escape the effects of the crash. On October 23, 1930, there was another severe break in the stock market, and Alleghany led all other stocks in the plunge. In little more than two months it fell from 56 to 10. Still blind to disaster, O. P. was in Boston trying to secure control of the Boston & Maine Railroad as a foothold for the Van Sweringen system in New England. His bankers, aware of the financial loss to which they themselves were exposed, summoned him to New York immediately. On the evening of October 23, the Van Sweringens met with representatives of the Morgan firm and Guaranty at the home of Thomas W. Lamont. The brothers were told they were on the verge of personal bankruptcy and that only a tremendous loan could avert it.

Morgan and Guaranty had already underwritten more than $200,-000,000 in Alleghany and the Van Sweringen Corporation (the real-estate counterpart of the Alleghany Corporation) securities during

---

[27] The Missouri Pacific controlled the Texas & Pacific and the New Orleans, Texas & Mexico (the Gulf Lines) and had a half interest in the Denver & Rio Grande Western.

the preceding year and a half, in addition to providing financing to the individual Van Sweringen roads. With the hope of rescuing their investment, they felt they had no realistic alternative but to rally to the brothers' aid.

After a week of negotiation, it was finally arranged that Morgan would head a syndicate which would supply a "rescue" loan to the Van Sweringens of $39,500,000. From then on, although there was the appearance of Van Sweringen control, the banks were in charge.

On October 31, the day the "rescue" loan was made, there began a series of conferences between representatives of the eastern big four—the Central, the Pennsylvania, the B & O, and the Van Sweringen roads. After a year of conference and compromise, they agreed on an eastern railroad consolidation plan, for which all the parties jointly applied to the I.C.C. on October 1, 1931.

According to a Senate committee report:

> It appears that the agreement was finally clinched as the result of pressure from President Hoover and J. P. Morgan & Co. respectively, the most powerful political and financial authorities in the country. In addition to the prestige of the Presidency, President Hoover's exhortation was lent weight by the terribly depressed economic conditions. The Government and the financial interests alike were desperately striving to check the onrush of the depression, and the railway executives could hardly afford to be pictured as allowing their individual desires to obstruct any move which might be considered helpful in turning the tide.[28]

The Van Sweringens' downfall became more certain in the fall of 1931, when they were unable to pay even the interest on the "rescue" loan. A Morgan office memorandum at that time recounted:

> We and the Guaranty Co. had a talk with the Van Sweringens . . . we have told the Van Sweringens that we see no point to our advancing additional money merely to pay ourselves interest. They have agreed to this and recognize that we are, in effect, the owners of all of their properties and that we shall have to determine policies as to what properties are to be protected, they to help in whatever way possible

[28] Report No. 1182, "Investigation of Railroads, Holding Companies, and Affiliated Companies," Committee on Interstate Commerce, U.S. Senate, 1940, Pt. V, p. 2963.

in carrying out our policies by virtue of their familiarity with the business and assets, particularly the real estate.[29]

When governmental aid became available, the Van Sweringens rushed to use it. In January 1932, the Reconstruction Finance Corporation was established by Congress to provide emergency financing to ailing corporations, particularly railroads. The Van Sweringens, in the words of O. P. at a Senate committee hearing in 1933, were "on the [R.F.C.] doorstep waiting for them to open."[30] Their railroads borrowed a total of $75,000,000. Of this amount $23,100,000 was pumped into the Missouri Pacific alone. At the very end of the Hoover Administration, in March 1933, Congress passed an amendment to the bankruptcy law, Section 77, designed to expedite reorganization of railroads in financial difficulty. The first to avail itself of this new law was the Van Sweringens' Missouri Pacific, which filed a petition in bankruptcy on March 31—less than three years after the brothers had taken it over.

In May 1935, the $39,500,000 "rescue" loan came due, along with an additional $8,500,000 in interest. No interest had been paid after July 1931, and the banking syndicate could have declared the loan in default when the next interest payment came due in the fall of 1931. Instead the banks had chosen to wait. In 1935, however, the Van Sweringens' position had so deteriorated that foreclosure became imperative. The best thing for the syndicate was to withdraw as discreetly as possible. The foreclosure sale was announced in a newspaper advertisement on Friday the thirteenth of September, 1935, by J. P. Morgan & Company on behalf of the banking syndicate. The collateral which the syndicate held, with its controlling interest in Alleghany, would be auctioned off on Monday, September 30. There was strong intimation in the news stories that, with the

[29] Report No. 714, "Investigation of Railroads, Holding Companies, and Affiliated Companies," Committee on Interstate Commerce, U.S. Senate, Pt. III, p. 960.

[30] Testimony of O. P. Van Sweringen, President of the Alleghany Corporation, June 8, 1933. Hearings before the Committee on Banking and Currency, U. S. Senate, on S. Res. 84 (72d Congress) and S. Res. 56 (73d Congress), "Stock Exchange Practices," 1933, Pt. II, p. 766.

sale, the banking relationship between J. P. Morgan & Company and the Van Sweringens would be terminated.

The Van Sweringens did not willingly give up their twenty-three-thousand-mile railroad empire. They issued a statement that they and their associates had "completed arrangements to bid for the collateral at the sale." The prime associate turned out to be a seventy-three-year-old Muncie, Indiana, mason jar manufacturer, George Ball, a director of Nickel Plate since 1932.

The auction itself was one of the most picturesque events, if not the most extraordinary, in American financial history. A railroad empire which had once been worth $3,000,000,000 was being auctioned off in the dingy offices of Adrian H. Muller & Son at 18 Vesey Street in New York. Facing the cemetery of St. Paul's Chapel, the rooms were known as the "security graveyard." Among the four hundred who crowded the auction room were some of the most respected representatives of American finance: George Whitney, a partner of J. P. Morgan & Company; Lansing Reed and F. A. O. Schwarz, partners in Davis, Polk, Wardwell, Gardiner & Reed, attorneys for the creditors; George E. Roosevelt of the executive committee of the Guaranty Trust Co.; Joseph M. Hartfield of White & Case, counsel for the First National Bank; O. P. Van Sweringen, the debtor in chief, whose brother was back in Cleveland mortally ill; George A. Ball, the Van Sweringens' new ally; Colonel L. P. Ayres, Alleghany's director and spokesman at that time for the Van Sweringen interests.

The rest of the room was filled out with four hundred other people. Some were "Wall Street" types of varying interests in the proceedings, but by far the majority were mere spectators.

To those who were aware of what was going on, a certain tension was observable in O. P. Van Sweringen. It was apparent even to the casual observer that he did not have the look of resignation generally associated with the hopeless bankrupt. The critical moment arrived almost with the sound of the auctioneer's opening gavel—the first block of securities to be auctioned carried with it control of Alleghany. The Midamerica Corporation, formed by Ball specifically for the purpose, bid $2,802,101 for this critical lot. The auctioneer hesitated while one of his associates leaned toward the Morgan partners, apparently awaiting a sign. None came. Down banged the gavel, signaling the sale of Alleghany control. From the sudden relaxation visible in Van Sweringen's face, it was now understood by most of those present that the Alleghany empire was his again.

The rest of the auction—an anticlimax—moved to its conclusion. When the auctioneer's hammer fell for the final time, George Ball, through his newly formed Midamerica Corporation, had bought the bulk of the Van Sweringen empire for $3,121,000. The banking syndicate had lost $34,750,000. J. P. Morgan & Company and Guaranty Trust had each lost a little over $9,000,000.

The crowd milled around to congratulate O. P. Now out of breath with excitement, he was still able to say contritely, "I'm sorry it had to be done this way. I'd rather have paid the bills."

The Van Sweringens had managed to persuade Ball to put up the money necessary to buy control of Alleghany and to give the two brothers a remarkable option which in effect would return control to them. For ten years the brothers would have "sole and exclusive" control of Alleghany. And if they were ever able to settle the huge claims enforceable against them—a total of over $70,000,000 was owed New York and Cleveland banks—they could buy the controlling stock at Ball's cost plus 5 percent interest per year.

However, the Van Sweringen brothers did not live long enough to have a chance to recapture their empire. M. J. died in December 1935 and O. P. died eleven months later.[31]

With the Van Sweringens' death, Ball lost all interest in Alleghany and decided to sell. The last vestige of Van Sweringen influence in railroading was about to disappear.

---

[31] M. J. left an estate of only $3067, plus insurance. O. P.'s estate amounted to about $700,000, mainly the proceeds from M. J.'s insurance.

3

The Battle for the C&O Railway Company

IN APRIL 1937, stories appeared in the papers announcing that George Ball[1] had sold control of the Van Sweringen empire to a three-man syndicate—Robert R. Young and Frank F. Kolbe, partners in what the *New York Times* called "one of the lesser-known firms in Wall Street," and Allan P. Kirby of Wilkes-Barre, Pennsylvania, described as "virtually unknown in Wall Street."

The purchase price was $6,375,000, a cash down payment of $4,000,000 and a note for $2,375,000 payable in two years. Of the $4,000,000 cash payment, $3,000,000 came from Kirby, $700,000 from Young, and $300,000 from Kolbe. The syndicate bought, along with other Alleghany securities, 1,933,809 shares of Alleghany common stock, about 43 percent of Alleghany's 4,500,000 shares, which carried working control of the corporation. Behind the two-year note were pledged 1,200,000 shares of the common stock as collateral; the syndicate, however, retained full voting rights in this stock.

The three members of the syndicate agreed among themselves that Young, Kolbe & Co. was to exercise full voting rights and that Young, with a 70 percent interest in the firm, was to manage the affairs of the company. From that moment on, wherever Young sat was the head of the Alleghany table.

Young was born in Canadian, Texas, February 14, 1897. His father was a small-town banker who belonged to the old-fashioned school in his requirements of respect and discipline in children. Young early rebelled against this discipline, complicating his family

[1] It was actually the George and Frances Ball Foundation, a charitable institution which Ball had just formed for tax purposes.

relationships. It cannot be without significance that he was a very slight boy and even as an adult measured less than five and a half feet and weighed only one hundred thirty-five pounds.

His mother died when he was a boy of about eleven. The last time he saw her, he remembered fifty years later, she was being carried out of the house on a stretcher, to be put on the midnight train to Kansas City and the hospital. After her death, his father, either unwilling or unable to control the boy, tried to place him in an orphanage in Denver. It was a traumatic experience for young Bob, and nowhere in any of his writings about his life did Young refer to it.

Once Young's father, who was foreman of the grand jury in Canadian, had a "kangaroo" indictment handed down against young Bob for breaking into the men's club to play billiards (Young's father was also head of the men's club). A fine was deducted from Bob's allowance. Some time later, Young wondered how he could be fined on an indictment without a trial or at least a plea of guilty.

When he was a teen-ager, his father sent him to the Culver Military Academy, still regarding him as a disciplinary problem.

Young was not yet a calculable personality. At the University of Virginia, he dropped out of school in the middle of his second year because, in his own words, he "became too interested in such extracurricular activities as poker, crapshooting, billiards, and bull sessions." Young's father, unhappy about his son's scholastic failure, offered him a job in his bank. Despite the fact that Young was only eighteen, had just married the former Anita O'Keeffe,[2] and had only the prospects of a small inheritance from his grandfather, he refused to be patronized. Instead he went to work for the du Pont Corporation at Carneys Point, New Jersey, as a powder monkey at twenty-eight and one-half cents an hour. Later he explained how he happened to start out with du Pont. While still a student at the University of Virginia, he was passing a bulletin board where notices of summer jobs were posted, and his attention was drawn, as he remembered long afterward, "by an unseen force" to the du Pont letterhead with

[2] The O'Keeffes were a talented family, and Mrs. Young's sister, Georgia O'Keeffe, is probably one of the most honored painters in the world.

"the familiar du Pont red oval of the ammunition cases," as evocative to him as the smell and grip of his Winchester.

In a short time he worked his way into the treasurer's office where he drew himself to the attention of top du Pont executives in a manner typical of his intense enterprise and his attractive personality. Even though his field was finance, he undertook on his own to prepare a written criticism of du Pont advertising, which he decided was violating every fundamental of the art. Young later said that "far from being original, the ideas had virtually been lifted out of the Alexander Hamilton Institute Volume X." He had taken a two-year correspondence course in business administration, and, although he had been too busy with his job to send in his answers to the course's packaged questions, he had read all twenty-four volumes from cover to cover. From this beginning, Young was to develop the art of advertising to enlist public opinion as few businessmen ever have.

During this time, in the early twenties, he lost his inheritance from his grandfather as a result of speculating in securities. Although the inheritance amounted to only several thousand dollars, it was a staggering loss to Young and drove him to study everything he could find on the stock market.

In 1922 Young shifted to General Motors at $100 a week. By 1928 he had become an assistant treasurer and was earning $35,000 in salary and bonus.

One of the men in General Motors who had come to recognize Young's talents was John J. Raskob, chairman of the finance committee. In 1928, Raskob accepted the chairmanship of the Democratic National Committee to direct Al Smith's campaign for the presidency of the United States. A few months later he resigned from General Motors—some suspected as a result of unfavorable reaction in the corporation to his assumption of a major position in Democratic politics. Pierre S. du Pont, chairman of the board of General Motors and head of the du Pont clan, left with Raskob, and the two men opened up offices in the just-completed New York Central Building at 230 Park Avenue. Raskob had always been given much credit for pushing the du Ponts into their successful gamble in motors. Now Raskob and Pierre du Pont were going into a new venture, a private

Robert R. Young and Mrs. Young, the former Anita O'Keeffe, at one of their homes. On the mantelpiece is a picture of their only daughter, killed in an air crash.

(Courtesy of C & O Railroad)

investment company called Equishares. Young joined them as treasurer of the company in the summer of 1929. During those halcyon days of pre-crash 1929, Young turned bearish, but he was apparently unable to convince Raskob of what he considered "the flimsy underpinnings" of the great bull market. Raskob was quoted in the August 1929 issue of the *Ladies' Home Journal* as saying that "not only can anyone be rich but ought to be rich"—all one had to do was put his savings in common stocks. Raskob's unbridled optimism did not impress Young, who sold short. After the crash, when most businessmen were losing their fortunes, Young made his. He not only added considerably to his personal wealth but, more important, gained a reputation as a shrewd financial analyst, particularly among his former associates in the General Motors organization.

Equishares did not fulfill its promise and, in February 1931, was liquidated and its holdings distributed to its stockholders, including Young, on a prorata basis. Raskob then turned his energy to the completion of his brainchild, the Empire State Building. With the self-assurance gained from his prediction of the stock crash, Young became a full-time investor for himself and a few General Motors executives. In late 1932 he purchased a seat on the New York Stock Exchange at a record low price of around $30,000 and formed an investment partnership, Young, Kolbe & Co., with Frank F. Kolbe, who had been a General Motors financial analyst before resigning in 1929 to devote his time to stock speculation. Young, Kolbe was in no sense a general brokerage firm. The seat on the Exchange enabled them to save commissions as they traded for themselves and their few clients.

As early as 1932 Young and Kolbe thought they saw something in the Alleghany Corporation. Intrigued by its potential "leverage," the promise of great returns from small investment, they began to accumulate Alleghany preferred stock, buying for themselves and for their General Motors clients, including Alfred P. Sloan, president; Donaldson Brown, vice president, finance; and John Thomas Smith, vice president and general counsel. Before the year was out, Young and Kolbe and their General Motors clients owned the largest block of Alleghany preferred. With this kind of stock ownership, Young approached the Van Sweringens for representation on the Alleghany board of directors. The Van Sweringens demurred and shunted him over to James Swan, who was president of the Guaranty Trust Company, by then the real power in the Alleghany Corporation. Because of the standing of the General Motors clients, Swan gave Young a very favorable reception. But, as Young later testified, "When we began to talk about an Alleghany directorship, his reception turned cold, and nothing came of it." It was Young's first rebuff from a banker since he had left his father in Canadian, Texas.

In 1935 Young and Allan P. Kirby were introduced by Walter Orr, a senior partner in the law firm of White & Case and tax attorney for both men. Acting on what turned out to be one of the most remarkable of hunches, Orr suggested that they would complement each other and that they examine the possibilities of cooperation. Kirby was heir to a chain-store fortune and had built a thriving Chrysler dealership in Wilkes-Barre, Pennsylvania. Unlike Young, he was a quiet and retiring man who avoided publicity. Young recognized in Kirby not only an enormous source of funds but also a conservative bastion on whom to rely. Kirby divined in Young the dynamics of success. It was the beginning of a close business association which was to leave an indelible mark on the business and economic history of the time.

In early 1937 it became apparent that Ball was ready to sell his controlling interest in Alleghany. Young and Kolbe started negotiations on behalf of a syndicate consisting of the General Motors clients, Allan P. Kirby, and themselves. The General Motors men were to put up most of the money and assume a dominating position; the Young, Kolbe firm was to have one-sixth of the deal, and Kirby a share proportionate to his investment. It was not long, however, before the purchasing group began to fall apart. Arrayed on one side were the General Motors clients, to whom Kolbe had attached himself; opposed were Young and Kirby. The General Motors group offered Young a broker's fee if he would withdraw. Obviously they had no understanding of Young's character.

The basis for the disenchantment of the General Motors group with Young has never been clearly expressed. There are indications that they felt he was "uncontrollable and unpredictable."

The first intimations that the group was trying to remove him from the deal were received by Young while he was wintering in Palm Beach. He rushed to New York to retain Joseph M. Proskauer, head of a prominent New York law firm, a former justice of the Supreme Court of New York, and president of the American Jewish Committee. Proskauer was close enough to the "establishment" to be respected by it and yet sufficiently removed so as to maintain a skeptical objectivity.

For their part, the General Motors group took the precaution of checking with Senator Burton K. Wheeler, chairman of the Senate Interstate Commerce Committee, then investigating railroad financing. Wheeler made it clear that he looked askance at a group of General Motors executives involved in the railroad business. This warning was not wasted. As a direct result, they withdrew completely from the deal[3] and abandoned their plans for "dumping" Young. As John Thomas Smith told Proskauer, the General Motors group "had no desire to stand the gaff of a Washington investigation" and added that Young, Kirby, and Kolbe (who had temporarily reassociated himself with Young and Kirby) were free to make a deal for Alleghany on their own. Young and his associates promptly entered into new negotiations with George Ball, and the deal was made.

What the syndicate bought was a railroad empire with a book value of $3,000,000,000 and with twenty-three thousand miles of track— a total surpassing all the railway mileage in Great Britain. The keystone was the rich coal-carrying Chesapeake & Ohio Railway. There were also the Nickel Plate, the Pere Marquette, the Wheeling & Lake Erie, as well as the bankrupt Missouri Pacific and Chicago & Eastern Illinois. Moreover, Alleghany controlled some two hundred other corporate affiliates in such diverse fields as real estate, coal mining, and trucking.

Still, in 1937 Alleghany was a financial nightmare. It had a debt of almost $80,000,000 in a series of three 5 percent bonds due in 1944, 1949, and 1950; interest on these three bonds alone amounted to about $4,000,000 a year. Moreover, Alleghany was about $22,-

[3] They did not leave Alleghany entirely, however. Their ownership of a substantial amount of Alleghany preferred stock left them in a very strategic position, which was important to Young because of their hostility.

000,000 in arrears on preferred dividends. No dividend had been paid Alleghany preferred stockholders since early 1931, and until the arrearage was paid off, not a cent could trickle down to the common stockholder. Alleghany common, which had sold in mid-1929 for $56 a share, had a net worth of less than nothing,[4] and its price of $4 on the New York Stock Exchange in mid-1937 represented a potential, not an actual, value.

This was the situation when on May 5, 1937, Young, Kirby, and Kolbe stepped into control of Alleghany. That first day all three were elected Alleghany directors, and Young was elected chairman of the board. (By coincidence the Alleghany annual meeting was held the day the syndicate acquired title to the controlling interest of the corporation.) The C & O board, however, was left intact, a decision Young was to regret later. Not until the first vacancy occurred in the fall of 1937 did Young go on the board.

From the beginning Young made it clear he was aiming for the eventual consolidation of all the Van Sweringen roads into the sort of big eastern system which the Van Sweringens had tried to establish in the 1920s, when the I.C.C. was still working on a consolidation plan. Two months after the purchase of Alleghany, Young was expressing the hope that they might be able to merge the Pere Marquette railroad corporately into the C & O and soon thereafter to take in the Nickel Plate. The Missouri Pacific, on the other hand, in Young's view, did not belong in an eastern system, and he indicated that control should be returned to St. Louis "where it belongs."

The first day of Young's control of Alleghany, one immediate obstacle faced the new purchasers, the grilling they expected the next day at the hands of Senator Wheeler's investigating committee. It was widely believed that Wheeler intended to initiate legislation eliminating holding companies like the Alleghany Corporation. During the hearings on May 6, Young insisted that he planned to reform Alleghany, to reorganize and simplify the complex pyramidal structure, and to reduce Alleghany's debts. The Senator in turn spoke critically of the financing of railroad securities by private negotiation

---

[4] Alleghany common equity was minus $100,000,000—or $21.90 a share "underwater."

dominated by the big investment bankers. He asked Young if he would commit himself to competitive bidding in railroad securities.

Young's response, "We are going to shop around and get the best price possible," did not satisfy Wheeler, who said, "That is quite a different thing. Shopping around is quite a different thing from opening it up to competitive bidding. I think, if you opened it up to competitive bidding, it would be exceedingly helpful if it could be done."

Young answered, "We are going to give very serious consideration to it. I do not want to make any commitments here, because I have been an owner for only about twelve hours."[5]

It was not long, however, before Young made competitive bidding his own crusade.

Young's first confrontation with J. P. Morgan & Company took place shortly after his appearance before the Wheeler committee. He received word from his lawyers, White & Case, that Thomas W. Lamont, the senior partner of the Morgan firm, wanted to meet Young and discuss the future of Alleghany. The Van Sweringens had always kept Lamont apprised of their plans, and the banker expected Young to do the same. Young, unwilling to compromise his independence, was reluctant to meet with Lamont. However, he finally gave in to his lawyers' repeated entreaties. He dropped in one day at "the Corner," the familiar name of the offices of J. P. Morgan & Company at 23 Wall Street.

It would have been an understandable reaction if Young was awed by Lamont. Barely forty years of age, Young was for the first time a principal in an important business venture. Lamont, approaching seventy, was already a legend on Wall Street. He was both condemned and praised during the thirties as one of the sixty men who ruled America. His life was part of the American dream. The son of a respected Methodist minister and a loving, intellectual mother, he was a graduate of the right schools—Phillips Exeter and Harvard.

[5] Hearings before Committee on Interstate Commerce, U.S. Senate, on S. Res. 71, "Investigation of Railroads, Holding Companies and Affiliated Companies," Part VII, p. 2310, May 6, 1937.

By the time he was forty, Young's age, he was already a Morgan partner, the pinnacle of the banking profession. He was renowned as a financial statesman, and had been decorated by the governments of France, Belgium, Greece, and Japan, and by Pope Pius XI, who had conferred on him the Cross of St. Gregory the Great.

In his personal life Lamont was known for his enormous number of friendships (his obituary described him as "a man who hated to see a friendship come to an end"), for his tolerance, and for his wide range of interests. One of his sons, with whom he had an affectionate and close relationship, a professor at Columbia University, was regarded as one of the leading apologists for the Soviet Union— even to the point of publicly defending the Moscow purge trials. Lamont had a friendly relationship with such world figures as David Lloyd George, Georges Clemenceau, and General Jan C. Smuts, and with such literary figures as John Masefield, Robert Frost, and Stephen Vincent Benét. He had been an overseer at Harvard for many years. For a time he was the financial support of the *Saturday Review of Literature*. In the worlds of finance and intellect, he moved with grace. He was amused by the "ostentatious display" of his wealthy peers and impatient with the frivolities of "conspicuous waste."

Young appreciated none of this. Instead he saw Lamont through the eyes of a Texas Populist, as the senior member of the House of Morgan, the embodiment of the eastern financial establishment.

Young and Lamont talked about Alleghany's future. Lamont pointed out that J. P. Morgan & Company and Guaranty Trust had originally financed most of the Van Sweringen enterprises and that they felt responsible to the investors for the future well-being of the empire. Young testified later before the S.E.C.,

He wanted to know what my plans were. I told him, "Well, Mr. Lamont, I am working on those plans daily with the Guaranty Trust Company . . . I thought you were informed."

He said, "No. You don't understand me. I want not only to be informed, but I want to help guide you in your policies."

I said, "Mr. Lamont, on the basis of the record down there with Senator Wheeler, I can tell you this: that if it becomes knowledge in Congress that I am sitting down across the table with you and going back and running this empire the way it has been run, and the way you apparently propose to continue to run it, there isn't the slightest hope of our escaping holding company legislation such as was passed in the public utilities and wiped many, many of those security holders out."

Mr. Lamont did not like that and he was clear that he did not like it, but I went on about my business. . . .[6]

Young resented what he regarded as Lamont's paternalism. The Young syndicate had invested their own money and were taking all the risk. He did not consider it Lamont's prerogative to impose his advice, let alone to chastise. So intense was his resentment that he often referred to this meeting as a turning point in his life. He repeated the story of the meeting frequently, even in testimony before congressional committees. He said later that Lamont made him feel "just like a country boy," that he "literally put me on the carpet, spanked me and raked me over the coals for having the temerity to be developing a . . . plan without discussing it with Morgan's." In reporting about this meeting to Allan Kirby, Young made a vow he was often to repeat publicly, that in time he would make Morgan's a tenth-rate bank.

Not long after this conversation with Lamont, Young's control of Alleghany's prime asset, the C & O, began to slip away. Although Young always charged Lamont and J. P. Morgan & Company with the responsibility for this loss of control, the underlying cause was a stock-market crash in the fall of 1937, the worst since 1929. Alleghany was peculiarly vulnerable to the vicissitudes of the stock market because of some very restrictive bond indentures, which the Guaranty Trust Company had written into the Alleghany bonds when they were issued in 1929 and 1930. Practically all of Alleghany's holdings, including its controlling block of C & O stock,[7] were pledged

[6] Testimony of Robert R. Young before the Securities and Exchange Commission, February 18, 1954, opposing the Proposal to Amend Rule U-50 regarding competitive bidding on securities.

[7] Technically the C & O stock was controlled by an intermediate corporation, the Chesapeake Corporation, which was in turn controlled by Alleghany Corporation—an arrangement which was typical of Van Sweringen corporate pyramiding. One of Young's early struggles was to simplify the complex financial structure of the Van Sweringen empire and eliminate the middle company.

as collateral behind the bonds. The indentures required that the market value of the collateralized securities be maintained at 150 percent of the par value of the bonds. If the value of the collateral fell below the 150 percent ratio, then the trustee of the bonds, the Guaranty Trust Company, had the right to assume receiver-like control of the collateral, with the power to impound all income and to exercise all voting rights—in other words, the right to take over control of the C & O from Alleghany.

Young had been in control of Alleghany and the C & O a very short time when Guaranty gave signs that it did not regard him as a proper or trustworthy individual to control such a vast empire, particularly one in which Guaranty had such a huge stake. William C. Potter, chairman of Guaranty, began to give serious consideration to "dumping that shoestring operator Young."

When the November 1937 appraisal date arrived, Guaranty Trust announced that the market value of the collateral behind all three bond issues had fallen below the 150 percent ratio.[8] It thereupon exercised the option of impounding all income and surplus cash; even funds for ordinary office expenses were cut off. Guaranty did not move immediately to exercise voting control of the C & O stock. But, obviously, it was not going to treat Young as generously as it had the Van Sweringens. When the collateral had fallen below the required ratio back in the early thirties, Guaranty had allowed the Van Sweringens to continue in practical control and to vote the impounded C & O stock at the annual stockholders' meetings. Young felt that he was entitled to the same kind of treatment, but the Guaranty Trust Company did not.

Things looked grim for Young and Kirby in late 1937. (Kolbe withdrew from the syndicate that fall and vanished from the Alleghany picture.)[9] They had suffered huge paper losses in their Alleghany investment; they had not acquired the complete control they thought

---

[8] Actually the market value of the collateral behind the 1950 bond issue, mainly stock of the bankrupt Missouri Pacific, had been under the 150 percent ratio continuously for years.

[9] From 1939 until 1959 he was president of the United Electric Coal Company, and he served as chairman from 1959 until 1962.

they were buying; they had received frosty treatment from the railroad and financial communities. The combination of troubles became more than Young could bear. His health collapsed. In his own words, he was "down in heart and in mind and in body and soul." A black and disabling depression temporarily overwhelmed him.[10]

While in this despair, he met one day with Walter Orr in the White & Case office, situated high above Wall Street. When he remained overly long in the lavatory, Orr became disturbed and went to see if anything was wrong. One look at Young's face and the wide-open window was enough to convince the lawyer that he had better accompany Young to Newport. Shortly thereafter Young was placed in a Newport rest home under the care of a psychiatrist.

While Young was hospitalized, a seemingly minor episode occurred which had enormous portent for the future. Allan Kirby made the trip to Newport, but, despite his crucial importance to Young's financial well-being, the physician barred him from the sickroom. Only Young's wife and nurse were permitted access. Kirby thereupon left without seeing his friend.

While some of Kirby's advisers felt he was treated cavalierly, Kirby himself was not offended, and he never abandoned his friend. Financial interests opposed to Young, however, made a cautious approach to Kirby and suggested through his lawyers that he drop his partner. Kirby wired his attorneys, "The answer is no. Play along with Young."

Young's melancholia did not last long. By early 1938 he had recovered and was prepared to come to grips with Guaranty Trust. The contest for control of the C & O first came into the open in March

---

[10] During his illness, he wrote poetry which has been described by Matthew Josephson, an authority on poetry as well as finance, as "in irregular meters and uncertain rhymes, though with a power of expression unusual in a man of stocks and bonds":

Sad are my thoughts, for I am forty, / Sad as the drifting leaves this autumn day. . . ./ Until today it seemed my path led upward, / But now I find myself upon a constant downward slope / Which gains in pitch until I see / Dim, distantly, a void / From which departed friends have turned tired faces, / And love has lost its zest, / The quest of fortune ended, / While none but liars house the halls of state.

1938, a month before the C & O annual stockholders' meeting was scheduled to be held. Young asked Guaranty for the power to vote the impounded stock at the meeting but was refused. Guaranty decided that it, not Young, would vote the shares.

War between Young and the bankers was now formally declared. The Alleghany Corporation filed a petition on March 30 in the U. S. District Court for the Southern District of New York for an injunction restraining Guaranty from voting the impounded stock and from delivering the proxies to anyone but Alleghany. Young claimed that the collateral behind the bonds had been incorrectly appraised and was actually above the 150 percent ratio. He further charged that Guaranty had been unduly influenced by J. P. Morgan & Company.[11] In answer, Potter filed an affidavit denying categorically that he or Guaranty had been pressured by J. P. Morgan & Company or by anyone else. He made it very clear that Guaranty would vote the stock for the election of its own candidates.

On April 6 Alleghany lost its case in the District Court.[12] The next day it appealed to the U. S. Court of Appeals, Second Circuit, from which it secured an order, signed by Presiding Judge Martin T. Manton, temporarily restraining Guaranty from voting the impounded stock until there was a final decision. Young had at least gained some time.

As the date for the C & O stockholders' meeting approached, it became apparent that the temporary restraining order would still be in effect and that neither Alleghany nor Guaranty could vote the contested stock. It would therefore be necessary to appeal to the sixty thousand stockholders for their proxies. The Guaranty Trust Company thereupon enlisted Earle Bailie, a partner in J. & W. Seligman & Company of New York and the head of two investment trusts owning substantial amounts of C & O stock, who was described by Matthew Josephson as "a big, breezy board-room orator who knew how to charm people and win proxies."[13] Two others were

[11] In Young's frequent references to "Morgan–Guaranty Trust," he meant a cabal; he had not the slightest idea that in 1958 the two companies would merge and become the Morgan Guaranty Trust Company.

[12] *Alleghany Corporation* v. *Guaranty Trust Co.,* 23 F. Supp. 203.

[13] Matthew Josephson, "The Daring Young Man of Wall Street," *Saturday Evening Post,* Pt. II, Aug. 18, 1945.

lined up as Guaranty allies: John B. Hollister of Cincinnati, who was an old Harvard Law School chum of Bailie and a partner in Senator Robert Taft's firm, Taft, Stettinius & Hollister; and John L. Dickinson, an attorney from on-line Charleston, West Virginia, known to be friendly to Guaranty. It was Guaranty's intention to replace friends of Young on the board with Bailie, Hollister, and Dickinson. These three men formed what was called "the Bailie Committee" and started soliciting proxies from C & O stockholders for the committee's election to the board. When Bailie indicated he would limit his solicitation in order to keep down the costs, Guaranty convinced him to broaden solicitation to all stockholders, agreeing to share the costs.

Young's former General Motors clients and erstwhile allies, John Thomas Smith and Donaldson Brown, joined the Bailie forces. They felt that they had a score to settle with Young; that Young had eased them out of the Alleghany picture earlier, with Senator Wheeler acting merely as his vehicle.

Young was now in his first proxy fight, and many of the techniques which he developed were to reappear in the future, refined and sharpened. He started a campaign to win over the support of the small stockholders. He charged that owners of C & O stock being held in "street names" (stock listed in the names of Wall Street firms instead of the names of the actual owners) were not always receiving C & O management appeals for proxies.[14] He put solicitors to work telephoning and mailing out proxy material. He appealed to the C & O personnel by charging that Guaranty—and its alleged close associate J. P. Morgan & Company—were temporarily in control of C & O and wished to put in a "new and untried management." He issued statements which put Guaranty on the defensive, charging it with seeking control of the C & O for special corporate benefit. With a knack he was to demonstrate in future battles, he goaded Guaranty into abandoning its traditional reserve. Guaranty executives joined in the exchange of charges and countercharges, some of uncharacteristic virulence. These were

[14] There were rumors at the time that the Securities and Exchange Commission might look into these charges. However, the same problem still existed in 1954 during Young's struggle for control of the New York Central.

reported extensively in the press. Young adopted the technique of the open letter, which, although addressed to the adversary, was actually intended as an appeal to the small stockholder. Aware of the anti–Wall Street bias of the 1930s, Young never lost an opportunity to point out the role of top representatives of the Wall Street bankers in the C & O. The battle came to be referred to in the newspapers as Young's "tilt with Wall Street." Perhaps the single most important factor in this proxy fight campaign was Young's reliance on the power of the newspapers and his ability to win the reporters' interest and sympathy.

On April 19, the scheduled date for the stockholders' meeting, Young had accumulated proxies representing 41 percent of the common stock of the C & O. Although the Bailie Committee had a minority of the vote, it did have a tactical weapon. The C & O bylaws required proxies for over 50 percent of all outstanding stock to establish a quorum. The Bailie Committee, by withholding its proxies, was therefore able to forestall the annual meeting, which was rescheduled for May 10. Again the meeting failed, and for the same reason—lack of a quorum. Young's slate in the meantime had actually lost 4 percent of the proxies because of revocations—due, Young charged, to the Bailie Committee's misleading use of the title "Committee for the C & O Railway Company" on its letters of solicitation to stockholders. A third day, May 19, was set for the annual meeting.

Neither side could be sure how the court would rule on Alleghany's pending appeal to keep Guaranty from voting the impounded stock. This uncertainty plus the possibility of a protracted standoff, with its disastrous consequences for all concerned, finally drove both sides to the conference table. On May 18 the opposing factions settled on a "compromise," the terms of which, it was agreed, would not be affected by the outcome of Alleghany's suit. According to the compromise, all of Young's management slate would be retained on the board but, in addition, the board was to be enlarged to include all three candidates of the Bailie Committee.

The question of whether Young actually lost control of the C & O at this point was later to be closely examined in an I.C.C.

investigation. In May 1938 the newspapers carried stories proclaiming Young the victor. At first blush this would seem to be true, but as a practical matter, both sides knew that there were members on Young's slate upon whom Young could not count. Some were holdovers from the Van Sweringen and Ball boards. There were some whose strict impartiality confused the issue of "who was running the railroad." And the May 1938 "compromise" had added to the board three open opponents of Young.

On June 9 the Court of Appeals ruled against Young, sustaining the lower court's refusal to enjoin Guaranty from voting the impounded C & O stock.[15] But, as agreed to by the parties, the compromise was unaffected by this decision.[16] Young, however, could not be restrained from issuing a statement that the court denial was only a skirmish in Alleghany's campaign against Guaranty.

While the issue of whether or not the compromise caused Young to lose control of the C & O was to be a matter of important contention later on, he still retained significant power, much more than the opposition would have liked. In his role as a member of the finance and executive committees of the C & O, he instituted one of the most important developments in the history of railroad financing.

In the fall of 1938, the C & O was considering a refunding

---

[15] *Alleghany Corporation* v. *Guaranty Trust Co.,* 97 F. 2d 367.

[16] Over fifteen years later, Young provided an extraordinary bit of testimony to the S.E.C. about this case. This may explain why the parties agreed not to be bound by the federal court's decision when they reached their "compromise" on May 18. Young testified that Manton, the first federal judge to be convicted for corruption, had sent his intermediary to meet with him at the Ritz-Carlton Hotel. It turned out to be William J. Fallon (nephew of "the Great Mouthpiece"). "This bag man told me that for $250,000 I could have the decision. The Judge had read our complaint and felt that the merits of the case were on our side but that the banks were calling his loans and he was sorry but if I did not come across with $250,000 the decision would probably go to the Guaranty Trust Company. I immediately communicated with General Donovan, my counsel. There was a conference the next day in which the proposed arrangement was discussed further. A phonograph record was made of the conversation." Donovan thereupon submitted the entire matter to the authorities, who had already begun an investigation of Manton.

operation involving a $30,000,000 5 percent bond issue. Morgan and Kuhn, Loeb had for practical purposes always acted as the investment bankers for the C & O, and there was no reason to think that there would be any change. Accordingly, when the C & O was ready for the bond issue in question, Elisha Walker of Kuhn, Loeb, and Harold Stanley of Morgan Stanley & Company[17] were scheduled to appear at the next board meeting to make their usual representations. As in the past, the performances were expected to be little more than a repetition of previous appearances before the board by the bankers.

Robert R. Young, however, had made up his mind that things were to be different. He had not forgotten his exchange with Senator Wheeler about competitive bidding or his confrontation with Lamont the year before.

As part of the upheaval in Wall Street resulting from congressional investigations and the influence of the Securities and Exchange Commission, some independent bankers began to consider challenging the domination of railroad financing by Kuhn, Loeb and Morgan. Cyrus Eaton, head of Otis & Company, a Cleveland investment banking firm, struck up a warm friendship with Robert Young shortly after the latter's take-over of the Alleghany Corporation. Their views on the "Wall Street Club" were almost identical. Eaton brought Harry Stuart, head of Halsey, Stuart & Co., a Chicago investment banking firm, into the picture and together they supplied Young with a firm bid in writing for the new C & O financing which they knew Kuhn, Loeb and Morgan would not meet. With this document, Young had a trump card for the next C & O board meeting.

For the convenience of those directors who lived in the area of New York City, including Young, the C & O provided a private car to transport them to the November board meeting in Cleveland. Traveling along were Harold Stanley and Elisha Walker. In the conversation on the car, the bankers indicated that their offer would contain the same terms as in previous C & O financing, so that their submission would be little more than a formality. Con-

---

[17] The investment banking spin-off of J. P. Morgan & Company required by the Banking Act of 1933.

siderably more important to the bankers, however, was their failure to agree on whether Kuhn, Loeb or Morgan Stanley's name would occupy the preferred left side of the prospectus and in the "tombstone" ads.[18] When the private car was uncoupled in Cleveland, the bankers still had not resolved whose turn it was to have top billing. During the entire trip, Young never said a word about the Otis and Halsey, Stuart bid he carried in his pocket.

At the board meeting on the following day, when the agenda reached the matter of the $30,000,000 refinancing, Young drew the competitive bid from his inside pocket. From the point of view of the railroad, it was an unusually favorable offer. Eaton and Stuart had committed themselves to underwrite the issue on the basis of $100 to the railroad for a $100 bond bearing interest at 3.5 percent. The underwriters thus would charge no discount. When the offer of Kuhn, Loeb and Morgan Stanley was presented, it was not even close.

When the board indicated that it would prefer to continue its relations with Morgan Stanley and Kuhn, Loeb, Young issued a warning. In the event that the less advantageous bid of the New York firms was accepted, then Young, as a stockholder and on behalf of all other stockholders, would hold the directors personally liable for the difference. Because of Young's litigious reputation, such notice was not regarded as an idle gesture. A recess was called to enable some of the directors to check with their own lawyers

[18] Thirty years later, the February 1968 issue of *Fortune* carried the following about Morgan Stanley:

"Perhaps the best indication of Morgan Stanley's pride in its standing on Wall Street is its policy on the positioning of the firm's name in tombstone ads. An ad of this kind lists the names, in descending order of importance, of the underwriters that participated in a security issue. First comes the manager (or the co-managers), then, in alphabetical order, the firms that took on the largest blocks of the issue. Below these appear arrays of smaller participants. When Morgan Stanley is the manager, its name appears first as a matter of course. When it is a co-manager, it almost always insists on first position. When it is neither—when it is a mere participant, however large— Morgan Stanley almost always insists that its name be omitted from the tombstone ad. In the eyes of the partners, it seems, the only suitable position for Morgan Stanley is at the top."

on the merits of Young's threat and the extent of the directors' personal liability. When the meeting was resumed, the directors, apparently now aware of their own exposure, made it clear that if Walker and Stanley wanted the business, they would have to submit a competitive bid.

The bankers were incredulous. To enter a competition for the underwriting of securities was totally alien to their way of doing business. Walker would not even consider the suggestion. Stanley, after conferring with his office in New York, could only come back with a bid of $95.50 per $100 bond at 3.5 percent interest. Now it was the C & O directors' turn to be stunned. In effect, because of the discount of 4.5 percent, Morgan Stanley was charging $1,350,000 more than the insurgent bankers to undertake the financing.

When the time came to vote, the directors, chastened by the advice of their lawyers, voted to accept the bid of Stuart and Eaton. Bailie and Hollister, still obdurate, were the only two directors to vote for the Morgan Stanley offer.

Young believed that the principle of competitive bidding had prevailed and that in the future it would be the way the C & O would conduct its financing. Actually another skirmish would have to be fought in January 1941, before the principle would finally be established.

Success gave Young confidence. In 1939 he won competitive bidding battles in the refinancing of bonds of the Cincinnati and St. Louis terminals. He engaged in a public letter-writing campaign, urging the terminal companies to open their bond issues to competitive bidding. When the smoke had cleared, Morgan Stanley and Kuhn, Loeb had lost two more battles; Halsey, Stuart was awarded the St. Louis Terminal financing, and Lehman Brothers, the Cincinnati Terminal financing. The St. Louis Terminal battle opened the eyes of a senator from Missouri, Harry S. Truman, who was at that time studying railroad financing as a member of the Senate Interstate Commerce Committee.

Young's successful introduction of competitive bidding provided a powerful example to the United States government. In 1939 the Federal Power Commission adopted a compulsory competitive bidding regulation[19] for electric companies under its jurisdiction, and the same year, upon the recommendation of the F.C.C., Congress imposed a compulsory competitive bidding regulation in the marketing of telephone securities.

The Securities and Exchange Commission was next to take up the matter of competitive bidding in the form of its proposed Rule U–50 under the Public Utility Holding Company Act. Upon the recommendation of its staff that a rule should be adopted requiring competitive bidding in the sale of securities of public utility holding companies, the S.E.C. scheduled hearings for January 27, 1941.

Shortly before the hearings, Cyrus Eaton, on behalf of himself and Robert Young, paid a visit to Thurman Arnold, head of the Antitrust Division of the Department of Justice. He informed Arnold that negotiations were going on between the C & O board members and Morgan Stanley to overturn the previously adopted principle of competitive bidding. He urged that the Department of Justice also take an interest in the matter of competitive bidding in security financing generally. At the moment the most effective way to do this, he said, would be to take a position at the S.E.C. hearings on the proposed Rule U–50. Arnold assigned one of his assistants, Fowler Hamilton, to attend the hearings.[20]

When Hamilton filed his appearance at the S.E.C. hearings on

[19] 18 CFR, Section 34, 1 a.

[20] Hamilton was chosen because only six months earlier he had filed an antitrust complaint against the Pullman interests and had included among the defendants George Whitney, president of J. P. Morgan & Company; J. P. Morgan himself; Richard K. Mellon of the Mellon National Bank of Pittsburgh and a director of the Pennsylvania Railroad; Harold Vanderbilt, a director of the New York Central; and Henry S. Sturgis of the First National Bank of New York.

Another of Arnold's assistants present at the meeting with Eaton urged an investigation of the investment bankers. "The money trust is the worst trust of all because it commands all the other trusts." He pointed out that, with Eaton and Young ready to testify, the Department of Justice had an opportunity that might never be granted again. A decade later, in fact, Young and Eaton were witnesses in the famous antitrust suit against the seventeen major investment banking firms.

January 27, it did not go unnoticed. The *Wall Street Journal* reported:

The presence of a special representative of the Department of Justice's antitrust division created considerable interest at the conference. . . . Questioned later regarding his appearance, Mr. Hamilton explained that the Justice Department keeps a watchful eye at all times on situations where there have been representations that monopoly exists.

The hearings turned out to be in the main a debate between Harry Stuart, Cyrus Eaton, S.E.C. Chairman Jerome Frank, and Senator Truman, on one side, and Harold Stanley of Morgan Stanley, Benjamin Buttenweiser of Kuhn, Loeb, and Emmett F. Connely of the Investment Bankers Association on the other. Chairman Jerome Frank and his supporters had their way, and in April 1941 the S.E.C. adopted Rule U–50.

The next government stronghold to fall to the principle of competitive bidding was in the area of railroad financing. In March of 1943 Senator Shipstead of Minnesota, impressed by the example of Young, Eaton, and Stuart, and helped by Arne Wiprud of the Antitrust Division of the Department of Justice, introduced a bill that would make competitive bidding a requirement in all railroad financing. Opposition began to form in almost every sector of railroad finance. Even the Interstate Commerce Commission submitted a report to the Senate Interstate Commerce Committee objecting to the purposes of the bill. The Commission claimed that the circumstances of each particular case should determine whether competitive bidding should be required, concluding, "There is no need at this time for any legislation requiring the sale of railroad securities at competitive bidding."

Young and his allies, Otis & Company and Halsey, Stuart & Co., took issue with the Interstate Commerce Commission, generating sufficient pressure to induce the Commission to order an investigation.

When the hearings began before the I.C.C. in the fall of 1943, the lineup could almost have been predicted. Appearing against compulsory competitive bidding were representatives of the Morgan Stanley & Company; Kuhn, Loeb & Company; the Metropolitan

Life Insurance Company; the Equitable Life Assurance Society of the U.S.; the Investment Bankers Association of America; the National Association of Securities Dealers, Inc.; the First Boston Corporation.[21] Significant segments of the railroad industry were also in opposition: the New York Central and a number of other individual railroads; the Association of American Railroads; the American Short Line Railroad Association.[22]

Appearing in support of compulsory competitive bidding were representatives of Young's C & O, Nickel Plate, and Pere Marquette; Cyrus Eaton's Otis & Company; and Harry Stuart's Halsey, Stuart & Co.; the Railway Labor Executives' Association; and Senator Truman.

On May 8, 1944, the I.C.C. issued its decision, and Young had won another battle against the compact majority. The I.C.C. ruled that there must be competitive bidding, with a few exceptions, on railroad securities issued in excess of $1,000,000. The I.C.C. report concluded, "While the charges and intimations of monopoly, banker domination, and lack of arm's-length bargaining have not been sustained, the fact is that many railroads continue to give most of their business to one or the other of two leading investment banking firms [Morgan and Kuhn, Loeb] and have failed or refused to investigate the possibilities of other avenues of financing." Now all federally regulated industries were subject in varying degrees to competitive bidding in financing.

In the meantime, the struggle for control of the C & O between Guaranty Trust and Young continued unabated. At the February 1939 nominating meeting of the C & O board of directors, almost one year after the proxy fight, all the C & O directors present except Young voted to enlarge the board again and to elect two

[21] Morgan Stanley was represented by Theodore Kiendl of Davis, Polk, Wardwell, Sunderland & Kiendl; Kuhn, Loeb by Leonard D. Adkins of Cravath, De Gersdorff, Swaine & Wood; the Metropolitan, by its treasurer, Harry C. Hagerty; the Investment Bankers Association, by Arthur H. Dean of Sullivan & Cromwell.

[22] The New York Central was represented by Jacob Aronson, Central vice president, law, and Willard F. Place, vice president, finance; the A.A.R., by John Dickinson, general counsel for the Pennsylvania Railroad.

new directors whom Young opposed. Young believed this was retaliation from "the Morgan-Guaranty sphere of influence" for forcing competitive bidding in C & O financing. The victory which the newspapers earlier had proclaimed for Young was beginning to look empty.

Two months later, in April 1939, an even more ominous development took place. At a directors' reorganization meeting, Young was precipitously and without notice removed from the key executive and finance committees of the C & O. The war between Young and Guaranty Trust had once again flared in the open. The press featured this resumption of battle, and the *New York Times* reported that "the action of the directors in removing Mr. Young from these two important posts, and thus excluding him from the inner circles of the management of the company, was unexpected, and apparently most so to Mr. Young's representatives at the meeting." This action stunned Young, who considered it a direct assault by New York investment bankers.

On May 5, 1939, Alleghany's two-year note to Ball for $2,375,-000—the balance of the purchase price for Alleghany control—came due. Young and Kirby made a decision which, on the face of it, appeared to be an admission of defeat. Rather than pay more millions for a property that seemed to be slipping away, they surrendered the collateral, 1,200,000 shares of Alleghany common. Only 800,000 shares remained in the hands of Young and Kirby. The seventy-six-year-old Ball, in Wall Street's view, was back in control of the Van Sweringen empire.

Still, the epitaphs for Young and Kirby were premature. Two days earlier, on May 3, at the annual stockholders' meeting of Alleghany, the Young-Kirby slate had been elected to serve for another year. The only way Ball could establish control for at least another year would be to launch and win a proxy fight. This would be even more difficult than appeared on the surface. Ball's stock was tied up in litigation, and neither he nor anyone else could vote it. The previous November, Young and Kirby instituted suit against Ball for $5,000,000, charging fraudulent speculation in violation of the Securities Exchange Act of 1934.[23] They accused Ball of inflating the value of Alleghany stock at the time the Young syndicate bought it. As a result of this litigation, the key block of 1,200,000 shares was in limbo, and neither side could vote it.

A reversal in Young's fortunes was becoming apparent. Guaranty, pressured by Young's public charges of conflict of interest, resigned as trustee of two of the three Alleghany bond issues in the spring of 1939. Continental Bank & Trust Company and Marine Midland Trust Company became the new trustees of these bond issues.

Earle Bailie had not yet given up, however. In January 1940, stories which Young regarded as planted by Bailie began to appear in the press indicating that the C & O directors were getting ready to drop Young from the board and replace him with Kirby. This was the familiar gambit of trying to split Kirby from Young. Kirby was offered not only Young's C & O directorship but also the choice of membership on either the executive or the finance committee. However, as in the past, Kirby remained steadfast. "Your proposal," he wrote the board, "is a proposal that ignores the wishes of [Alleghany] and tells the corporation whom it may have and whom it may not have on the board of the railroad whose largest stockholder it is."

Young and Kirby now began to mobilize for another proxy fight. They asked the C & O management to make available the most recent list of C & O security holders. They published an advertisement in the *New York Times* for stock proxy solicitors. They sent letters to all the C & O directors advising them of the probability of a proxy fight. Then, on February 19, 1940, the night before the C & O directors' annual nominating meeting in Richmond, Virginia, most of the interested parties started checking into the rambling old Jefferson Hotel. Young and his party occupied one wing; Bailie and his forces, another. As Carl E. Newton

---

[23] This was the largest suit to have been filed under the Securities Exchange Act. Moreover, Kirby and Young filed additional suits against Ball for an additional $3,000,000.

of Donovan, Leisure, Newton & Lumbard, who was then counsel to Alleghany, later recalled, "There were many conferences and meetings and moving around in the hotel that night, and I don't think anyone can say exactly who met whom or in whose room. It seemed that the whole Jefferson Hotel was taken over by various elements in this situation." He said that the Young forces were determined "to stop Bailie once and for all from making any further attempts to impair Alleghany's control."

Finally, at 3 A.M., Bailie, by now convinced that he was facing the probability of another big proxy fight, to say nothing of a chain of lawsuits, agreed to a compromise. Young was to remain on the slate, the board was again to be enlarged, and three new directors were to be added: Harvey D. Gibson, president of Manufacturers Trust Company,[24] "an independent representative of Alleghany"; Harry C. Thompson, vice president of Continental Bank & Trust Company, trustee of Alleghany's 1949 bonds; and James G. Blaine, president of Marine Midland Trust Company, trustee of Alleghany's 1950 bonds. Although the new directors were in Young's camp, Young still did not have a clear majority of directors upon whom he could rely.

An indication of Young's continued uncertain position was indicated by a one-paragraph item in the *New York Times* on January 21, 1941. Written as a speculative story under the heading "C & O Refunding," it observed that reports were circulating in Wall Street that the C & O was planning to refund the $30,000,000, 3.5 percent bonds which Halsey, Stuart, and Otis & Company had underwritten in 1938 as the result of Young's competitive bidding fight. The fact that there were discussions with "certain underwriters" rather than a request for competitive bids "aroused considerable interest in investment circles yesterday." Actually the finance committee of the C & O was consulting with Morgan Stanley on a negotiated basis. Though Young had been removed from this committee in 1940, he learned of these negotiations and leaked the story to the *New York Times*. Within a day the worst fears of the C & O direc-

[24] Also chairman of the New York World's Fair Corporation (1939).

tors hostile to Young were realized. On January 22, at a board meeting in Cleveland to discuss the refunding plans with a member of the firm of Morgan Stanley, Young showed up with his lawyer, Carl E. Newton. In his most strident manner, Young made it clear that, should the new financing be awarded by negotiation rather than competitive bidding, he as a C & O stockholder would hold every member of the board so voting personally liable. The presence of Carl Newton sitting beside Young provided this notice with more than ordinary substance. The discussion of the new financing was terminated. The *New York Times,* under a two-column head "C & O Refinancing Halted by Young Forces Who Demand Competitive Bidding for Issue," reported the next day:

> While the official announcement after the meeting was that there was "no action," the Young forces were satisfied yesterday that there was no immediate prospect of the C & O selling the proposed issue without competitive bidding.

Young's fortunes now took a dramatic turn upward.[25] By August 30, 1941, he succeeded in eliminating the restrictive bond indentures. This meant that the shackling 150 percent ratio requirement was dropped and the trustees relinquished the impounded C & O stock. The owner of the controlling block of C & O stock could now vote this stock and take over control.

There was one last problem. Who was the owner of the controlling block of stock, Alleghany or Ball? The stock was still tied up in the Alleghany fraud suit against Ball. In March 1942, Ball, now a weary seventy-nine, made a settlement out of court, agreeing to pay over $4,000,000 in Alleghany securities, including almost all of the controlling block of stock Young and Kirby had surrendered to him in 1939. For Young and Kirby it was also a financial windfall. The $4,000,000 recovered from Ball in effect reimbursed them for their initial payment five years before, and

---

[25] However, in 1941 his only child, Eleanor Jane, died in a plane crash. She was described by society writers in 1937 as "the most beautiful debutante in the country." Young never recovered from this loss, which periodically plunged him into uncontrollable grief.

they again owned and could vote the controlling block of C & O stock.

Finally, in April, at the annual C & O stockholders' meeting, Alleghany was able to gain a clear-cut majority on the C & O board. Now there could be no doubt of Young's control. He became chairman of the C & O board and of its finance committee. He replaced six "unfriendly" directors. The removal of John B. Hollister was particularly satisfying to Young. (His other archenemy, Earle Bailie, had died in the fall of 1940.)

A few months later, Young was able to ease George D. Brooke from the C & O presidency.[26] The new president was Young's lawyer and friend, the forty-four-year-old Carl Newton, who since 1938 had steered Alleghany so successfully through all manner of difficulties.

Nevertheless, Young's struggle for control of the C & O was not yet over. Back in 1940 two pieces of legislation had been enacted which were to have a significant impact on Alleghany's future. One was the Investment Company Act of 1940, which brought investment companies under the regulation of the Securities and Exchange Commission; exempted, however, were companies subject to the Interstate Commerce Commission regulation. The second was the Transportation Act of 1940, which, among other things, added to the Interstate Commerce Act a punitive provision, the new Section 5 (4), making it unlawful for anyone to acquire control of two or more carriers except with I.C.C. approval after the effective date of the Act, September 18, 1940.

Under which of these government agencies was Alleghany to be regulated—the relatively conservative, old-line I.C.C. or the crusading, "New Dealish" S.E.C.? It seemed to Young and Kirby at the time that Alleghany had no choice. They believed Alleghany must register under the S.E.C.

Alleghany had never been brought under the jurisdiction of the I.C.C. The 1933 amendment to the Interstate Commerce Act aimed

---

[26] The next year Brooke turned up as chairman of the board of the Virginian Railway, where he was to have a chance to strike back at Young in 1947. See p. 112.

at "non-carriers" like Alleghany had not been retroactive; since Alleghany had acquired control of no railroads after 1930, it had no occasion to come before the I.C.C. The 1940 amendment was not retroactive either, and Alleghany had still acquired control of no new roads. Alleghany was therefore registered with the Securities and Exchange Commission on November 1, 1940, as a "closed-end, non-diversified management investment company."

In early 1944, when Young and Kirby believed their hold on the C & O lines was secure, they were shocked to learn that the I.C.C. was launching an investigation to determine whether Alleghany had lost control of the C & O lines before September 1940, and then regained control after that crucial date without going through the necessary formality of I.C.C. approval. The issue, simply stated, was whether Alleghany's control of the C & O lines was illegal. Young always maintained that this investigation was instigated by his old opponents in the battle for control of the C & O. In 1947 in a speech to the National Press Club, he specifically named John B. Hollister (whom he made a point of identifying as a law partner of Senator Robert Taft). "Now in 1942 we tired of Mr. Hollister's company, and his continued hob-nobbing with the bankers to the injury of our railroad, and replaced him on the C & O board. Whereupon he hurried down here to the Commission and readily persuaded them to bring action against us for taking illegal control of the C & O lines."

Young and Kirby were further dismayed to learn that the I.C.C. had referred the case to the Department of Justice in April of 1944 for possible criminal action against them. There could be little doubt that the Commission meant business when, in its letter to Attorney General Francis Biddle, it included the warning, "The matter is presented at this time so that there may be ample opportunity for consideration before the expiration of the statutory period for criminal prosecution."

Young visited Attorney General Biddle, and, while there is no record of their discussion, the Department of Justice vetoed any criminal action against Young and Kirby. Instead, the meeting marked the beginning of a uniquely cooperative relationship, particularly on matters of antitrust enforcement. Young and the Department of Justice joined forces in opposing the Reed-Bulwinkle bill, designed to exempt railroads from antitrust prosecution in collective rate making. Even more significant, in the antitrust suit against the Western Association of Railway Executives, *et al.* (the A.A.R., J. P. Morgan & Company, Kuhn, Loeb & Company, and the major western railroads, including the Missouri Pacific), the Department of Justice and Young issued a joint communiqué:

> The Attorney General and Mr. Robert R. Young, chairman of the board of the Alleghany Corporation, have conferred on certain questions relating to certain of the charges in the government bill of complaint pending against the A.A.R. and various Western railroads, particularly with reference to the "Western Agreement" under which it is claimed that rates were fixed by the railroads without the authority of the I.C.C. Alleghany Corporation has a substantial investment in the MoPac Railroad, which has been named a defendant in the government's pending case against the A.A.R. and various Western railroads. The complaint filed by the government in that case charged collusive rate fixing and agreements to limit services and suppress technological improvements.
>
> Mr. Young expressed himself as having the view that the public interest and the development of competitive enterprise in this country could be served by a modification of certain practices within the railroad industry.
>
> As a result of the conference between the Attorney General and Mr. Young, representatives of the Department of Justice and of the Alleghany Corporation have begun a series of conferences, with the purpose of formulating a constructive solution to the problem discussed.[27]

Undaunted by the Attorney General's decision to take no criminal action against Young and Kirby, the I.C.C. persevered in its own civil investigation. Assigned by the Commission to hear the case[28] were Commissioner Charles D. Mahaffie and Assistant Finance Director C. E. Boles.

The issue turned on the technicality of time: were Young and Kirby ever out of control of the C & O after passage of the Transportation Act of 1940? Young's entire battle with Guaranty Trust

[27] *New York Times,* October 27, 1944, p. 27, col. 5.

[28] The Alleghany control case was actually consolidated with another proceeding, the "C & O Purchase" case, and was known by that name.

over control of the C & O was reviewed during the hearings. The key point was to determine if Young ever lost control of the C & O and, if so, when.

The I.C.C. position was that Alleghany had lost control to Guaranty Trust in 1938 and did not reacquire control until 1942. Alleghany's lawyer, George S. Leisure, insisted that Alleghany had controlled C & O continuously since early 1929 and therefore was not subject to the 1940 amendment.

To buttress the I.C.C. contention that Young did not have control between 1938 and 1942, John B. Hollister and John L. Dickinson testified that they had been elected C & O directors in 1938 despite Young's opposition and remained in office until 1942, when they were not re-elected.

Two C & O vice presidents, Edward Thomas and W. H. Wenneman, testified that Young held a commanding role on the board of directors between 1938 and 1942. As proof, they cited Young's role in the introduction of competitive bidding in C & O financing during those years.

I.C.C. attorney Joseph J. Doran introduced into evidence a letter Young had written to Guaranty Trust in 1939 which Doran sought to show was an admission by Young that Alleghany had lost control of the C & O to Guaranty Trust and was trying to win it back. He questioned C & O president Newton at length about the last paragraph of the letter, in which Young wrote:

> Please take notice that in the event that you fail or refuse to bring about such resignations [of Bailie, Hollister, Dickinson], you and your agents and associates will be held liable and accountable to Alleghany Corporation . . . for any and all damages and injuries that may be suffered by reason of such failure or refusal in addition to the damage already suffered by Alleghany Corporation . . . by your action in seizing control of . . . the C & O Railway Co. and other properties last year."

Newton explained that Young had written the letter because he feared that the Guaranty Trust, having its "toe in the door," might try to take over control of the C & O.

On March 6, 1945, after taking the testimony of all sides and weighing the evidence, Boles issued his proposed report. His find-

ings were that Alleghany had lost control of C & O at the annual
stockholders' meeting in the spring of 1938 and did not reacquire
control until the annual stockholders' meeting in the spring of
1942—Alleghany was not in control of C & O on September 18,
1940, when Section 5 (4) was adopted. He concluded, therefore,
that Alleghany, Young and Kirby were now in illegal control of
C & O, Nickel Plate, and Pere Marquette and must divest themselves
of these roads.

In support of this drastic conclusion, Boles pointed to a number
of circumstances which existed between 1938 and 1942. He cited
the election of Bailie, Hollister, and Dickinson to the C & O board
in 1938, the 1939 enlargement of the C & O board to include two
new directors, and, even more significant, the removal of Young
from the C & O finance and executive committees. He pointed to
the continued presence of Young's opponents on the C & O board
until 1942 and the running battle between the two factions, particularly on the subject of competitive bidding. He referred to
allegations by Young and Kirby that Ball had defrauded them
in the sale of the Alleghany stock because it did not carry control
of C & O as Ball had represented. Furthermore, Alleghany's C & O
holdings were in the hands of trustees until August 1941 because
of the restrictive bond indentures. It was not until the spring of
1942, Boles concluded, that Alleghany had clear control of the
C & O when, for the first time since 1938, it had a majority on
the board.

If the Commission adopted Boles's recommendations, the result
would be disastrous for Young, Kirby, and Alleghany. In Young's
words, they would be effectively "railroaded out of railroading."

Young read Boles's proposed findings and recommendations with
growing rage, but he recovered sufficiently to charge Boles with
a narrow view of the law and an incorrect interpretation of the
facts. How could Boles say Young had lost control of the C & O
when, during the time in question, he had actually enforced his
views on competitive bidding? He implied that Boles was out of
sympathy with all Young's views—that he was prejudiced.

As violently as Young felt toward Boles, however, he was

still a realist. Under the pressure of the report and the "unfriendliness" of some of the Commission members, he came forward with a compromise settlement. Alleghany would limit its control to "the single transportation system generally known as the C & O lines"—subject to the right of Alleghany to apply to the I.C.C. for control of other carriers. Alleghany and C & O, moreover, would deposit with the Chase National Bank of New York all voting stocks of carrier corporations not affiliated with the C & O system which they already owned or which they might acquire in the future.

There was only a negligible amount of such stock in Alleghany-C & O hands at the time. The C & O owned Erie Railroad stock, which was to go into the Chase trusteeship. Alleghany owned Missouri Pacific Railroad stock, but this road was still in reorganization under the Bankruptcy Act. In the event Missouri Pacific emerged from bankruptcy and Alleghany gained voting control, the Missouri Pacific stock would also have to be put in the trusteeship.

The proposed compromise settlement also provided that there would be no interlocking directors between Alleghany or C & O and any company whose stock was deposited with the Chase. However, these provisions could be modified with I.C.C. approval.

The I.C.C. issued its decision on June 5, 1945.[29] It accepted the proposed compromise and allowed Alleghany, Young, and Kirby to retain control of the roads which formed the C & O system. They would remain in railroading.

The Commission further softened the effect of Boles's findings by acknowledging in its decision the contributions of Young's management to the C & O, Nickel Plate, and Pere Marquette: Young had succeeded in cutting down indebtedness which burdened the system, simplifying the corporate structure by eliminating unnecessary companies, and securing through competitive bidding the best prices possible for bonds and other securities issued by the system companies. The Commision noted that the C & O, Nickel Plate, and Pere Marquette were operating, under Young's man-

[29] 261 I.C.C. 239, "C & O Railway Company Purchase, etc.," June 5, 1945.

agement, at a level of efficiency higher than that of the average of Class I railroads as a whole and that over the preceding twelve years all three had consistently kept ahead in that respect.

The *New York Times* reported that "some observers saw the decision as a moral victory for Robert R. Young and Allan P. Kirby." At the time Young did indeed regard it as a victory, particularly when compared to Boles's recommendation. But the Chase trusteeship was to have profound consequences.

One result of the Alleghany control case was the decision of the I.C.C. that Alleghany was henceforth to be considered a carrier subject to I.C.C. regulation. In October 1945, the S.E.C. accepted the I.C.C. ruling and exempted Alleghany from registration under the Investment Company Act. But it stipulated that the exemption would be revoked if Alleghany ever ceased to be considered a carrier. Now Alleghany was primarily answerable to the I.C.C., and Young and Kirby were to find themselves often in that regulatory arena.

With the conclusion of the control case, it seemed to Young that the way was finally clear for the realization of his ambition to merge the members of the C & O railroad family into the East's third largest trunk line system—a system substantially like the C & O–Nickel Plate system envisioned by the Van Sweringens in the twenties. But this consolidation never came about, even though in the late summer of 1945 the directors of the four roads—the C & O, Nickel Plate, Pere Marquette, and Wheeling & Lake Erie— voted approval of such a consolidation. Young had miscalculated the strength of a group of Nickel Plate preferred stockholders, who were opposed to the terms under which their stock was to be exchanged for C & O stock.[30] They made it clear they would fight

---

[30] The 1945 Alleghany annual report contained the following statement on the proposed exchange of Nickel Plate stock for C&O stock: "Not only was Chesapeake and Ohio's offer more than fair, but it was also in excess of anything that the Nickel Plate stockholder may ever hope to receive. Before this proposal could be submitted to the stockholders or to the Interstate Commerce Commission, organized opposition developed. It was led by a number of foreigners, now residents of America, who acquired Nickel Plate shares in recent years at low levels. These holdings have appreciated

the consolidation at the Nickel Plate stockholders' meeting, before the I.C.C., and in the courts. The merger was dropped.[31] The long-dreamed-of C & O–Nickel Plate system was dead.

substantially in anticipation of an offer by Chesapeake and Ohio for Nickel Plate stock. Unwilling to meet the unpredictable terms of this holdup group, Chesapeake and Ohio was reluctantly compelled to withdraw its proposal for unification of the four roads."

[31] In 1947 Alleghany and C&O sold their holdings in Wheeling & Lake Erie to the Nickel Plate. The Pere Marquette was merged into the C&O in June 1947. In November 1947 the C&O divested itself of its 57 percent interest in Nickel Plate common stock by distributing it to the C&O stockholders in the form of a special dividend. In December 1949 the Wheeling & Lake Erie was merged into the Nickel Plate.

4

The Battle for the Pullman Company

IN THE SPRING OF 1945, while waiting for the I.C.C. decision in the Alleghany control case, Young began preparing a position to which he could retire in the event of a setback. Among the options under consideration was the purchase of the Pullman Company, which owned and serviced, for practical purposes, all the sleeping cars of the country.

The Pullman Company fitted squarely into Young's hopes and plans for the future of railroading. Frequently he had expressed the opinion that the mind of the typical railroad executive was as antediluvian in operations and innovations as that of the banker who sat on the board and dominated him. V–E Day, marking the end of World War II in Europe, was approaching, but, according to Young, the railroad industry had "not the wit nor the imagination" to realize that an entirely new passenger plant would be needed to take care of the anticipated postwar travel boom. While the railroads slept, the airlines would fill the void. There was a real fear that the pre-emption could be permanent. Betrayal of the stockholders once again was in prospect.

Young was already formulating in his mind concepts of lightweight passenger cars and dramatic new fuels to be used in even more dramatically new locomotives. He thought in terms of the elimination of tipping which, from redcap to porter to steward, had irritated generations of travelers; the introduction of credit cards; and more efficient ways of processing reservations. Furthermore, why shouldn't passenger trains have radios, motion pictures, and libraries?

Of all of Young's dreams for passenger service the one he

dreamed the hardest was for a transcontinental service in which coast-to-coast travelers would not have to change trains or stations at Chicago, St. Louis, or New Orleans. With control of the Pullman Company he could smash the invisible barricade that ran down the middle of the country from Canada to Mexico.

So intrigued did Young become with the opportunities offered in controlling the Pullman Company that he decided to make its acquisition a major effort.

The Pullman Company was for sale as the result of a federal court decision in 1943 holding that the Pullman interests were in violation of the antitrust laws. The case had grown out of the New Deal antimonopoly crusade sparked by Thurman Arnold. The complaint filed on July 12, 1940, charged the existence of an illegal monopoly in the manufacture, ownership, and operation of the sleeping cars of the United States. Named as principal defendants were Pullman, Inc., the parent company, and two wholly owned Pullman subsidiaries, the Pullman Company, owner and operator of the sleeping-car business, and Pullman-Standard Car Manufacturing Company, the manufacturer of sleeping cars. Prominent among the defendants were the directors of the companies cited, including Harold S. Vanderbilt, J. Pierpont Morgan, George Whitney, Richard K. Mellon, H. S. Morgan, and Henry S. Sturgis

The Pullman empire had risen from modest beginnings. George M. Pullman, a house mover in Chicago, suggested in 1858 to the Chicago & Alton Railroad that, as an experiment, he remodel two-day coaches into sleepers, including the addition of upper and lower berths. So successful was Pullman that he soon expanded his operations to the Michigan Central, the Chicago, Burlington & Quincy, and the Chicago & North Western. In 1887 he found it desirable to incorporate and formed Pullman's Palace Car Company. Two years earlier the New York Central had formed its own sleeping car company to compete with Pullman. In time the New York Central Sleeping Car Company evolved into the Wagner Palace Car Company, by far Pullman's major competitor. However, Pullman, as noted in the West Shore fiasco,[1] did not take kindly

[1] See p. 16.

to the competition. In a more successful undertaking he began an aggressive campaign of acquisitions. By the end of the century, the Pullman Company, following its founder's plans, had swallowed all of its competitors, including even the Wagner Company. It now had the sleeping car business firmly in its grip.

The monopoly of sleeping car service then led to a monopoly of sleeping car manufacture. The Pullman Company accomplished this by the simple expedient of refusing to service the cars of any manufacturer other than those of its own affiliate, Pullman-Standard. No railroad dared oppose the power of Pullman by purchasing sleeping cars from any other manufacturer and thereby risking the loss of service.

While any railroad presumably could cancel its contract with Pullman and operate its own sleeping car service, according to the government this was an illusory power. The Pullman Company so arranged and staggered its contracts with the railroads that "in practical effect there is no cancellation privilege." For verification, the government pointed out that in recent years no such contract was ever canceled.

Pullman could exert an even more persuasive and direct influence on the railroads. Most sleeper traffic moved over the tracks of several railroads. As the complaint noted,

A substantial part of all sleeping car travel involves the use of connecting carriers. Even if a railroad could prepare to operate its own sleeping car service, it would be unable to send its sleeping cars over the lines of connecting carriers with which the Pullman Company has contracts, or if these Pullman contracts were abrogated, without then entering into numerous complicated contracts for exchange of cars.[2]

It was the Pullman Company, therefore, that had the final word on whether sleeping cars could interconnect between different railroads. The implication was clear that the Pullman Company was responsible for the lack of coast-to-coast sleeping car service, a lapse that compelled generations of travelers crossing the country to change trains and stations at Chicago, St. Louis, Memphis, or

2 Complaint, *U.S.* v. *Pullman Company, et al.*, Civil Action No. 994, U.S. District of Pennsylvania, pp. 11–12.

New Orleans, lugging their baggage with them. The government's complaint further alleged:

The Pullman Company has plenary power to deprive railroads of sleeping car service and to force undesirable rolling stock and onerous terms on recalcitrant railroads. No railroad of any size can afford to be deprived of Pullman service or to be discriminated against. . . . This power of The Pullman Company is so great that its very existence, apart from any threats or positive action by The Pullman Company . . . is alone sufficient to force railroads . . . to comply with policies favored by The Pullman Company. . . .

Defendants have stifled competition in the manufacture, sale, lease, and operation of modern lightweight, streamlined, high-speed trains and rolling stock . . . and defendants have unreasonably retarded the growth and development of a supply of modern passenger coach and sleeping cars in the United States.[3]

In addition, Pullman's power was strengthened through interlocking directorates between the Pullman companies and certain railroads, suppliers, and investment and commercial banking interests.

At the close of the long list of charges, the government demanded as relief the divorce of the business of operating sleeping cars from the business of manufacturing these cars "in such a manner and to such extent that the efficiency of a single operating pool of sleeping car equipment under responsible and unified management may be preserved and maintained and that effective competition may be created and maintained in the future in the manufacture and sale of sleeping car equipment. . . ."

After the usual legal preliminaries, which included a number of abortive attempts to settle the case by a consent decree, the Pullman case went to trial on November 3, 1941, before a three-judge expediting court in the United States District Court for the Eastern District of Pennsylvania in Philadelphia. The judges assigned were Circuit Judges Herbert Goodrich, Albert Maris, and John Biggs.

Fowler Hamilton, after presenting a detailed explanation of the various counts in the complaint, concluded:

[3] *Op. cit.*, p. 12.

Finally we will also endeavor to demonstrate that one of the factors that sustains the manufacturing monopoly is the cluster of corporations with which Standard is affiliated, through interlocking officers and directors, as a result of its connections with such power groups as J. P. Morgan & Company, First National Bank of New York, Mellon Securities Company; such powerful railroads as the New York Central and Pennsylvania; and such powerful industrial concerns as United States Steel, du Pont, Montgomery Ward, Aluminum Company of America and United States Gypsum. We will argue that no company interested in securing either trade or finance would care to incur the ill will of so powerful a group.

During the protracted trial, Hamilton constructed an impressive case in support of the government's allegations.[4] He sought to demonstrate that the banking interests represented on the Pullman board of directors were able to exert influence on certain major railroads, particularly the New York Central and the Pennsylvania. The Central was pictured as a Morgan road and the Pennsylvania as a Mellon road. Pullman director and defendant Henry Sturgis, vice president of the First National Bank of New York and a director of the Erie Railroad, also came under government fire for his railroad-banker affiliations.

On April 20, 1943, the three-judge court handed down its decision.[5] It held that the defendants had illegally monopolized the manufacture and operation of the sleeping cars of the nation.

The sum total, it is clear, constitutes a complete domination by the defendants of a limited but important market. They have full control, they have the power to exclude, they have exercised the power and they, by all this, violated the provisions of the Sherman Act.

But the court held back on delivering the *coup de grâce* for the Pullman companies. It was not yet ready to spell out the nature of the relief. Instead it set forth a number of points to be considered at a future hearing. Among these were the possible separation of the business of the Pullman Company, which serviced the sleeping cars, and Pullman-Standard, which manufactured them; the right of

[4] One of the judges later described it as a classical prosecution of an antitrust case.
[5] *U.S.* v. *Pullman Co., et al.*, 50 F. Supp. 123.

any railroad to operate and own its own sleeping car business; compelling the Pullman Company to "furnish through-line sleeping car service to any railroad or group of railroads." This concern the court emphasized:

> We cannot conceive that the travelling public would submit to sleeping car changes each time the traveller left one railroad line and continued his journey on another.

Briefs were then filed by the parties submitting proposed decrees. The government strongly contended that Pullman, Inc., be compelled to dispose of the manufacturing business as the most effective remedy. On January 22, 1944, Judges Goodrich and Maris decided the issue, with Judge Biggs dissenting in part.[6] The court found unanimously that the public interest required a "complete separation in ownership and direction of the business of manufacturing and the business of operating sleeping cars." But the majority, with Biggs dissenting, held that Pullman, Inc., should be permitted to decide whether to divest itself of the manufacturing or operating subsidiary. It rejected the government's contention that the public would best be served by requiring Pullman to dispose of its manufacturing affiliate.

Relief should be remedial, not punitive. "Separation is a necessary element in the remedy. But there is no reason, in protection of the public interest, why the separation needs to be made more difficult than necessary for the defendants nor against their judgment of what is in their best interests."

Judge Biggs disagreed. "In my opinion we should decide what company or companies should be divested." He supported the government's recommendation that Pullman, Inc., should be compelled to sell its manufacturing business. He reasoned that Pullman, Inc., would most likely choose to sell the service company. In that event the new management might not be sufficiently skilled to prevent dislocations "of a service the maintenance of which at this time and under present circumstances [World War II] has taxed the skill and ingenuity of even the present highly trained directing personnel of Pullman Company." Moreover, Biggs feared that the ending of the

---

[6] *U.S.* v. *Pullman Co., et al.*, 53 F. Supp. 908.

monopoly would be delayed by the difficulty in finding a proper purchaser for the service company.

It will be difficult to find a purchaser for Pullman stock unless it be the railroads or interests representing them. In any event there must be delays in effecting the sale. Pullman Company stock will be found to be not readily salable whoever the purchaser may be.

On May 8, 1944, the court entered final judgment[7] and gave Pullman, Inc., ninety days to decide which branch of the business it would sell.

Following the news of this order of the court, the stock of Pullman, Inc., took a spurt upward on the New York Stock Exchange. Pullman, Inc., satisfied to be given the choice of which company it would keep, then accepted the decision of the court as final and abandoned any attempt to appeal the verdict to a higher court. To no one's surprise, the board of directors of Pullman, Inc., meeting on July 19, 1944, elected to divest itself of the sleeping car service. Accordingly, on August 30, 1944, Pullman's president, D. A. Crawford, addressed a letter to "The Railroads Now Being Furnished With Sleeping Car Service Under Contract With The Pullman Company," suggesting that they form a buying group to take over the business of the Pullman Company. The sale to the railroads would "provide opportunity for the continuance of the centralized pool system of sleeping car operations under a going, experienced operation." The railroads would represent the best group to maintain the high standards of service. The main reason, however, was the unquestioned financial responsibility of the railroads. Since the offers by the potential buyers were not for "all cash" but involved a deferred payout, the sufficiency of their credit would be a matter of concern to Pullman, Inc. For legal and financial reasons, the assets rather than the stock were for sale.[8]

---

[7] *U.S.* v. *Pullman Co., et al.,* 55 F. Supp. 985. Judge Biggs still dissented in part.

[8] The offer by Pullman was set forth in twenty-two pages plus exhibits. It specifically did not include the Pullman interests in the Railroad Rolling Stock Patents Corporation formed jointly by the New York Central Railroad, the Pennsylvania Railroad, the Chrysler Corporation, and the Pullman Company.

The Pennsylvania Railroad promptly replied that it would not accept Pullman's offer but instead would plan to own and operate its own sleeping car service. Pennsylvania's persistence in this decision would be a serious blow to the continuation of the sleeping car pool.

For the moment the railroads took no discernible action, although they appointed three Special Pullman Committees, from the East, South, and West, to study the offer. However, until the regional committees understood the antitrust ramification as well as the financial and technical considerations involved, it was determined to maintain a cautious interest. It was not ready to risk the government's wrath by substituting itself for Pullman.

On September 30, Pullman, Inc., presented to the court its plan to sell to the railroads, but the plan would not come up for court hearings until the following March. Fowler Hamilton appeared for the Department of Justice in opposition to Pullman's plan, characterizing it as simply a "gesture of compliance," an evasion of the decree and a violation of its spirit as well as its legal force. Hamilton then demanded that if it did not produce a sales contract for the servicing business within a year, the court require Pullman, Inc., to sell its manufacturing business.

On March 22, 1945, the court, without ruling on the offer to the railroads, gave Pullman, Inc., one year to dispose of the stock or assets of the Pullman Company. The court ordered Pullman to treat with "the railroads or any other persons" in such a sale.

Pullman, Inc., repeated its offer to the railroads on May 12, but this time it called for the sale of the stock instead of just the assets. But, in the words of Pullman President D. A. Crawford, this offer was met "with prolonged inactivity on the part of the Special Pullman Committees. . . ."

The time had now come for Robert Young to make his appearance once again. "Alarmed at the jeopardy in which the continued policy of delay was placing the Alleghany system," he decided to make a place for himself in the Pullman picture. He called on Gustav Metzman, president of the New York Central, and George Whitney, president of J. P. Morgan & Company. Young was not unmindful of the fact that Harold Vanderbilt and George Whitney were directors both of the New York Central and Pullman, Inc.—and, in Young's opinion, the dominant figures in both. From Whitney and Metzman, Young learned that the railroads had no real plan regarding the sleeping car business. Distressed, Young asked Whitney to arrange a meeting with Crawford. This Whitney did.

At the meeting Crawford confirmed the fact that the railroads had presented no plans to purchase the sleeping car business. As Young later related,

I then told Mr. Crawford that with V. E. Day [May 8, 1945] behind us and V. J. Day not far away I could not, as a railroad official, sit idle and see the sleeping car situation deteriorate further. Therefore, if it was necessary to break the deadlock and get action, we were prepared to organize a syndicate to purchase the Pullman Co.'s equipment and offer a new and progressive pool service for the benefit of the railroads of the country.

Crawford agreed with Young on the urgency for action but demurred on opening negotiations with him. He had authority from his board to deal with the railroad group and no other.

Crawford made it quite clear to Young, however, that he was hopeful that the railroad's Special Pullman Committees would form a buying group shortly. In the meantime, Crawford told Young, the inactivity of the railroad group was caused by the conflict between two schools of thought. One was headed by the Pennsylvania, which believed that the pool of sleeping cars should be broken up and the individual railroads should run their own service. The other was headed by the New York Central, which urged that the pool should be maintained.

Young offered to "break the deadlock." Would Crawford go back to his board and see if he could secure authority to negotiate with Young?

At the June meeting of the Pullman board, Crawford reported on Young's proposal, which included a request for a thirty-day exclusive option. Crawford also reported to the board that Pullman had been previously approached by some other groups with requests for similar options. Among these were Glore, Forgan & Company; Morgan Stanley & Company; and Standard Steel Spring Company. Crawford recommended, and the board concurred, that the request for an option by all the purported buyers, including Young's, be denied and their offers tabled for the time being.

Shortly thereafter, Pullman sent out a formal notice to all the railroads supplied with sleeping car service that their contracts would be terminated at the end of 1945; that while the sale of the Pullman Company was still in abeyance, short-term contracts would bridge any gap.

Willard F. Place, vice president, finance, of the New York Central, acting for the three regional committees, then called a meeting for August 14 in Washington, D.C. The group voted to recommend to the court that the sale be delayed for another eighteen months beyond the March 1946 deadline—or to about September 1947. The rationale behind this request was that nothing should be done until the war was over. Later, at a hearing before the I.C.C. on the matter, Young was to note sarcastically that August 14 was the day Japan surrendered. Place's exasperated reply was, "How were we to know the war would end on that day?"

The recommendation by the regional committees was enough to convince Young that delay was to be the gambit of the railroads in frustrating the court's decree. On August 27, 1945, Young and Kirby, once again in conjunction with Cyrus Eaton's Otis & Company, formally petitioned the court with a proposal to submit a bid to purchase the Pullman Company.

The petition was filed by Thurman Arnold, former head of the Antitrust Division, under whom the government's antitrust suit against Pullman had been instituted. Since then he had been appointed a judge of the United States Circuit Court for the District of Columbia. In June 1945, he had resigned from the bench to enter the practice of law. With Arne Wiprud, former head of the Transportation Section of the Antitrust Division, he formed the law firm of Arnold and Wiprud. Robert Young, Allan Kirby, and Otis & Company were among their first major clients. Because Arnold had signed the complaint in the Pullman case, he first refused to take the case, even though Young and Eaton argued that five years had elapsed since he and his associates in the Antitrust Division had initiated the suit, and more than two years had elapsed since he had resigned from that division. But Young and Eaton finally convinced Arnold and Wiprud that it was their obligation to fight through to a successful conclusion the battle begun by the government. Otherwise the government's "victory" would have been in vain.

Arnold's first move was to file a petition to the court that his clients would meet the Pullman offer made earlier to the railroads. The Pullman fleet of heavyweight sleeping cars was obsolete. To meet the competition of other modes of transportation, the antiquated cars would have to be scrapped and replaced. The Young-Kirby-Otis group would expend $500,000,000 to do so. Because of a single ownership, the advantages of the pool would be retained. The petition then noted that

through-line sleeping car service is a "modern essential" in rail passenger service for, as the court points out, it is inconceivable "that the traveling public would submit to sleeping car changes each time the traveler left one railroad line and continued his journey on another." Yet that is just what any passenger traveling by railroad between the East and the West is compelled to do today at the Chicago, St. Louis, and New Orleans gateways. The challenge of national air transport will encourage national rail passenger services with no delays or changes at these gateways.

To make the coast-to-coast service truly attractive, libraries, radios, telephones, motion pictures, and other innovations, including credit cards and no tipping, would be provided, as Young had earlier envisaged.

Of critical importance was Young and his associates' readiness to act immediately. Only by prompt action could the railroads meet the competition of air and bus for the postwar passenger market.

No sooner had Arnold filed the petition to purchase the Pullman Company than Young fired off a telegram to the presidents of all the railroads involved, seeking meetings to discuss new sleeping car contracts in the eventuality the Young offer prevailed.

Although Young was rebuffed by most of the railroads, the Pennsylvania Railroad officials did agree to meet with him. President Martin W. Clement informed Young at a meeting on September 12 that the Pennsylvania felt it necessary to own and operate its own sleeping cars. Clement said he was opposed either to all the railroads or any one railroad interest—including Young—owning the entire sleeping car service.

On September 19 Willard F. Place sent a memo to all the participating railroads of the regional committees expressing the view that, while individual operation and ownership might be the ultimate solution, the Young-Otis offer precipitated a crisis calling for prompt action: ". . . the railroads appear to be faced with the necessity of immediate action as a result of the petition made by the syndicate of Otis & Company. . . ." The railroads must act together. Individual purchasing of sleeping cars would take too long and would be too complicated.

Place's memo brought results. Before September had ended, the railroads had formed a governing committee—called the Place Committee after its chairman—to organize a buying group.

After learning of the governing committee's formation, Young asked for an immediate meeting. On September 27 Young and William Daley, President of Otis & Company, met with the Place Committee in the board room of the New York Central, on the thirty-second floor at 230 Park Avenue. It was Young's first visit to that august chamber, richly paneled in oak and presided over by portraits of the Vanderbilts.

Young told the committee that the railroads had not in the past taken advantage of their mass purchasing power. If the railroads would cooperate with him, it would be to the advantage of both. "I am here to break a deadlock and give such service as I can and will handle it the railroads' way if they insist, even though it means only sweeping out the cars." The Place Committee listened to Young with impassive politeness. Its only response was to agree to send him the minutes of the meeting.

Spurred by Young's offer for Pullman, a number of other interests also acted. On October 13 Glore, Forgan & Company made a bid for the entire capital stock of the Pullman Company. Shortly thereafter the Standard Steel Spring Company filed a comparable offer.

On October 18, a month after Place's warning, twenty of the main railroads of the country, constituting 80 percent of the sleeping car business, entered into a memorandum agreement setting up an unincorporated Buying Group of railroads.

By October 27 the Buying Group completed its arrangements and, acting through Place, made a formal offer to purchase the capital stock of the Pullman Company, but with conditions concerning methods of computation of depreciation and deferred maintenance. Because of this reservation, Pullman declined the offer, despite its preference to sell to the railroad group. Nevertheless, the Buying Group pushed ahead, and a petition was filed with the court in its name by four leading railroad lawyers: Jacob Aronson, vice president, law, of the New York Central; John Dickinson, general counsel of the Pennsylvania; Emmet McInnis, general counsel of the Atchison, Topeka & Santa Fe; and Sydney E. Prince, general counsel of the Southern.

The Pullman board of directors met to consider the various offers. Harold Vanderbilt, George Whitney, and Henry Sturgis this time did not participate because of their conflicting interest as directors of railroad companies. In any event, the Pullman board took no action on any of the proposals.

In early November the court heard the merits of and objections to the proposals to buy the Pullman Company. Over fifty lawyers appeared on behalf of the various parties, including the government. It soon became clear that the battle had narrowed down to two contestants—the railroad Buying Group, supported by Pullman, on one side, and Young-Kirby-Otis & Company, supported by the United States government, on the other.

Central's Gustav Metzman, testifying for the Buying Group, in answer to a question from Central's Jacob Aronson, acting as counsel for the Buying Group, contended that if any organization other than the railroads was awarded the Pullman Company, "the railroads are at the mercy of an outside organization which is imposed upon it against its will for the performance of one of its own functions. If such an outside organization is armed with the ownership of the only presently available sleeping cars, the railroads are robbed of the opportunity of protecting their important financial interests and public service obligations. . . ."

Holmes Baldridge, attorney for the government, charged that sale to the Buying Group would merely substitute one monopoly for another. What is more, the larger railroads like the Pennsylvania and the Central would have the power to discriminate against the smaller roads. Thurman Arnold, on behalf of Young and Otis & Company, echoed this theme, emphasizing the dominant position of the New York Central and the Pennsylvania and the interlocking relationship of the directors of Pullman and the banking institutions.

Young, testifying for his group, concentrated on the kind of service to which he believed the public was entitled. He would inaugurate a $500,000,000 program for new equipment. If the airlines could spend $750,000,000 for new equipment, "the railroads should blush if they aren't ready to spend $500,000,000."

Young charged that the entire capacity of the sleeping car manufacturing industry probably did not exceed four cars a day. He would change all that by ordering thousands of new cars, thereby stimulating new companies to enter the field. The railroad industry and the public would benefit by the expansion. New enterprises would spread from the new travel opportunities as "ripples spread over a pool."

Young did not stop with this picture of what might appear to be a brave new world of travel. He also had a knack for immediate reality. He now made an all-cash offer of over $75,000,000 for the Pullman Company without conditions. Such an offer, clearly better than any other, placed Pullman and the railroads in a delicate position.

Young's dramatic act, in the words of C. R. Harding of the Southern Pacific, a member of the Governing Committee, "swept away the bargaining position" of the railroad Buying Group. One day after the court hearing, the railroads capitulated. In a letter to Crawford signed by F. G. Gurley of the Atchison, Topeka & Santa Fe, Metzman of the Central, and Ernest E. Norris of the Southern, they withdrew the conditions of Willard Place's letter of October 27 and instead stated,

. . . we beg to supplement said letter of Mr. Place as follows:

The undersigned, acting on behalf of the Buying Group of railroads, hereby accept your said offer of May 12 to sell the stock of the Pullman Company, paying for the same in full in cash. . . .

Pullman promptly notified the court that it had accepted the new offer of the Buying Group. Young followed immediately with the announcement that he would carry the fight to the I.C.C. and, if necessary, to the Supreme Court.

Young then introduced a new dimension to the controversy. He carried the fight to the public. On November 16, over the name of the Chesapeake & Ohio Railway and the Nickel Plate Road, he placed a quarter-page advertisement in fifty-five key newspapers, with the headings:

WHY SHOULDN'T AMERICA HAVE THROUGH SLEEPING CAR SERVICE FROM COAST TO COAST?

CHESAPEAKE & OHIO AND THE NICKEL PLATE STAND READY TO JOIN WITH OTHER RAILROADS TO START THIS SERVICE WITHOUT DELAY!

INVISIBLE LINE DIVIDES AMERICA.

When Young had informed his staff about his idea for this advertisement, the lawyers for the C & O Railway, under whose auspices the ad would appear, pointed out that it contained elements that could be regarded as contempt of court. The Pullman issue was before the court, and such an advertisement could be construed as improper pressure. They compelled Young, therefore, to avoid any mention of the antitrust action or the applications to the court for the purchase of the Pullman Company. The implied criticism of the Interstate Commerce Commission also bothered the lawyers.

Young knew, however, that he had within his grasp a matter of great public interest. He sent a proof of the ad and a letter inviting comment to every member of the U.S. Senate and House of Representatives as well as to over six hundred prominent businessmen. He also sent them to major newspapers and magazines. The response was encouraging, with only one unfavorable editorial.

For the remainder of the year 1945, the battle continued in the courts. With Pullman and the Buying Group now in agreement, they turned to an attack on Young and Otis & Company. They pointed out in oral arguments and in briefs that the Young-Otis group would merely continue the monopoly; that Young would favor his own railroads—the C & O, Nickel Plate, and Pere Marquette. What is more, here was a deal involving a purchase price of over $75,000,000 and a promise to spend $500,000,000 for new equipment. In the face of this, Otis & Company had a net worth of only $1,500,000.

Young and Otis & Company hammered away at the Buying Group, charging the "New York Central, Pennsylvania, Morgan" interests with a sit-down strike against expanding sleeping car service and with slowing down the aggressive promotion of passenger travel.

The government's attorney, Holmes Baldridge, argued that the Young-Otis offer was preferable, particularly because of its $500,-000,000 plan for new equipment and a guarantee to maintain the sleeping car pool. "This pool appears to be essential to the smaller roads if they are to offer adequate sleeping car service." Baldridge was not unmindful of the problem of Young's control of several railroads and the opportunity for favoritism. But he noted that Young had already testified "that in the event the court should decide" in their favor, Young and Kirby "would consider retirement from the railroad field." To permit the railroad Buying Group to take over the sleeping car business, Baldridge warned, would result "in a more vicious monopoly" than the one Pullman held for half a century. His argument was emphasized by a recital of the interlocking directorates of the Pullman Company, New York Central Railroad, Pennsylvania Railroad, Erie Railroad, J. P. Morgan & Company, Bankers Trust Company, New York Trust, First National Bank of New York, Guaranty Trust Company, Chase National Bank, National City Bank, Equitable Life Assurance Society of the United States, Metropolitan Life, Mutual Life, New York Life, and Prudential Life.

Thurman Arnold confirmed that Young and Kirby, should they prevail, would sever their ties with Alleghany and its affiliated railroads, including the C & O, although he added that in his opinion such a step was not necessary.

Aronson, not to be outdone by Arnold, announced that George Whitney and Harold Vanderbilt, directors of the Central, had already surrendered their directorship in Pullman and sold their Pullman holdings. Aronson further announced that Henry Sturgis had also resigned as director of Pullman. And Richard K. Mellon, a director of Pennsylvania, was ready to give up his Pullman directorship "if the court feels it is an impediment to approval" of the Buying Group's offer.

Aronson couldn't help making the observation that the Department of Justice hadn't opposed the railroads until Arnold's alignment with Otis and Young. An element of bitterness on both sides was becoming apparent.

On December 18, the court unanimously approved the sale of the sleeping car business to the railroads because they were "the natural and obvious people to be in the sleeping car business" and had the "legal responsibility for providing sleeping cars."[9] However, the government's stand was not entirely ignored. The court added certain significant conditions.

> We think there is very great danger to the public interest if the railroads by interlocking directorates, or whatever means there may be, continue the kind of tie-up which we found to exist and talked about in our original opinion in this case. We are, therefore, going to impose three conditions in the order confirming this sale.
>
> (1) . . . there shall be no interlocking directorates between Pullman Standard, Pullman, Inc., and the railroads. . . .
>
> (2) We shall require the Pullman Company if and when it buys new sleeping cars to purchase them under competitive bidding. . . .
>
> (3) . . . the railroads, in purchasing sleeping cars following consummation of the transaction under consideration, shall also purchase them from manufacturers following competitive bidding. The railroads are not defendants in this lawsuit and we know that perfectly well. But they are, for their own business purposes, coming in to deal with the business and property of a company that has got into serious trouble under the Sherman Act. We do not want the practices established under the monopolistic regime to carry over into the operation in the hands of the new owners. The requirement for competitive bidding will, we think, shut off the last possibility of any untoward influence of Pullman Standard following sleeping cars into the hands of the people who now take over.

[9] *U.S.* v. *Pullman Co.*, 64 F. Supp. 108.

Aronson then requested of the court that the Pullman Company be allowed to continue the sleeping car service until March 31 while arrangements were being made for concluding the purchase. He also asked for a modification on the ban on interlocking directorates. The former was granted; the latter, denied.

The decision was a blow to Young; and, while he had not by any means given up, he nevertheless chose discretion. The C & O, Nickel Plate, and Pere Marquette elected to become members of the Buying Group, "but only in the event that the court decision permitting the Buying Group to acquire the stock of Pullman becomes final." A Supreme Court test was still ahead.

In the meantime, Young, gratified by the public response to his advertisement "Why Shouldn't America Have Through Sleeping Car Service from Coast to Coast?" drafted another one with the same theme. On February 11, 1946, there appeared in fifty-four key newspapers a half-page advertisement headed "Are Chicago and St. Louis Part of America—or Not?" Once again, with railroad lawyers nervously breathing down his neck, Young merely pointed out that

Why Should St. Louis Be a Stepchild?

Chicago has just won through sleeping car service. It is being denied to St. Louis—on the Washington to Texas run. The same old excuses are being offered!

The campaign to get through sleeping car service for St. Louis has bogged down.

The phantom "Chinese Wall" which divides this country—a wall that no traveler can cross without changing trains—has been cracked. *But only at Chicago!*

This breach at Chicago followed a series of Chesapeake & Ohio advertisements backed by powerful support from the American press. The C & O pointed out, among other things, that a hog can cross the country without changing trains, but a citizen can't.

On March 18, within a week from the time this last C & O advertisement appeared, the four biggest railroads running through Chicago finally promised through service. On March 31, the first through cars actually rolled into a Chicago station.

Through Service for Chicago— but Excuses for St. Louis!

travelers going through Chicago or St. Louis (or through Memphis and New Orleans for that matter) had to change trains and "pay an exasperating toll in delay, inconvenience, and bother." He called it an unsolved mystery.

> No one has ever given an adequate explanation as to WHY. . . .
> We invite the support of the public, of railroad people and railroad investors everywhere—for this essential improvement in rail transportation.

Again, as in the case of the first ad, Young undertook a mass mailing—with the same gratifying response.

On March 4, 1946, Young–Otis & Company, Glore, Forgan & Company, Standard Steel Springs, and the government appealed the district court's decision to the Supreme Court, and the district court extended indefinitely its order permitting the Pullman Company to operate the sleeping car business. This meant nothing would change until the Supreme Court took action.

On the same day that the Pullman case started on its journey to the Supreme Court for final disposition, Young published still another ad. This one contained a cartoon of a self-satisfied, cigar-smoking pig riding a train as a distraught human family looked on. The heading told the whole story: "A Hog Can Cross the Country Without Changing Trains—But YOU Can't!" The ad continued,

> The Chesapeake & Ohio and the Nickel Plate Road again propose to give humans a break!
> It's hard to believe, but it's true.
> If you want to ship a hog from coast to coast, he can make the entire trip without changing cars. You can't. It is impossible for you to pass through Chicago, St. Louis, or New Orleans without breaking your trip!
> There is an invisible barrier down the middle of the United States which you cannot cross without inconvenience, lost time, and trouble.
> If you want to board a sleeper on one coast and ride through to the other, you must make double Pullman reservations, pack and transfer your baggage, often change stations, and wait around for connections.

> Last year alone, more than 560,000 people were forced to make annoying, time-wasting stopovers at the phantom China wall which splits America in half!

A Hog Can Cross the Country Without Changing Trains —But YOU Can't!

The Chesapeake & Ohio and the Nickel Plate Road again propose to give humans a break!

It's hard to believe, but it's true.

If you want to ship a hog from coast to coast, he can make the entire trip without changing cars. You can't. It is impossible for you to pass through Chicago, St. Louis, or New Orleans without breaking your trip!

There is an invisible barrier down the middle of the United States which you cannot cross without inconvenience, lost time, and trouble.

560,000 Victims in 1945!

If you want to board a sleeper on one coast and ride through to the other, you must make double Pullman reservations, pack and transfer your baggage, often change stations, and wait around for connections.

(Courtesy of Library of Congress)

End the Secrecy!

Why should travel be less convenient for people than it is for pigs? Why should Americans be denied the benefit of through train service? No one has yet been able to explain it.

Canada has this service . . . with a choice of two routes. Canada isn't split down the middle. Why should we be? No reasonable answer has yet been given. Passengers still have to stop off at Chicago, St. Louis, and New Orleans—although they can ride right through other important rail centers.

The Chesapeake & Ohio, whose western passenger terminus is Cincinnati, stands ready now to join with any combination of other railroads to set up connecting trans-continental and intermediate service through Chicago and St. Louis, on practical schedules and routes.

Through railroad service can't be blocked forever. The public wants it. It's bound to come. Again, we invite the support of the public, of railroad people and railroad investors—for this vitally needed improvement in rail transportation!

Young struck a note to which he knew the public would respond. Annoyed by the near collapse of railroad service as a result of the war, the public greeted Young as a new kind of railroad man.

A proof of the ad with a letter of explanation was sent not only to members of the U.S. Senate and House but to every cabinet member and undersecretary, to the more than forty thousand persons listed in *Who's Who,* to practically every important radio and television commentator, and to almost every newspaper and magazine.

The ad hit the jackpot. A flood of mail resulted, almost four thousand letters from every sector of society, the business world, labor, and politics. Only five expressed disagreement which could be described as strongly in opposition. On the other hand, many volunteered help and asked what they could do about the problem.

It was from the press that the most meaningful reaction was registered. While the "hog ad" appeared as a paid advertisement in a mere handful of the daily papers and financial journals, it appeared as part of a news story in over two thousand papers, and most of these ran favorable editorials in addition. *Time* ran the cartoon in its news columns together with a story entitled "Bob Young's Privileged

Porker—Human Passengers Might Not Soon Be As Lucky." *Barron's, Business Week,* and the *Wall Street Journal* followed in the same vein. With the Associated Press, United Press, International News Service, and Scripps-Howard sending out news stories, it turned out to be a saturation item. Hardly a radio commentator failed to mention it. Even today, twenty-two years after the event as of this writing, it is still a frequently cited episode fixing the identity of its author.

When Young first drew up the "hog ad," the lawyers for the C & O once again objected. They pointed out that Young was bidding for the Pullman Company as a personal matter and not on behalf of the C & O and therefore such an ad in the name of the railroad would have unfortunate effects. For instance, it undoubtedly would be obnoxious to the I.C.C. and insulting to the railroad industry. And other Young associates reminded him that the contempt of court problem was ever-present. In the light of subsequent history, the most curious objection to the advertisement came from the advertising agency. They had reluctantly gone along with Young on the previous ads, but this one they insisted was going too far. Nevertheless, Young convinced them to go along and not resign the account.[10] There were, on the other hand, enthusiastic supporters. The law firm of Arnold & Wiprud and Young's personal assistant and counsel, William C. MacMillen, Jr., urged Young to stand his ground.

As the years rolled by and memories faded, many persons have come forth to claim authorship of the "hog ad," including some who had predicted the direst consequences. The simple fact is that the "hog ad" was the product of Young's genius in the advertising medium.

---

[10] The "hog ad" may have been Robert Young's first problem with the C & O lawyers and his advertising agency, but it was by no means the last. When the advertisement "How Can Slave Railroads Serve the Public?" (see p. 2) appeared, *Advertising Age* of June 2, 1947, noted, "This newspaper ad was prepared a couple of months ago by Robert Young and Kenyon & Eckhardt for insertion by the Chesapeake & Ohio. It was too 'frank' even for the C & O. Somewhat modified, it has been turned over to Mr. Young's Federation for Railway Progress to be placed—probably soon—through its agency, Walter Weir, Inc."

Young was not one to miss a chance to capitalize on his huge advertising success. He asked one of his advertising agencies to determine the most irritating aspect of Pullman service as far as the traveling public was concerned. After making a survey of 250 businessmen in New York, the agency advised Young that the most disturbing feature of Pullman service related to the inability to get reservations on sleeping cars. The result was a considerable black market in Pullman reservations. The necessity of paying a premium "under the table" for Pullman accommodations was apparently a sore spot for most businessmen. Armed with this knowledge, Young placed an ad entitled "Let's Get the Black Market's Hand Out of the Traveler's Pocket" in sixty-seven newspapers and a number of magazines. This ad labeled the "under-the-table" sale of sleeping car space a "national scandal" and proposed as a solution that last-minute cancelation of reservations be penalized. Readers were urged to write their views to the newspapers.

While the "hog ad" was impossible to top, the black-market ad still hit a very responsive chord. It proved the value of pretesting. The *New York Times* alone received more than two hundred letters on the subject.

In June and July, Young followed these ads with two others: "Let's Get That Mule Off the Tracks!" and "Why Must Sleeping Car Passengers Put Up With 'Rolling Tenements'?"

Despite the huge and favorable response to his advertising campaign, Young failed to enlist public opinion as an ally in his quest for the Pullman Company. Few readers related the ads to Young's legal battle to take over the sleeping car service. The legal restraints made the purpose of the ads too obscure. The campaign therefore did not direct the public to support Young's cause before the Commission and the courts. But it succeeded beyond anything Young ever hoped for in establishing him as a hero to the traveling public disenchanted with railroad service.

In the meantime, the Pullman case was nearing a legal solution. At the end of July, the Buying Group applied for I.C.C. approval[11]

[11] Under Section 5 (1) of the Interstate Commerce Act, which prohibited pooling arrangements except with I.C.C. approval.

of its plan for pooling earnings and services. The I.C.C. set November 19, 1946, for oral argument. Young would appear, as would representatives of the Buying Group. The railroads were learning not to underestimate him.

Why must sleeping car passengers put up with "rolling tenements"?

**9 Out of Every 10 Sleeping Cars Now in Service
Belong in Museums! What Can Be Done About It?**

5

The First Battle for the Central

YOUNG'S CHANCES of taking over the Pullman Company were running out. Of course, still possible was denial by the I.C.C. of the Buying Group's application for approval of their acquisition of Pullman. Should the I.C.C., however, approve the application—which appeared likely—an appeal to the Supreme Court would represent Young's last chance.

Throughout the Pullman case, Young used the combination "Morgan-Vanderbilt-Central" as an epithet. He charged this group with more than control of the Pullman Company; he charged that it dominated the entire railroad industry. Young fervently believed this and realized that such power could not easily be thwarted. The signs did not point to victory.

With this in mind, Young was already preparing for a battle on still another front. If he couldn't capture the Pullman Company, why not a leapfrog assault on the citadel of power? Why not aim for the Central itself?

In the early fall of 1946, rumors began to spread through Wall Street that Young was embarked on "something big." A few newspaper stories speculated on the possibility that Young might be mounting a "take-over of the New York Central." One of the stories went so far as to identify the Duke of Windsor as a Young backer in such an attempt. Another indicated the Central would be Young's first link in a transcontinental line, so that a human passenger as well as a hog could "cross the country without changing trains."

The possibility of the C & O's taking a significant ownership interest in the Central was a matter that concerned the Antitrust

Division of the Department of Justice. Assistant Attorney General
Wendell Berge, although friendly to Young's aspirations, asked one
of his sharpest transportation experts, Samuel Karp, to keep the
entire matter under observation. Karp, in fact, had already made an
appearance before the I.C.C. in the Pullman matter.

In the meantime, the price of Central stock was steadily falling—
from a high of $35 at the beginning of the year to a low of $13 as
the year drew to a close. The financial difficulties which Central was
suffering, along with the entire railroad industry, were clearly a main
factor in depressing the price of the stock.

On September 19, 1946, the leaders of the railroad industry were
testifying before the I.C.C. that the immediate future of the rails was
very grave. Walter Franklin, vice president, traffic, of the Pennsylvania Railroad, emphasized the seriousness of the situation by stating
grimly that his railroad would have the worst financial year in its
history, with a staggering deficit of $27,000,000 for the first seven
months of 1946, "even after carry-back credits." Gustav Metzman
confirmed the general malaise of the railroads. The New York Central would have a deficit in net income of almost $32,000,000, and,
even with a huge carry-back tax credit of almost $20,000,000, the
deficit would still be $12,000,000. He compared this figure with the
total in 1945, when the Central had a net income of over
$24,000,000.

Still, in spite of Metzman's bleak news, it would be difficult to buy
a block of stock in the Central large enough to challenge control
without driving up the price. The falling market seemed to give the
lie to the rumor that Young was buying into the Central. But the
rumor persisted.

The report received a measure of confirmation when, on November 29, 1946, *Investor's Reader,* the organ of the largest brokerage
house in Wall Street, Merrill Lynch, Pierce, Fenner & Beane, appeared
with an article entitled "Bob Young Eyes the New York Central," an
unusually detailed speculation on Young's purchase of Central,
including the source of funds for buying the stock, the allies
Young would enlist, and other apparently reliable information.
The article was given further substance by the inclusion of an author-

ized interview with Young concerning his views on railroad finance. As a matter of fact, Merrill Lynch, Pierce, Fenner & Beane knew full well what it was talking about. *At that very moment it was acting as Young's agent in the purchase of the Central stock.* In fact, Young, through the Alleghany Corporation and the C & O, was now by far the largest stockholder in the New York Central, with an interest many times larger than that of the Vanderbilts.

The Central could not have been unaware of what was going on. To keep secret from Central's management the large transfers of Central stock would have been a technical impossibility. But the reaction of Central's management to Young's maneuver could not be measured with certainty. Whether or not a battle was shaping up was a matter of intense interest in many quarters. On the day the Merrill Lynch interview appeared, Young was scheduled to be cross-examined by Jacob Aronson in the I.C.C. Pullman hearings.

The manner Aronson adopted during the examination would provide some indication of the attitude of the Central management toward Young. Would Young's control of the largest single block of the New York Central stock lessen Aronson's antagonism toward him? He had given Young a rough time in the federal court in Philadelphia in the matter of the Buying Group application. The development stirred up more than ordinary interest among the press.

As expected, Young aimed his testimony over the heads of the examiner and counsel and at the public. His remarks were peppered with such phrases as "Wall Street banker control," "abuse of stockholder rights," "irresponsible management," "rolling tenements," "antique equipment," and "black market." With equal determination and vigor, Aronson made it clear by word and manner that he would not be intimidated. He subjected Young to a vigorous, almost unfriendly cross-examination, continually demanding that Young cease his "flippancy" and answer the questions presented to him. Aronson, not Young, he thundered, would control the questioning. Once during the hearing, Harold Vanderbilt, under pressure to catch a train to Florida, asked the examiner for permission to testify out of turn, a request which was granted. When

Young with courtly graciousness offered to step down from the witness stand to make room "for my friend and neighbor Mr. Vanderbilt," Aronson, pointedly turning his back to Young and facing the audience, commented acidly, "You will step down because the examiner has ordered it."

The atmosphere was charged; the open antagonism of Young and Aronson had overtones for the future. The Pullman case became secondary. The first shots fired in anger for control of the Central had now been heard.

While there could be no doubt that the railroads took very seriously Young's bid for Pullman, not everyone believed that Young was really serious about swallowing the New York Central. The November 23 *Business Week*, under the heading "Tired of Railroading?" reported that "Wall Street, rightly or wrongly, thinks the railroad field generally has lost much of its former attraction for Young." By December 7, however, *Business Week* expressed suspicions, based on a report of the ownership in "street names" (a device whereby an investor could conceal his stock ownership by listing it in the name of a brokerage house) of 218,000 shares of Central.

On January 8, 1947, Young's buying campaign of Central stock was publicly confirmed. The Alleghany Corporation reported to the I.C.C. that it had purchased 162,500 shares of Central's capital stock, representing 2.5 percent of the ownership. "This," according to *Business Week*, "is Young's retort—or part of his retort—to the railroad men who guffawed a couple of months ago when he declared that he might try to buy up control of the Central."

On January 29, 1947, Alleghany increased its Central holdings on behalf of C & O to 250,000 shares, or approximately 4 percent. This prompted Cyrus Eaton to remark:

From now on you can count New York Central as a Robert R. Young property. . . .
The New York Central needs the youth, color and imagination of Robert Young and I believe he will be welcomed by the rank and file of the New York Central stockholders.

The C & O is the best railroad in the world, and there is no limit to what it can do with New York Central.[1]

Accumulation of Central stock by the C & O through the Alleghany Corporation continued, so that by March it totaled 400,000 shares. Of course, in accordance with the conditions of the 1945 I.C.C. decision concerning Alleghany's control of the C & O roads, the Central stock had to be deposited with Chase National Bank as trustee.

The holdings of the Young interests in the Central now dwarfed the 65,000 shares held by Harold Vanderbilt, hitherto Central's largest individual stockholder. Young's intentions were no longer a mystery. He wanted the Central.

On February 1, 1947, the I.C.C. examiners filed a proposed report supporting the railroad Buying Group's bid for Pullman, and on March 31, 1947, the Supreme Court, by a four-to-four vote with Justice Robert Jackson not sitting, sustained the lower court's award to the Buying Group.[2] Young had lost his battle for the Pullman Company.

Whether or not Young anticipated such a setback, he had nonetheless two weeks earlier confronted the Central officially with his massive accumulation of Central stock. Young called on Gustav Metzman, Central's chief executive officer and president, for the second time in two years. This time he demanded representation on the board.

How the Central would respond fascinated Wall Street. No one familiar with Young's history seriously considered the possibility that Central would let him get his foot in the door.

A stunned Wall Street, therefore, read on March 28 an announcement issued to the press by the New York Central: *"Subject to the necessary authorization of I.C.C.,"* Metzman would recommend to the Central board the election of Robert R. Young, C & O chairman, and Robert J. Bowman,[3] C & O president, as directors of the Central.

[1] *New York Times,* January 30, 1947, p. 33L.

[2] *U.S.* v. *Pullman Co.,* 330 U.S. 806.

[3] Bowman served as president of the C & O for a relatively short period of time, from April 1946 to October 1948.

The Chesapeake and Ohio Railway Company as the beneficial owner of 400,000 shares of capital stock of the New York Central has requested that it be accorded representation on the board of directors of the New York Central. It has long been the New York Central's policy to recognize the propriety of representation on the part of such large holdings.

There was more than mere suspicion among skilled watchers that this was no surrender and that the Central was pinning its hopes of defeating Young on a strategy that would avoid the violence of a proxy fight and substitute instead the legal shoals of the I.C.C.

Aronson, as the chief legal officer, had charted Central's strategy. His role in the Pullman case as chief counsel for the Buying Group indicated the regard held for him by the industry. He was considered, for good and established reasons, one of the most skillful and experienced practitioners before the I.C.C. In his judgment, the state of the law, the character of the I.C.C., and Young's own personality would block Young's aspirations for the Central. The risks inherent in the decision were great, but it was a time for risks. Few corporate stakes have ever been so large. Young's daring would have to be matched.

Within days of Metzman's invitation, both Young and Bowman filed applications with the I.C.C. requesting authorization to sit on the board of the Central while remaining directors of the C & O. At the same time the C & O and Alleghany filed a petition requesting release of the 400,000 shares of the New York Central stock from Chase's voting trust and permission for Young and Bowman to sit on both the Central and C & O boards.

The applications of Young and Bowman were filed under Section 20a (12)[4] of the Interstate Commerce Act. They requested, in effect, that an exception be made to the general prohibition against interlocking directorates. The Commission had the power

---

[4] Section 20a (12): "After December 31, 1921, it shall be unlawful for any person to hold the position of officer or director of more than one carrier, unless such holding shall have been authorized by order of the Commission, upon due showing, in form and manner prescribed by the Commission, that neither public nor private interests will be adversely affected thereby."

to grant such an exception upon an affirmative showing that "neither public nor private interests will be adversely affected thereby."

Young recounted his successes in rehabilitating Alleghany, the Nickel Plate, and the Pere Marquette. The implication was clear that Young, with the Commission's permission, would do the same for the Central. After all, the Central and the C & O were ideal partners with an obvious community of interests.

Chesapeake would bring to the system the large originated tonnage of coal which Central so sorely lacks, and Central in return would contribute its large originated tonnage of manufactured and miscellaneous products, thus providing a generally stabilized and balanced traffic. . . .

No other proposal offers so much promise for a restoration of a sound transportation system in the Eastern territory as this one of unification of the relatively prosperous Pocahontas roads with the present major systems in trunk line territory.

Moreover, the Central as a prime passenger road would prove a better vehicle for Young's innovations than the C & O had been.

Probably the most arresting point made by the petition was in the area of finance and economic well-being. The financial difficulties of many railroads, of which Central was a leading example, were worsening. The deep concern of the I.C.C., the Congress, securities holders, and other interests involved in rails was manifest. Here was a telling point—the financial comparison of the healthy C & O with the ailing Central. Young pointed with pride to the fact that the C & O had a proven capacity to earn a high level of return on investment and that this record had continued over a long period of years.

In comparison, the analysis of the Central's finances was grim. The management of the Central were proud men; despite the current difficulties, their railroad was a blue chip of American industry. The patronizing tone of the petition must have been rankling. Unfortunately the recital of the Central's deteriorating finances was accurate.

Central's financial picture and its credit standing have been impaired, since 1930, by lack of adequate earning power . . . its volume of business and revenues fell off sharply in 1946, and it had a net deficit in income of approximately $9,500,000 in that year. . . . The impairment in its credit standing is also manifested by the relatively low prices at which its high interest bearing bonds are selling in the market.

After the filing of the petition and applications by the Young forces, Metzman held his counsel, saying nothing for public consumption. The mass communications field was not one in which to engage Young, no matter how great the provocation. Metzman had made his offer to Young and the formal proceedings were still several months away.

Within a month after the filing, the I.C.C. delivered Young what he considered a low blow. It appointed, as an examiner to hear the matter, C. E. Boles, assistant director of the Bureau of Finance. This was the same Boles who two years earlier had proposed that the Commission require Alleghany, Young, and Kirby to divest themselves of their railroad holdings. Young had never bothered to conceal his conviction that Boles had been unfair, and now he was not mollified by the explanation that Boles's appointment was a logical one: the new proceeding, after all, was technically an extension of the 1945 case, since the C & O and Alleghany were petitioning the I.C.C. to modify the provisions in that decision. The new case even bore the same I.C.C. docket number and title, "Finance Docket No. 14692, Chesapeake & Ohio Railway Company Purchase, etc."

Despite reports of Young's attitude, the Commission stood its ground. Boles was an experienced hand in railroad finance, with a thorough knowledge of the Interstate Commerce Act. Moreover, he was intimately familiar with the workings of the Commission, with which he had been associated since 1921. He was not apt to be overly impressed by either the eminence of counsel or the lofty positions of the various witnesses. What is more, he had previous experience in a hearing involving many of the same parties. A relatively quiet man, Boles had already shown that he could run a hearing on an even keel. This was important, since all preliminary indications pointed to a bitterly fought proceeding.

Young was dissuaded from demanding the disqualification of Boles only with difficulty. His counselors pointed out that even

Memo From The C&O To The New York Central

Why not have a through coast-to-coast train instead of merely "through sleeping cars"? Passengers could be spared all that stalling in Chicago — and save hours of traveling time.

Memo No. 2 From The C&O To The New York Central

A plea for the long-neglected commuter. Why not give him now the improvements that can be made immediately? Why not start by mailing his commutation ticket?

A word to the public:

It is an unusual circumstance when the largest owner of a business must present their ideas to the management in the public press instead of in a Directors' meeting.

But though the C&O is now the largest owner of the New York Central, we may not, under the law, vote our stock, our officers may not sit on the Board of Directors, nor may the C&O have any voice in the Central's affairs, until the Interstate Commerce Commission approves.

This may take several months. Meanwhile we are making our recommendations in this way. What you will find here is merely a sample of the kind of thinking the C&O would like to contribute to the Central in the interest of the railroad and of you the traveler.

This is the second of a series of "Memos to the Central." The first one urged through trains without layovers for coast-to-coast travelers.

Memo No.3 From The C&O To The New York Central

Why should travelers have to <u>stand in line</u> or send to the station for sleeping-car tickets? The C&O invites you to adopt our new "Centralized Reservation Bureau."

A word to the public:

It is an unusual circumstance when the largest owners of a business must present their ideas to the management in the public press instead of in a Directors' meeting.

But though the C&O is now the largest owner of the New York Central, we may not, under the law, vote our stock, our officers may not sit on the Board of Directors, nor may the C&O have any voice in the Central's affairs, until the Interstate Commerce Commission approves.

This may take several months. Meanwhile we are making our recommendations in this way. What you will find here is merely a sample of the kind of thinking the C&O would like to contribute to the Central—in the interest of the railroad and of you the traveler.

This is the third of a series of "Memos to the Central." The first two urged through trains without layovers for coast-to-coast passengers—and some immediate improvements in commuter service.

To the New York Central:

The old-fashioned way of getting sleeping-car accommodations—a way that hasn't changed since General Grant rode the rails—is a downright nuisance to the traveler.

This is a model of C&O's new substitute for the ticket line. All the traveler does is make a local phone call!

A Thank-You Memo From C&O To New York Central

The C&O, largest owners of the Central, have publicly made three recommendations for improving the Central's service. All three have been <u>acted on</u> or <u>promised</u>!

Part of Young's barrage of gadfly advertisements.

if the attempt to disqualify were successful, any other examiner would lean backwards to avoid the suspicion of truckling; the move might boomerang. The C & O lawyers pointed out to Young that Boles had had no personal bias in the Alleghany control case but had instead expressed his findings as he honestly saw them. In fact, his findings were not without some merit. To impugn his impartiality, if not his integrity, would sit badly with many staff members of the I.C.C. The C & O would have to live with these individuals as well as the Commission for many more years on many other matters. Common sense dictated restraint.

Young reluctantly followed their advice, but thereafter the C & O legal staff was able to exert little restraining influence.

Young promptly accepted an invitation to address the National Press Club in Washington, D.C., on May 8. No forum could have served his purposes better. The I.C.C. was not apt to overlook his remarks, made in their own backyard.

To liven up the anticipation for that speech, Young, in testimony three days earlier before the Senate Banking and Currency Committee, referred critically to the former Reconstruction Finance Corporation officials who had turned up in the management of the bankrupt B & O Railroad. He left the Committee as well as the press table in a state of amazement with the closing paragraph of his prepared remarks:

In my opinion, the handling of this situation by the Baltimore and Ohio management and the R.F.C. was either dishonest or incompetent. One does not expect incompetency in financial matters from the R.F.C. or former R.F.C. officials.[5]

A charge of corruption, even if expressed obliquely, is rarely overlooked in Washington.

When Young appeared before the National Press Club, the luncheon meeting was sold out. Anyone familiar with Young's history and character would not have expected him to try to influence the railroad establishment or to try to make friends of the so-called

[5] Testimony of Robert R. Young before the Senate Banking and Currency Committee, May 5, 1947.

Wall Street bankers and lawyers. But in view of the fact that he was about to supplicate the I.C.C. to make an exception, to depart from its traditional ground, the speech appeared to be incredibly rash. Some of his own advisers felt deeply concerned.

Young opened his remarks by asking why prominent bankers and lawyers, apparently with more important things to do, seek the poor-paying, time-consuming position of railroad director.

High up among other reasons is the direct banking patronage. It is estimated that the railroads have on deposit over one billion one hundred million dollars, mostly in a few New York banks. . . .

In addition there are the banking fees: for trustees of equipment issues, agents for stock transfer, payment of bond coupons—the most sought after of all banking emoluments. Railroads pay out annually nearly three million dollars for these services, again mostly to a few New York banks.

. . . There are melons as well. The railroads buy steel, equipment, paint, lumber, coal and other supplies to the vast sum of two thousand million dollars a year; thus accounting for one-third of the heavy industry of America.

The top Morgan law firm, Davis, Polk . . . has collected millions of dollars in legal fees from no less than fifteen recent railroad bankrupts. Mr. Davis, you will remember, was once Democratic Presidential nominee.

Do not believe that political lightning cannot strike twice in the same place. Who is to be our next Republican Secretary of State? Why, Mr. Dulles[6] of Sullivan & Cromwell, counsel to Kuhn, Loeb, Dillon, Read, and numerous railroad bankrupts or alleged bankrupts, including B & O.

Now I am not questioning Mr. Dulles' integrity, for he is Chairman of the Federal Council of Churches, a burden he unselfishly assumed in that critical year abroad, 1937, on top of his duties as Counsel to such harried foreign governments as Poland, Belgium and Britain. A man with all those responsibilities, including numerous Democratic foreign assignments, can hardly be expected to know what his left hand doeth.

. . . this railroad lobby is stronger than the government . . . it dictates foreign and domestic policy.

[6] Young, like almost everyone else, was conceding the election of Thomas E. Dewey in November 1948, and assumed John Foster Dulles would be Dewey's Secretary of State.

It was Mr. Dulles' client, Earle Bailie of Tricontinental, and Senator Taft's "along the line" partner, John Hollister of Cincinnati, who Morgan-Guaranty selected in the following year [1938] to undertake against us the hottest proxy fight in all history. That fight continued for five long, bitter years, first through Judge Manton's Court and then down through the C & O, the Cincinnati Union Terminal, the St. Louis Union Terminal . . . and other sensational competitive bidding engagements, and led finally to the S.E.C.'s public utility rule, and later, grudgingly, to the I.C.C. rule. Later when Judge Manton was tried, who do you think appeared as his character witness? John W. Davis.

Now in 1942 we tired of Mr. Hollister's company, and his continued hobnobbing with the bankers to the injury of our railroad, and replaced him on the C & O board. Whereupon he hurried down here to the Commission and readily persuaded them to bring action against us for taking illegal control of the C & O lines.[7]

. . . the Commission persecuted us with lengthy proceedings, filling 40 rooms of the Carlton Hotel in wartime with witnesses, and, as any one familiar with Commission flexibility could have predicted, produced an Examiner's report finding us guilty. . . . So our goose was cooked. Instead of going down in history as a champion of through travellers over hogs, Morgan had finally got us; and we were to be forced out of C & O.

But we have not been given to quitting when Morgan, or his "along the line" men, had our nose in the dust. With your [the press's] help and others, the Commission was forced to yield to public opinion, agreeing most reluctantly to let us stay in C & O if we would deposit the voting power of Alleghany's other railroad stock—*with an approved bank.*

. . . and our self-styled statesmen have the crust to display the scales of Justice on our public buildings. . . .

With this speech Young left no doubts as to the kind of a war he would wage. The barrage continued almost to the eve of the hearings.

At Central's annual stockholders' meeting on May 28, President Metzman defended his invitation to Young and Bowman—an invitation issued despite Young's unremitting attacks on the I.C.C. and the Wall Street bankers and lawyers, despite Young's charge that the Central board did not represent the interests of the stock-

[7] He was referring to the I.C.C. Alleghany control case, 1944–1945.

Future crises were looming larger as Young—founder of the Federation for Railway Progress—delivered one of many speeches on railroad passenger trains losses.

(Courtesy of C & O Railroad)

holders, and despite Young's patronizing attitude toward the management of the Central. When a stockholder referred to Young as a little Napoleon and demanded to know why the offer of two directorships had been made, Metzman referred to the C & O's ownership of 400,000 shares, representing over 6 percent of all the stock in the Central. The matter was simple. "They are the only group of 6 percent stockholders we have."

At the same meeting, Metzman gave out the doleful news of a $10,449,268 net deficit for 1946.

Despite Metzman's statement, Young was suspicious of Central's offer of the two directorships. On August 27, 1947, hardly two weeks before the hearing opened at the I.C.C., in an interview with Robert S. Allen reported in the "Washington Merry-Go-Round," a column carried by over seven hundred newspapers, Young dropped a clue to future action in the event he lost the current battle.

Robert R. Young, crusading railroad tycoon, today served notice on Wall Street banking interests that he is prepared to wage a no-quarter battle in the stock market to gain control of the New York Central Railroad system.

. . . The slight, 50-year-old Texan declared his plans are all set to stage such a fight in the event the Interstate Commerce Commission refuses to allow him to retain his New York Central directorship. . . .

"When the Morgan banks 'invited' me to join the New York Central's board," Young said, "they apparently figured they would be powerful enough behind the scenes to have the I.C.C. subsequently block me. I don't think the I.C.C. will do that, but if it does, then I'm all set for these Wall Street bankers.

"I will resign from the chairmanship of the Chesapeake & Ohio and the Alleghany Corporation (top holding company of Young's railroad empire) and fight it out in the open market. It will not be difficult for me to buy 50,000 shares of the New York Central stock and to get the stockholders behind me. Wall Street fought me once on competitive bidding and lost. And they'll lose again this time.

"As a result of that other fight, Morgan Stanley, the investment banking unit of J. P. Morgan, dropped from first to tenth place in the investment banking field. If they fight me for control of the New York Central, they will know I come into power with a chip on my shoulder and take deposits away from the banks that are balking me. And they know me well enough to know that I don't make idle threats!"

One week before the hearings were to begin, in an interview with the *New Republic* magazine, Young cast serious doubts on whether he would get even-handed justice from the I.C.C. When asked "How soon do you expect a decision from the I.C.C. on your bid for places on the Central's board of directors?" he replied, "They should have an answer by the first of the year. In fact, we should have had it already, but they are probably trying to figure out some way of doing what the bankers want them to—as they always have."[8]

Young's speeches, public statements, and advertisements appealed to the public's general dissatisfaction with the railroads and anything connected with them, including regulatory commissions. Young came to the hearing room as a crusader with a cause. Citations and precedents, laws and regulations were just so many complications invented by lawyers, impediments to the rendering of justice.

Despite his public statements, the strategy Young evolved in the battle for the Central was founded on the conviction that the Interstate Commerce Commission was now ready to make a major break with the past. The worsening financial plight of the railroads—particularly of the Central, as compared with that of the prosperous C & O—the deterioration of the railroad plant generally, the public dissatisfaction with passenger and freight services, and the apparent success of his own public relations campaign caused Young to conclude that the I.C.C. was ready to move forward.

Such a strategy posed enormous legal hazards, particularly when complicated by his public statements. But the risk was Young's and he insisted on taking it.

Young's case rested chiefly on a showing that unification of the C & O and the New York Central would promote the national transportation policy, by leading to a balanced system in the East capable of competing with the Pennsylvania–Norfolk & Western–Wabash system, and equally important, by saving the Central from financial ruin.

Yet Young wanted to keep his risks to a minimum. He was

[8] David Munro, "An Exclusive Interview with Robert R. Young," *New Republic*, September 8, 1947, p. 26.

not certain of the immediate value of unification with the Central, particularly because of the latter's precarious financial condition. A precipitous misstep might prove a disaster to the keystone of his empire, the C & O. A trial period—a companionate marriage as it were—therefore presented significant advantages. Moreover, Young was anxious not to repeat the fiasco of the C & O–Nickel Plate–Pere Marquette–Wheeling unification attempt, when a clique of Nickel Plate preferred stockholders proved sufficiently obstreperous to thwart Young's plan. There was no reliable evidence that the Central stockholders would be any more compliant than the preferred stockholders of the Nickel Plate had been in Young's 1945 merger attempt. There was, in fact, reason to believe that the reaction would be more violent. Certainly, serious opposition would come from management and the Vanderbilts. Avoiding the issue of a legal unification made sense.

Another serious complication centered on the legal concept of control. All the remedies and innovations in the Central which Young believed necessary could not be accomplished without control. Control of two or more carriers, however, like unification, required I.C.C. permission pursuant to a formal proceeding under Section 5 (2).[9] Young and his lawyers had no intention of entering the thicket of a control proceeding. To overcome this legal impediment then, the C & O lawyers would try to show that Young's plans for improving the Central could be instituted without control. They would attempt to show that Young and Bowman's presence on the Central board, buttressed with the power to vote the 400,000

---

[9] Section 5 (2) (a): "It shall be lawful, with the approval and authorization of the Commission . . . for two or more carriers to consolidate or merge their properties or franchises, or any part thereof, into one corporation for the ownership, management, and operation of the properties theretofore in separate ownership; or for any carrier, or two or more carriers jointly, to purchase, lease, or contract to operate the properties, or any part thereof, of another, or for any carrier, or two or more carriers jointly, to acquire control of another through ownership of his stock or otherwise; or for a person which is not a carrier and which has control of one or more carriers to acquire control of another carrier through ownership of its stock or otherwise. . . ."

shares of stock, would be sufficient to influence the Central management.

Further complicating the difficulties was the acute problem posed by Section 7 of the Clayton Act, which provided in part:

No corporation shall acquire, directly or indirectly, the whole or any part of the stock . . . of two or more corporations engaged in commerce where the effect of such acquisition, or the use of such stock by the voting or granting of proxies or otherwise, may be to substantially lessen competition between such corporations . . . or to restrain such commerce . . . or tend to create a monopoly of any line of commerce.

If the I.C.C. were to release the Central stock from the Chase voting trust as the C & O and Alleghany requested, would the result be substantially lessened competition? Since there were areas in which the C & O and the Central competed, would the requirements of Section 7 of the Clayton Act be satisfied?

That these problems would be forcefully presented was made apparent by the active opposition of a number of powerful interests, led by the Virginian Railway Company. The Virginian, the smallest of the three coal-carrying Pocahontas lines,[10] ran from Norfolk westward across the southern part of Virginia, through the southern West Virginia bituminous coal fields to Deep Water, West Virginia, where it connected with the Chesapeake & Ohio and with the New York Central by the Deep Water Bridge over the Kanawha River. There had been a substantial exchange of traffic between the Virginian and the New York Central since the completion of the Deep Water Bridge in 1931. The C & O threat to the Deep Water connection with the Central and the consequent risk of loss of traffic was the most important objection presented by the Virginian. It would take no great effort by the Virginian to show that they would be "adversely affected." Young suspected the Virginian of other motives. He had concluded that the Virginian was dominated by Mellon interests and was there-

[10] So called because of the main area of operation of these roads, the Virginia tidelands, where the Indian maiden Pocahontas lived in the early seventeenth century.

fore part of the investment banking conspiracy. What is more, he knew that the chairman of the Virginian, George D. Brooke, whom Young had removed from the C & O presidency in 1942, would relish an opportunity to strike back. Although Brooke did not appear as a witness at the hearings, Young suspected that he was doing everything possible to frustrate Young's plans.

The hearings opened on September 15, 1947, to a packed room. Two sure signs of the impact of the case were the crowded press table and the large number of I.C.C. employees and officials not connected with the proceedings who lined the rear of the room.

C & O counsel Joseph C. Kauffman, after the disposal of such formalities as noting appearances, presented his opening statement.[11] He came to grips immediately with the ambiguities of "unification." "There has been a suggestion," he noted, "that the petitioners have some further purpose regarding the New York Central than that which has been disclosed in the petition and applications." Admitting that this was true, he then went on to say:

> If what is meant is that the petitioners are looking forward to a closer association with that company than that for which their authorization is presently sought and that they are hopeful that this closer association may develop into unification of the two companies, I want to say . . . What we are doing in this proceeding is to make at least such a *prima facie case*. . . . This represents but the first step in an association of these two carriers. . . . We are confident that results of an affiliation between the Chesapeake and Ohio and the New York Central will show the desirability of a closer association . . . and eventually of their unification in a later proceeding under Section 5 of the Act. But that will be another proceeding on another day. . . . Whether such an application may be filed and if so in what form, and at what time cannot now be predicted.[12]

This statement brought the Virginian counsel, Wilbur LaRoe, to his feet with a strong objection. To permit the C & O to make

[11] That first day he eliminated one major legal hurdle to the C & O's petition when he announced the C & O would distribute its Nickel Plate stock to the C & O stockholders on a prorata basis.

[12] Hearings, I.C.C. Finance Docket No. 14692, "C & O Railway Company Purchase, Etc.," September 15, 1947.

a preliminary case in support of unification without a formal consolidation proceeding would lead to a prejudgment of the consolidation issue. For one thing, a number of parties interested in
objecting to a consolidation were not present, since this was not,
after all, a consolidation proceeding. For instance, the governor
of each state affected in a proper proceeding would have to be
notified. This had not been done. The examiner must not permit
this proceeding to result in a *fait accompli* for unification. There
was a proper way prescribed to accomplish this end, and the C & O
should be compelled to follow it. The Commission rules and the
law relating to unification were clearly defined, and to accept Kauffman's proposal would be patently illegal. The examiner should rule
out all evidence and testimony relating to unification. LaRoe's
argument was impressive and clearly effective.

Boles did not rule on LaRoe's objection at this time, saying
instead he would permit Kauffman to develop his case "and see
how it goes."

Kauffman launched his presentation, calling President Robert
Bowman of the C & O as his first witness. Bowman opened by
saying that he and Young, if approved as directors, would set
about promptly to restore the Central's financial and credit position. He thought that the advantage of an association between the
C & O and Central had been obvious since 1906[13] and that if the
two roads had been unified then, "the benefits flowing therefrom
would have been so apparent that no one today would question
the propriety of that alliance in the public interest."

He conceded that, while it was possible that some competition
would be lessened by the C & O–Central association, in a broader
sense it would actually lead to "more constructive competition."

"We think," he said, "that the kind of railroad competition
which is in the public interest can best be promoted by establishing
strong transportation systems capable of furnishing a full measure
of competition among themselves. Consolidation or unification of

[13] He was referring to the time when the Pennsylvania and Central jointly
held the C & O and the Central tried to buy the Pennsylvania's C & O holdings. See footnote, p. 23.

rail carriers does not necessarily interfere with competition if it be conducted along constructive lines."

Bowman considered that in its main aspects "this proposal involved an end-to-end unification," and that the complementary aspects of these two systems were "much more important than their competitive aspects." With the Clayton Act in mind, Bowman played down those points where the Central and the C & O competed for traffic.

Turning to the ways in which the private interests of the two railroads would benefit from the proposed relationship, he saw the alliance providing Central with the coal tonnage it had always lacked and giving the C & O badly needed outlets for its ever-expanding coal business. The C & O would also welcome manufactured and miscellaneous products from the Central. The result would be a more balanced traffic for both.

Bowman made a valiant effort to overcome the Virginian's anticipated argument that its interests would suffer. "It is not the intention of the C & O management to cause any of the present routes or service arrangements via either C & O or New York Central to or from any connections, to be disturbed," he said. The C & O was entirely agreeable to the Commission's making it a condition that all present routes in connection with both roads be maintained.

Bowman had to admit, on cross-examination by LaRoe, that he "would hope" that the granting of the application would result in taking traffic away from other railroads, including the Virginian. After all, he would expect his organization to work hard to get all the business it could. Wasn't this, LaRoe pointedly asked, a violation of the Interstate Commerce Act, since it would adversely affect the Virginian?

LaRoe also wanted to hear Bowman on the possible violation of the control section of the Act. How could Young and Bowman put through all their ideas and recommendations for the Central without assuming control? Bowman said that he would get the Central board to follow their ideas through "salesmanship"—a term that opposing attorneys pounced on. It appeared and reappeared in the cross-examinations but never was explicitly defined. More than one observer compared the exchange to something out of *Alice in Wonderland*.

Bowman was followed by Ross Marshall, senior vice president of the C & O, who gave a general dissertation on consolidation in the eastern region, emphasizing the need for a Central–C & O unification. He compared the revenue trends of the Central and the Pennsylvania to show how the relative position of the Central had declined since 1930.

When Ross Marshall's cross-examination began, he made one potentially damaging admission—that the C & O had no more use for the Deep Water Bridge in 1947 than it had in 1930, when it had none. Since this was a critical connecting point between the Virginian and the Central, Marshall tried to recover by echoing Bowman's promise that all routes and services would be maintained.

As the testimony of C & O witnesses continued, the cross-examination by LaRoe and the other opponents became more effective and the admissions by the C & O witnesses more damaging. Under direct examination, they expressed the C & O position with clarity and competence. Cross-examination proved to be an ordeal. They found difficulty in denying that the Virginian Railway would be adversely affected, particularly the Deep Water connection with the Central. They also had difficulty with the problem of the diversion of traffic from the Virginian to the C & O. So, too, the elimination of competition between the C & O and Central could not easily be dismissed. Equally troublesome was the problem of reforms to improve the Central without exercising control. The word "salesmanship" seemed the best they could do. Again and again during the cross-examination C & O witnesses fell back upon a semantic differentiation between salesmanship and control. On this issue the witnesses' testimony did not have the ring of conviction.

Curiously enough, it was the academic witnesses presented by the C & O who came closest to the spirit of Robert R. Young in this proceeding. Dr. Julius Grodinsky, associate professor of finance at the University of Pennsylvania and author of *Railroad Consolida-*

tion, Its Economics and Controlling Principles, expanded the point
of the need for competition between systems, even at the sacrifice
of some competition between individual roads.

"A price—in the form of less competition—must sometimes be
paid to achieve lower costs and lower rates," he said. "This was
tacitly recognized by the I.C.C. in the approval of the acquisition
of the Wabash by the Pennsylvania. . . . This consolidation involved
—what is so important in the public interest—the absorption of
a weak road by a strong road, with a rise in the standard of service."

Dr. William N. Leonard, associate professor of economics at
Rutgers University and author of *Railroad Consolidation Under
the Transportation Act of 1920*, dealt not only with the benefits of
railroad policy of the United States but also with the evils of the
separation of ownership and control. For instance, he pointed
out that the Central board ownership interests had dwindled from
19 percent in 1920 to 1.5 percent in 1946. Young and Bowman,
he said, would bring ownership back to the Central's board of
directors. He testified that in large part the efficiency of C & O management was attributable to the presence of an ownership interest
"willing to take the time and expand the effort required to give
proper attention to the conduct of the business." He quoted from
the I.C.C.'s 1945 decision in the Alleghany control case, which
praised Young's management.

The hearings were now in their third day. The testimony of the
witnesses so far had been building the technical case for the I.C.C.'s
breaking with the past.

Then it was the turn of Robert R. Young himself.

Young testified that when he decided to come out of premature
retirement, he looked for the "easiest berth" he could find, the
"berth where I could make the greatest record with the least effort,"
and had chosen the railroad business.

Young told how he had saved the Nickel Plate and Pere Marquette from going "down the rathole of reorganization," meeting
a maturity of $16,000,000 "without any funds." He not only saved
the two roads but he "saved every stockholder in those properties."
Through his efforts, the Erie was the last railroad to go into reorgani-

zation and the first to come out, and "it was the only railroad which had preserved any equity for the stockholders." Now Young would save the Central stockholders from ruin. The Central stock was "being kicked around in the Street for virtually ten cents on the dollar."

Nothing was being done about large-scale railroad consolidation, and he had "resolved that, as far as Alleghany was concerned, something would be done." His studies had convinced him that "the most logical railroad consolidation in America from the standpoint of the physical factors, the possible savings and the intangible factors of general benefit to the railroad industry" would be a merger of the C & O and New York Central and that it "would come nearer to approaching an ideal than a merger between any other two railroad systems in the country."

He had been "gratified and pleased" when, a few months after C & O's acquisition of Central stock, he and Bowman had been invited to join the board. He had expected some difficulty about that.

He would try to "sell" the Central on the idea of new lightweight trains which would operate safely at speeds of one hundred miles an hour. With that type of equipment, he believed the Central would be more prosperous than the C & O. Other railroads were still refusing to order new passenger equipment "in the face of proof that people will patronize decent trains."

The Central was "the most strategically located road in the world." He would absorb losses on branch-line passenger service by operating more through-trains.

With regard to conflict of interest, he went on, "I make it a rule to engage in no outside business adverse to the railroads . . . my only hope of remuneration is in appreciation of my securities."

This led into an attack on bankers: some bankers served the people well—"my father was a banker"—but bankers "at the top, in New York" served only themselves. The New York bankers active in the railroads, he testified, were J. P. Morgan & Company, in the New York Central; the Mellon interests, in the Pennsylvania, the Virginian, and the Pullman Company; and Harriman & Company, in the Union Pacific. He noted that the Virginian "hadn't

Memo No. 5 From The C&O To The New York Central

Great advances in comfort, convenience and speed are promised travelers by a revolutionary train design. Will the Central join us in developing "Train X"?

To the New York Central:

The C&O's Research Department has been working on the design of a train so new that it may change all our present ideas of comfort, convenience and speed.

Since the New York Central's passenger business is so much larger than ours, why not join forces in this development?

The C&O is making the suggestion not only in the interest of all railroad progress, but also as the New York Central's largest stockholder.

"Train X" a Completely New Concept

"Train X" represents the most revolutionary change in railroad car design in half a century.

The coaches are much shorter than at present—the train would *flow* around curves. There should be far less wrenching and side-away than with present-day long cars.

Each coach is built on a trailer principle and each is integrated to the train. Because heavy, cumbersome trucks are not needed, the train can ride much lower

"Train X" will have shorter, trailer-type, integrated coaches. It will flow around curves!

Young's desire to modernize train travel was epitomized by "Train X," which he described glowingly to the public and which his research men at the C&O actually developed. Below, Young and his colleagues examine the train's undercarriage.

(Courtesy of C & O Railroad)

said anything about the Mellons yet," in his opinion, the real power behind that railroad. What is more, "those three banking houses, controlling our railroad system and the A.A.R.," wanted to see shortages in equipment and steel and "all those other things" because they could wield greater power over the economy and satisfy more banking clients that way.

Cross-examination did not dampen Young's ardor. Pressed by LaRoe about a news story quoting Young as saying that C & O's Central holdings would give the C & O complete working control of the Central, Young said he meant that the stockholders, as opposed to the bankers, would control. "The stockholders saved me from the bankers in the C & O" and "they're the people I represent."

Young's interest in the Central was not a sudden impulse. He had been "ambitious to be in the Central for years" but had not thought seriously of it until Bowman's suggestion that they needed the Central in order to provide more outlets for C & O's coal and to diversify its traffic.

LaRoe asked Young whether he thought that, if his application were granted, his "effective persuasion would accomplish all the improvements he had in mind.

"Without a doubt. I'm so confident about it, I'm just dying to get there."

Did C & O references to a "happy marriage" mean that unification was the ultimate aim?

Young replied that "we would hope that we like this girl well enough after we have been going with her for eight or ten years perhaps to marry her."

He thought that if the Central were saved from the "tender mercies of reorganization," the Central stockholders would "probably be more grateful than the Nickel Plate stockholders turned out to be."

If the C & O were out of the picture, would Young still be interested in the Central? LaRoe pointed out that newspaper reporters had quoted Young as saying that if the I.C.C. turned down the proposals, he would resign from C & O and Alleghany and go for the Central on his own. If the I.C.C. "turns us down—the most I have ever said to any reporter is that I *could* resign from Alleghany and Chesapeake and Ohio and buy 50,000 shares of New York Central and go on the New York Central board without jurisdiction of the Commission. I did not say I *would* do it, and I do not know what I would do. That would depend upon just how far down the road this railroad situation may be at the time."

Boles then interrupted to question Young as to how he would relieve the Central board of alleged banker control. Young, with an air of something less than self-effacement, responded: "I think our mere presence there will relieve it." Then, with his mind on the requirements of the Interstate Commerce Act, Boles asked:

If you were to go on the New York Central board and these directors were still connected with the banks, and they did not approve of your policies, would you move to get men on who would approve of your policies?

Young: Well, then, we might come to you and ask you for control. We probably would.

Boles: But you would make no move of that kind until you had asked for control?

Young: Absolutely not.

This pledge from Young closed the C & O's case, and the spectators believed that the fireworks were over.

It became increasingly clear that Boles regarded the strict construction of the Interstate Commerce Act as ruling in this proceeding. So did the intervenors and objectors, who concentrated their fire on the deviations from a strict construction of statutes. For this reason they hammered home the concept that "control" and "unification" were subject to specific definition and the section of the act pertaining to them should be strictly construed. No amount of semantic switches from control to salesmanship, from unification to "trial marriage," should divert the examiner or the Commission from its appointed duty to enforce the Interstate Commerce Act.

The proponents resolutely based their case on the general transportation policy of the United States and the proposition that the

time had come for a departure from past precedents in order
to make that policy viable. Control, competition, and conflict of
interest should not become inflexible concepts, frustrating the
intent of Congress. In this sense, a policy of constructive consolidation should guide the Commission.

This was how the contest seemed to shape up at the halfway point
of the hearings.

President F. D. Beale of the Virginian opened the Virginian's
case on September 18. He said the New York Central–C & O
link would be contrary to I.C.C. policy, as set forth in the 1932
consolidation plan of the I.C.C. The New York Central–Virginian
route via the Deep Water Bridge had been "firmly established" and
should be "continued in full vigor." The New York Central was
the Virginian's one friendly connection and without it the Virginian would be completely bottled up and at the mercy of
its two strongest competitors. The soliciting power of the C & O
and Central combined would be overwhelming. The Virginian would
be so handicapped, in fact, that its service to the public would
be impaired immediately and its ability to furnish adequate and
efficient transportation service generally would be endangered.

One Virginian witness did explore the question of ownership
and control. W. R. Coe, vice president and treasurer of the Virginian, presented an exhibit ridiculing Young's claim of ownership.
The exhibit was entitled "Robert R. Young Interest in Assets of
New York Central System." It showed that Young's investment
in Alleghany represented 0.00006 percent of the New York Central
assets; Alleghany's investment in the C & O represented 0.00718
percent of Central's assets; and C & O's investment of 400,000
shares of Central common represented 0.215 percent of Central's assets.

So far the opposition case was exactly what Young, Bowman,
and their counsel could have expected, and Coe's testimony appeared
to be the climax of the presentation.

Then LaRoe dropped a bombshell. He presented two witnesses
to support the Virginian's opposition to Young's ambitions. Until
now the Central management, including those who were observing

the hearing and the top echelon on the thirty-second floor at 230 Park Avenue, had maintained a decorous detachment. This had been in the face of continual provocations by the Young lawyers, witnesses, and public relations men, to say nothing of the main irritant, Young himself. Not the least of these had been the patronizing tone of the C & O executives as they discussed the Central's desperate condition and what they would do to repair it. The implication was not too disguised that the management of the Central was wanting in talent. Now it was the Central's turn to repay Young and company.

The first witness called by LaRoe from the Central was J. P. Patterson, general freight traffic manager. His direct testimony was short but, for the Virginian and possibly some others, it was sweet. To Young the voice was Patterson's but the words were Metzman's, and they were written in Wall Street.

LaRoe asked Patterson whether the granting of the applications would benefit the New York Central. Would it increase the tonnage or revenues of the New York Central? Everyone in the room seemed to lean forward to hear the answer.

But Patterson opened with a preamble. Before he answered the question, he wanted to say, first, that he was under subpoena; second, that no influence had been brought to bear on him by any officer of the New York Central as to what his answers should be; and, third, his answers were his own as a minor stockholder of the Central.

He then answered LaRoe's question: "*No.*" To the Young entourage, at least, this represented a not unexpected double cross.

Asked to enlarge on this response, he said that he did not like the reference "to this trial marriage." He said, "The result of that kind of a marriage ends in disaster to the distaff side. . . . The reason it does is because with an announced principle as to the conclusion of the whole matter, we invite the combined opposition of all of our connections south of the Ohio River, and we will lose traffic in the net."

The first opportunity for the C & O's reaction to this appearance came at the end of Patterson's brief direct testimony.

Horace L. Walker, an attorney for the C & O, expressed "surprise," in view of the Central's official position. He asked for and received permission to defer his cross-examination until the following morning.

Next LaRoe called Willard F. Place. The tension at the C & O-Alleghany counsel table quickened perceptibly. Place could not be regarded as a petulant employee acting on his own against the declared policy of his company. Here indeed was an identifiable element in the policy-making machinery of the Central. His very appearance—calculated to harm Young's cause more than even the words that might follow—convinced everyone familiar with Central policies and operating patterns that the Central management would go to any extremes necessary to thwart Young's ambitions.

Place opened his remarks by explaining that he had been subpoenaed and that his appearance was not voluntary. His testimony was even briefer than Patterson's. It was also more restrained, in keeping with his senior position in the Central, and it was more damaging from Young's standpoint.

What effect would this so-called trial marriage have on the credit position of the New York Central? LaRoe asked.

Place replied with shattering directness. "I can't see how it would improve the credit position of the New York Central."

Young's lawyers, claiming to be taken by surprise, received permission to defer cross-examination until the next day.

The following morning opened with a dueling match between Patterson and Robert W. Purcell, vice president, law, of the C & O. Patterson was firm, and the main thrust of his replies on cross-examination was that "the ultimate unification as announced publicly is not a good thing for the New York Central."

Purcell's carefully phrased and sharply directed questions had an unnerving effect on Patterson, who felt compelled to make one point very clear: no official of the Central tried to influence his testimony. He neither asked for nor received any advice from them. Of course, they knew what his views were—but he told them that he did not want to know their views, since he would be testifying under subpoena.

Asked at what time he had concluded that the proposal would

not be in the interest of the New York Central, Patterson's reply brought a laugh from the audience. "A week ago Sunday night at home, talking it over with my wife, because I knew the implications of the answer."

It was then Place's turn for cross-examination. When asked whether he thought the C & O had done a good job of financial rehabilitation with the Nickel Plate and Pere Marquette, he agreed that it had. His demeanor reflected his high position in the Central. Unlike Patterson, he had discussed his testimony with Metzman and had been authorized to confirm Central's statement of policy of recognizing large holders of the company's stock by providing representation on the board of directors. Since the C & O owned 400,000 shares, the single largest block of stock, President Metzman accordingly had recommended the election of Young and Bowman to the board of directors of the Central, ". . . subject to the necessary approval by the Interstate Commerce Commission."

"I can state," said Mr. Place, "that that is the policy and the position of the New York Central. There has been no change in that from the time that was made to Mr. Young, and it stands today just as stated."

After Patterson and Place, the rest of the testimony was anticlimactic. More points were scored for the opposition in testimony by the city of Norfolk, the Norfolk Association of Commerce, the Chrysler Corporation, Packard Motor Company, and a Nickel Plate director, Oliver R. Grace—a leader in the 1945 Nickel Plate stockholders' revolt against the C & O–Nickel Plate consolidation, who said he hoped Young's one-man rule would not be applied to the Central.

After a few more witnesses and the tidying up of loose ends, the hearings ended. On November 10, briefs were filed and Boles retired to write his proposed findings and report for presentation to the Commission.

On December 10, Boles filed his proposed report with the Commission. The examiner recommended a complete rejection of the applications of Young and Bowman and of the petition of C & O and Alleghany. It was an utter defeat for Young.

As far as Boles was concerned, the bulk of the testimony and evidence presented by Young and his group about unification was irrelevant. The proponents had attempted to support their petition and applications "on the basis of benefits to the Chesapeake & Ohio, the New York Central, and the public which are supposed to flow from a set of conditions which by the applicants' own admissions may never come about, but which in effect would require the Commission to prejudge a matter which is not and may never be before it."

On the question of control, Boles found the testimony of Young and Bowman as well as the C & O's other witnesses unimpressive. No matter how it was to be viewed or explained, the release from the trusteeship of the 400,000 shares of Central stock to the C & O would give it control of the Central. This was a clear-cut violation of Section 5(2) of the Interstate Commerce Act.

Although petitioners and the applicants disclaim any intent presently to control the New York Central, the evidence as to their objectives and their plans for attaining them indicates that approval of their proposals would result in control. They have very definite plans about things that should be done to improve the New York Central's traffic and financial condition. . . . They hope to have enough influence on the New York Central's board of directors to effect changes in its policies and to bring about cooperation between its traffic department and that of the Chesapeake and Ohio. The testimony of the applicants themselves clearly indicates that they expect granting of the petition and applications to result shortly in the two carriers being managed in a common interest. . . .

Applicant Young anticipates making "very substantial changes in New York Central's policies" as a result of his presence on the board of that carrier. He expects to revolutionize the Central's passenger service and equipment as well as the high-speed freight-train service, to "put the New York Central back on its feet" and to "save it from the tender mercies of reorganization." While asserting that the New York Central is now dominated by a small clique of bankers in New York, he expects that his mere presence on the New York Central board will free it from the alleged banker control. . . . However, he does not contemplate any resignations would actually be necessary.

At this point what some observers judged to be Boles's distaste for Young appeared in a footnote: "The record developed in . . . [the Alleghany control case] shows that applicant Young, when he is in position to do so, will brook no interference with his plans."

On the issue of competition, Boles held that the effect of the release of the 400,000 shares to the C & O and the interlocking directorates sought by Young and Bowman "would be to substantially lessen competition between the New York Central and Chesapeake & Ohio," indicating a violation of Section 7 of the Clayton Act.

After reviewing the factual material presented by the applicants and petitioners, Boles expressed the view that "the remainder of their evidence consists largely of opinions, prophecies, speculation, and to some extent pure fancy. . . ." Boles gave great weight to the testimony of Patterson and Place of the Central. He repeated Patterson's views that no increase in tonnage or revenue would result and that in fact the proposed application would "invite combined opposition" of the other railroads affected. He agreed with Place's contention that the credit position of the Central would not be improved by the mere granting of the petition and applications.

As to the adverse effect on private interest, Boles pointed out that the Deep Water interchange between the Virginian and Central would be seriously injured. It could not continue "with full vigor." He noted the Virginian contention that it might lose other coal traffic "essential to its very existence."

The adverse effect on the Virginian would in turn affect other interests. Without the wholehearted cooperation of the Central, the usefulness of this route would be impaired, the service would deteriorate, and the benefits of the route would be lost to the public and to the Virginian. Industries served by the Deep Water route would likewise suffer. Norfolk and other cities would be deprived of competitive advantages afforded by the route, as would industries located in cities on this line, some of which set up their plants because of the service of the Deep Water route. The contention of the applicants and the petitioners that competition would not be lessened substantially, that a conflict of interest would not arise, Boles found unconvincing.

At the close of his proposed report, Boles's evaluation of Young's business and fiduciary character was presented in unvarnished terms.

As trustees of the Chesapeake & Ohio stockholders, the applicants have shown a *willingness to take great risks with the company's funds* [italics supplied], speculating on their ability to get on the New York Central's board by persuading the Commission to overthrow all its precedents, and further speculating on their opinion that they can do a better job running the New York Central than can its present management. The applicants have further speculated in severing all connection with the Nickel Plate in anticipation of the approval of their proposals. Little regard either for the public interest or for the private interests of the stockholders of the Nickel Plate was displayed by the petitioners or the applicants in thus severing a connection of long standing which the Commission had found to be in the public interest.

In case the Commission and the public were unaware of Boles's feelings toward Young, he added this footnote:

There is much in the record to indicate that purchase of the New York Central stock was made for the purpose of indulging a hobby of applicant Young and for the further purpose of satisfying his personal ambition "to be in the New York Central."

Boles then hurled a challenge. If Young had such faith in his own prophecies regarding the merits of unification of C & O and Central, then why wasn't he willing to rely on that faith and seek immediate unification?

If the applicants possess the great abilities, foresight and salesmanship attributed to them, there is no reason why they should not take their proposals directly to the stockholders of the two companies and persuade them as to the desirability of such unification, and having persuaded them, file an application for the necessary authority under Section 5 (2) of the Act. Failing that, there is nothing to keep from filing an application under Section 5(2) to acquire the limited control they now propose. In connection with such an application, due consideration could be given to provision for other carriers and to employees who might be adversely affected by the proposals.

The proposed report, viewed in its entirety, was a carefully reasoned document, despite its acerbic tone. Both its organization and legal development were professional, and the consensus around the Commission was that the conclusions reached were correct. It is doubtful that Boles realized how his judgments would look in a final document. What effect Boles's unusually severe language would have on the staid and proper Commission was a matter of intense speculation by both sides. Each was uneasy as to its real effect. The Commission itself could not help but be disturbed.

Young received the news of Boles's recommendation while traveling in his office car to his home town, Canadian, to receive the "Texan-of-Achievement" award from Texas Governor Beauford Jester. The substance of Boles's report was transmitted to Young while the train was stopped at Green River, Wyoming, which happened to be a communications point on the Union Pacific with excellent telegraphic facilities. So deeply affected was Young by this news that he got out of his car and paced the station platform in intense silence. To one associate he appeared to be in a black mood bordering on depression. After what appeared to his worried friend to be an interminable time, he regained control of himself and began thinking of the press release he should issue in answer to the I.C.C. examiner.

In the press release, he contemptuously dismissed Boles as a "bureaucrat." His main fire was directed against the "two-faced justice" of the I.C.C., one kind for Young and another for the investment bankers and insurance companies. Once again he seemed to be talking to the public, not the Commission.

Today's I.C.C. report is another decision against the public interest by a government bureaucrat whose duty it is to further public interest— a decision which I publicly predicted some time ago.

Difficult as it is for us to accept this decision, it is even more difficult for us to take the Commission's two-faced justice. This is a serious charge, but so are the facts.

(1) Harry Hagerty, a Metropolitan Life officer, was quietly granted the right, without a hearing, to sit on the board of the New York, New Haven & Hartford Railroad and the Erie Railroad, at the very time we were required to appear before the Commission in elaborate proceedings in a futile attempt to obtain a similar right. The Metropolitan Life Insurance Company is dominated by the investment bankers whose interests are adverse to those of the railroads.

(2) Last year, when by government order, the Pullman Company was offered for sale, we made a bid identical to that of the railroad cartel plus a commitment to spend a half-billion dollars to replace the entire obsolete fleet of 5,000 Pullman cars. Our bid to replace monopoly with competition was turned down with I.C.C. connivance. The result is that

the people must continue to ride for years to come in these same archaic Pullman cars at the same fares for which we would have provided new cars and new service.

(3) 27 years ago Congress instructed the I.C.C. to devise a plan for consolidating the railroads into a small number of systems. Today there are still 130 Class I railroads. Now we have proposed to lay the groundwork for a major consolidation—one which, according to transportation experts, is the most natural and beneficial of all possible American railroad consolidations. In no other way but consolidation can railroads meet spiraling costs without a dangerous increase in rates. But here again the I.C.C. violates its public duty and turns us down.[15]

The release concluded by predicting ultimate victory.

In addition, in an interview with a United Press reporter, Young said:

We have 400,000 shares of stock in the New York Central, the largest individual bloc. I trace the opposition to our application to the group of investment bankers headed by J. P. Morgan & Co.

These bankers are not interested in improving passenger service; they are interested in putting railroad deposits in their banks.

I will appeal this decision to the division of the commission which has jurisdiction, then to the full commission, and, if necessary, to the courts.[16]

Although Young ignored Boles's name in these attacks, his lawyers did not and took exception to the examiner's "intemperate language," claiming it indicated a predisposition against the proponents.

In a bill of exceptions filed with the I.C.C. January 8, 1948, the attorneys said: "The tenor of the report makes it clear that the examiner is against the petition and the petitioners, the applications and the applicants, and everything they propose." They charged that Boles had erred in ruling out a showing of benefits to be derived from ultimate unification. He had erred further in refusing to recognize the constructive purposes underlying the C & O proposals. He had also erred in finding that granting the proposals would result in acquisition of control of the Central. Moreover, Boles had em-

[15] C & O press release dated December 11, 1947. Statement appeared in *Railway Age*, December 13, 1947, "Mr. Young Comments on the Boles Report," p. 64.
[16] St. Louis *Star Times*, December 11, 1947.

phasized unduly the lessening of competition and had ignored the public benefits of the proposed alliance and had erroneously found that public and private interests would be adversely affected. He had ignored the national transportation policy in favor of railroad consolidation and the urgent necessity for measures that would lead the Central out of its difficulties.

While the word "biased" did not appear in the exceptions, it was clearly implied. The C & O counsel charged that in addition to using "intemperate language," Boles had taken certain of Young's testimony out of context and had ignored "even more pertinent testimony."

The C & O counsel took Boles to task for saying that Young had claimed all the credit for many reforms, when the record disclosed that he had consistently used the pronoun "we" in describing the campaigns.

Also objected to were Boles's statements that the applicants had shown willingness to take great risks with C & O funds and that Young "no longer intends to leave to experienced management the matter of operations. . . ." The fact of the matter was that the C & O had invested in Central shares only after "most complete consideration of the benefits that would flow to Chesapeake through an association with Central," and the changes that Young advocated were "at the level of policy-making and over-all management, the function which a board of directors is supposed to exercise but which in the case of so many railroad corporations have been so sadly neglected, or subverted to considerations not involving the best interests of the company."

There was only one more avenue of persuasion left: the oral arguments before the full Commission, which took place on February 27, 1948.

It was a lively session, with members of the Commission often interrupting the attorneys.

The commissioners' questions were pointed. Didn't the statute prevent the C & O from discriminating against its connecting carriers? Why did Young take all the credit for getting rid of the black market in Pullman reservations? Why was the C & O not asking for unification now? How could Young put his recommended innovations into effect without control? Hadn't Young said he would "go to the country," use advertising to rouse public opinion if the I.C.C. refused his application?

On May 10, 1948, the Commission handed down the decision. It accepted Boles's findings almost without exception and denied both the petition and the applications.

But the Commission's final decision carefully expunged almost all of Boles's acid characterizations of Young. Omitted were the phrases "brook no interference with his plans," "opinions, prophecies, speculation, and . . . pure fancy," "willingness to take great risks with the company's funds," "little regard either for the public interest or the private interests of the stockholders," "indulging a hobby for applicant Young," "satisfying his personal ambition." As far as substance was concerned, however, the defeat for Young recommended by Boles was not changed in the slightest detail. What is more, in less than three months the Commission further eased the implied criticism of Boles by promoting him to be director of the Bureau of Finance of the I.C.C.

For the moment, then, Young's assault on the Central was repulsed. But for how long?

6

The Second Battle for the Central

IN BEATING BACK Young, the Central had an opportunity to assess its tormentor and, more important, itself. Nevertheless, the Central's weaknesses were destined to persist. The repeated emphasis on the Central's financial and physical deterioration during the 1947 I.C.C. proceeding was a grim advertisement to the public and stockholders alike. None of the Central's financially powerful allies appeared enthusiastic about building a larger stock position to counterbalance the block of 400,000 shares still owned by the C & O and controlled by its alter ego, Young.

The gloomy atmosphere surrounding the victor was in contrast to Young's warm glow as defender of the stockholders against management and the Wall Street bankers, as champion of the public in its demands for better service and modern equipment, as the voice of progress. He was a public figure whose name and picture were now easily recognized—a priceless advantage for a politician and no less so for a corporate leader with great ambition. An index of this status was Young's appearance on the cover of *Time* magazine of February 3, 1947, as well as stories about him in every major publication. Moreover, Young and the C & O were prospering.

The main revenues of the C & O, of course, were coming from coal tonnage, which made it one of the most prosperous railroads in the United States. Young, however, was passionately devoted to raising the quality of passenger service as a personal monument. The public response to the "hog ad" spurred him on. The Central, joining together large centers of population like New York, Chicago, Buffalo and Cleveland, was the prime passenger road of the country.

Young charged that the Central's continued large deficits despite this built-in advantage were the result of non-owning, banker-controlled management which made practically no effort to increase passenger volume. The Central, Young was convinced, was made to order for his bold concept of what passenger service could and should be. He considered this one of the major areas for rehabilitation of the Central.

The attachment Young had for passenger service appeared in a number of innovations which he introduced to the C & O. He not only recommended these innovations to goad the railroad industry and to underscore its backwardness, but he actually put them into practice in the C & O. He instituted a "no tipping" policy, a method for picking up tickets on the train, a credit-card system, and motion pictures on trains. None, however, proved to be successful. When these had to be abandoned, Young was sure it was because the C & O was a coal-carrying freight road, with passenger business too small and unimportant to accommodate itself to these innovations. He was convinced that, with a passenger road like the New York Central, things would be different.

Young's interest in the Central continued to percolate. He gave a press interview in May 1948 indicating that he might buy control of the Virginian and then apply to the I.C.C. for a three-way merger of the C & O, New York Central, and Virginian. Young even hinted that enough Virginian stock to accomplish such an end had already been offered to him.

In August, Young was still discussing this possibility publicly. In an interview he kept up the pressure. "The Virginian is controlled by the Koppers Company of Pittsburgh, a Mellon outfit. It is my understanding that the Koppers people have felt for some time they are skirting very close to the edges of the Clayton Antitrust Act in keeping control of this railroad. If they feel that way, they should be willing to dispose of their stock. We'll be glad to buy the stock and clear up the situation for all concerned."[1]

Whether Young was conducting an "operation terror" or really

[1] Robert S. Allen, "Washington Merry-Go-Round," Washington *Post*, August 21, 1948.

meant what he was saying about buying the Virginian, no one could be sure. But Young's advertising campaign, his press interviews, and his conduct generally added up to an unmistakable warning. A crash effort by the Central was needed to shore up critical weaknesses before the inevitable next blow.

Betterment of Central's financial position and increased volume of traffic were fervently to be desired. But the state of the national economy and the mountainous problems of railroading were beyond management's capacity to overcome.

The depressing statistics were familiar to stockholders and analysts alike. The same discouraging theme of "profitless prosperity" ran through the annual reports of those years: huge volumes of traffic but low earnings; marginal dividends or none at all.

The annual messages from President Metzman were almost plaintive: "Again in 1949 the New York Central performed a large volume of work for relatively little return."

Passenger traffic losses, higher wages and costs, strikes and stoppages—all contributed to the Central's troubles.

In addition, the Central was being crushed by debt of monumental proportions, and it had to incur new debt each year to modernize and replace equipment. A typical year was 1950, when it retired more than $27,000,000 of old debt but incurred a new debt of almost $30,000,000 for dieselization and electrified locomotives.

Young, in the meantime, was conducting a major battle against his traditional "enemies," the investment bankers and the insurance companies, in the matter of the Missouri Pacific bankruptcy. He was fighting the bondholders in an attempt to preserve the equity of Alleghany's huge holdings of common stock, which would have become worthless under proposed reorganization plans. Young had been engaged in this struggle since he took over control of Alleghany. It went on in the I.C.C., through the courts, before congressional committees, and in the press. At a critical point in late 1951, when the I.C.C. was reviewing the Missouri Pacific reorganization, Young resorted to a hard-hitting advertising campaign. Even his supporters were surprised by the violence of his attack. It proved too much for his own advertising agency, which this time succeeded in resigning the ac-

Congress Be Damned!

THE CAPTAIN'S OBLIGATION
IS THE HIGHEST!

An Open Letter to the Directors of Certain Life Insurance Companies

count. Young had lost none of his capacity to shock. Two advertisements in particular—"Congress Be Damned!" and "The Captain's Obligation Is the Highest!"—outraged the opposition and some officials of the government agencies that were criticized.

The Missouri Pacific reorganization was under the jurisdiction of the U.S. District Court in St. Louis, presided over by Judge George H. Moore. When he read the "Congress Be Damned!" ad, he reacted with predictable outrage, both on and off the bench. What angered him most was the paragraph:

Judge George H. Moore of the U.S. District Court, St. Louis, Missouri, former Collector of Internal Revenue, on December 26, 1944, confirmed Frank Thompson as sole Trustee of the St. Louis–San Francisco Railway, operating out of St. Louis, and permitted his brother, Guy, to remain as sole Trustee of the Missouri Pacific, also operating out of St. Louis and competing with the Frisco. Thus, these two competing carriers have since been operated out of the same law office. Throughout the bankruptcies the two Thompson brothers and the New York Financial Group have consistently taken the same side.

At the time this ad appeared, a scandal regarding the corruption of some of the Collectors of Internal Revenue was making headlines. Even the Commissioner of Internal Revenue was on his way to jail.

Shaking with anger, Judge Moore shouted from the bench at T. C. Davis, who had signed the advertisement along with Young and Kirby, that it had been twenty-nine years since he was a Collector of Internal Revenue and that there was nothing unusual about the appointment of trustees of several bankrupt railroads from one law office.

In the advertisement "The Captain's Obligation Is the Highest!" Young put the pressure on the so-called opposition by listing the names of all the directors of the four largest life insurance companies opposing him. The implication of the ad was that, although these directors had a fiduciary obligation so far as the Missouri Pacific reorganization was concerned, they were "into the first life boat," leaving "trampled behind, naked and helpless, the tens of thousands of men, women and children who hold some 13 other Missouri Pacific security issues that can only be scuttled by your callous desertion of them." The list of these directors to which this message was presumably addressed was the aristocracy of American finance, industry, and commerce. Young, once again, was relying on the David-Goliath predisposition of the American public and identification with the small stockholder.

It was during a press interview that reporters covering the I.C.C. hearing on the Missouri Pacific reorganization in November 1951 were startled by a Young statement having nothing to do with the issue at hand. Young told reporters that he would shortly take over the New York Central. To remove any legal impediment, he would resign as chairman of the C & O. "Mr. Young indicated," according to the United Press story, "that if the I.C.C. approves, he will act before the next New York Central stockholders' meeting next May."[2]

Just as suddenly and without explanation, Young denied the story. He refused to say any more about it.

It would have been the height of folly for the Central directorate to ignore the warnings of an impending assault. By this time they knew that the 400,000 shares owned by the C & O were a ticking time bomb.

[2] *New York Times*, November 28, 1951, p. 45.

In August of 1952, the Central had to consider the appointment of a new president, since Metzman was approaching retirement age. Someone was needed with enough talent to tackle the Central's gargantuan problems of finance and traffic. Even more important, a president was needed who would be a match for Young in the combat which was sure to come. This time the Central would look outside its organization for such a man. To the surprise of some, the man chosen was William White, president of the Delaware, Lackawanna & Western. Metzman moved up to become chairman of the board.

White's rise up through the railroad ranks—befitting the Horatio Alger tradition of the poor American boy achieving the American dream—his self-education, and his forty years of solid railroad experience made him an imposing figure among his railroading peers. By birth, by training, by personality and appearance, he was the very essence of what the railroad business thought a railroad president should be.

Eleven days older than Young, he was born February 3, 1897, the oldest child of a master mechanic who had come to the United States from the Netherlands. He never graduated from high school, quitting when he was sixteen to help support his family by working on the Erie. His first job was as a twenty-dollars-a-month clerk in the freight auditor's office. He advanced with an intense drive and determination through jobs as secretary, office manager, trainmaster, assistant superintendent, division superintendent, assistant general manager, and general manager. It was at this point in his career, in January 1938, that he was hired away from the Erie by the Virginian Railway as vice president and general manager. Two years later, at the beginning of 1941, he went to the trouble-ridden Delaware, Lackawanna & Western Railroad, which chose him as president. With the Lackawanna he established his reputation as an executive troubleshooter, overhauling both the financial structure and the operating policy of the road. During his eleven years with the D.L. & W., the road's stock went up 157 percent—a record which would provide ammunition for the Central against Young, since C & O stock had declined 7 percent during the same period.

White also had the traditional affiliations that mark a captain of industry. He was, at one time or another, a director of the First National Bank of New York, American Telephone & Telegraph Co., Railway Express Agency, Inc., the New York Telephone Co., the National Biscuit Co., the Manufacturers & Traders Trust Company of Buffalo, the Association of American Railroads, and the Lehigh & Hudson River Railway Co. He was a Republican. He lived in Westchester County, New York, in "on-line" Scarsdale. His business, his hobby, his life was railroading.

By 1952 the Central had become a $2,500,000,000 property, carrying a funded debt of almost $800,000,000. With a gross revenue of almost $807,000,000, the rate of return on net investment was only 2.48 percent. This was a continuation of Central's trend of lagging behind the eastern railroads (whose average rate of return on net investment in 1952 was 3.80 percent) and all Class I railroads (4.16 percent). The road was carrying an annual deficit from passenger train operations of more than $50,000,000.

In White's first report to the stockholders, after he had struggled with Central's problems only a few months, he was soberly optimistic. Close control of expenses, together with improved unit revenues, had enabled the Central to overcome a moderate general decline in traffic and finish 1952 with earnings higher than in 1951, despite fractionally lower gross revenues. The company's needs for additional capital expenditures were still great, but there would have to be a tapering off until earnings were more substantial and working capital increased. Dieselization of the system was about 55 percent complete and would probably reach 60 percent during 1953. A firm of management engineers had been hired to go into all phases of the passenger deficit problem. Freight business other than coal was holding up well.

White had been in office less than six months when further ominous signs of the coming struggle for control of the Central appeared. White, fully briefed on Young's last attack, knew better than to underestimate him. As a matter of fact, the Central had been keeping a file on Young ever since his abortive attack in 1947.

News of the impending battle for control of the Central now

began to appear in newspaper reports. By January 1953 the mobilization of Young's forces could no longer be concealed. The first clear signs of such activity emanated from the C & O. President Walter J. Tuohy, who had succeeded Bowman when the latter retired because of illness, announced that the C & O had added 244,741 shares of Central stock to its basic holding of 400,000. The combined total of 644,741 represented an exact 10 percent of the 6,447,410 total shares of Central. Tuohy added that the immediate purchase, when added to the immense gathering of Central stock, "evidences our unbounded faith in the future of the railroad industry and reflects a further step in our company's planned program of diversification. . . ." He continued:

The New York Central is a major segment of the industry and has begun to tap its inherent potentialities. It is increasing its earning power by an expansion of its already large traffic base and a better control of costs. C & O's management believes that through closer association of interests, it will be able to contribute to this hopeful trend of the Central, as well as the industry as a whole—and all to the ultimate benefit of C & O's security holders.

But no one was diverted from his suspicions, least of all the Central's management or board of directors. They knew the real import of Tuohy's announcement. The battle for the Central had resumed. Any doubts were dispelled on March 28, 1953, when, after a formal speech before his Federation for Railway Progress, Young amplified his remarks in a press conference. He predicted that the C & O would control the Central in a year and consolidate in ten years. As an afterthought he said he would move its headquarters from New York to Cleveland. It would then be farther away from Wall Street.

No one, certainly no sophisticated observer, thought Tuohy spoke with conviction when, at the C & O annual meeting on April 30, 1953, he said that there were no immediate plans to merge with the Central.

Furthermore, the financial community, always supersensitive to the moves of a man like Young, knew the C & O was continuing to buy Central stock. By the end of July, the C & O conceded that an additional 155,259 shares had been purchased since the last announcement about C & O's Central holdings, which now totaled 800,000 shares. Within a few months C & O ownership had been doubled, from 6.25 percent to 12.50 percent.

In addition, in a move shrouded by complete secrecy, Young began buying for his and Kirby's personal accounts. In early December 1953, Young called in H. Hentz & Company and Pershing & Company, two relatively small brokerage houses on Wall Street. As a careful student of Wall Street morality, Young knew he could trust these firms. He asked that between them they purchase for himself and Allan Kirby 100,000 shares of stock each, at the same time maintaining absolute secrecy for whom they were buying. Young did not even chance telling his most intimate associates in Alleghany. So expertly did Hentz and Pershing perform that they accumulated the large block without causing any upward movement in Central stock. Neither did anyone learn for whose account the stock was being bought. Although in the 1946 purchase of Central stock Young had had an excellent experience with the large brokerage firm Merrill Lynch, Pierce, Fenner & Beane, in 1954 the secrecy of his undertaking dictated the choice of the smaller firms with their limited personnel.

By early 1954 Young was ready. On January 16, Harold S. Vanderbilt phoned White from Palm Beach with some unpleasant news. Robert Young had called on Vanderbilt that day—the two were social friends and neighbors—to report that he and Kirby had personally bought heavily into the Central. "They are getting out of the C & O," Vanderbilt told White, "because Young wants to be chairman and chief executive officer of the Central, and bring Kirby along."

In White's view the demand was sheer effrontery. He told Vanderbilt to inform Young that he would have an answer after the Central board meeting on February 10.

Three days later, on January 19, a series of announcements by Alleghany, the C & O, and Young himself made the headlines. They disclosed that all the Alleghany directors who sat on the C & O board, including Young and Kirby, had resigned from the C & O.

Further, the Alleghany Corporation had sold all of its holdings in the C & O, 104,854 shares, to its long-time ally, Cyrus Eaton. The C & O then elected Eaton chairman in place of Young and announced that "with this action, Alleghany Corporation and Mr. Young and Mr. Kirby are completely divesting themselves of control of C & O and are free to acquire control of another carrier."

Any remaining mystery was dispelled by the Alleghany announcement of the resignations from the C & O. The Alleghany Corporation, along with Mr. Young and Mr. Kirby, had become a "substantial stockholder in the New York Central Railroad." The Interstate Commerce Commission would, of course, be told formally of this and other developments.

Before the week was out, William White in a public statement disclosed that Young and Kirby had formally requested that, as substantial stockholders, they become members of the New York Central board of directors. The question would be brought up at the next meeting of the board. How much stock Young and Kirby personally acquired in addition to the C & O's 800,000 shares was not immediately known. But White, supported by the 1948 I.C.C. decision frustrating the C & O's attempt to take over the Central, could confidently add that "the board may consider it premature to answer [Young's] request until such time as legal questions within the jurisdiction of the Interstate Commerce Commission have been resolved." For the moment the language was temperate and within the confines of proper corporate protocol. Young had requested but had not yet demanded capitulation.

While the Central management had no way of accurately estimating the extent of Young and Kirby's holding in Central stock, they knew the block was substantial. There loomed even more ominously the 800,000-share block owned by the C & O. The Central knew Young would ultimately exercise its power one way or another in any full-scale battle for control of the Central.

Young then asked White and Place to join him for lunch in New York. On February 2, after a well-concealed trip from Palm Beach, Young met the two men at the Cloud Club in the Chrysler Building. Young was friendly, almost conciliatory. First he offered to retain

White as president of the Central and Place as financial vice president, with further inducements, including handsome stock options. White of course would have to relinquish to Young the position of chief executive officer and remain on as chief operating officer. Then Young suggested that it would be to the advantage of the New York Central (and to Young) to adopt the C & O bylaw which provided that the chairman of the board be the chief executive officer. He urged that White and Place use their influence with the board to support his request to be chairman. Finally, he requested a copy of the list of Central stockholders.

White replied that before a decision could be made on any of these requests, he would have to think it over and, in any event, report the discussion to the Central board. Young left the meeting in a confident mood, convinced that White and Place would accept his offer and that he could count on their neutrality should a proxy contest develop. When he reported to his staff about the luncheon, they were not so sanguine.

The stockholder list of forty-four thousand names did arrive the next day, and Young wrote to White acknowledging its receipt. Despite the odd fact that the package came tied together by a pair of old suspenders, Young regarded such a gesture hopefully. At least he would not have to go through a protracted and costly court fight to get the list.

Young and Kirby's major demands still required consideration by the board itself. To Young's consternation, he heard nothing more from White. On the day of the meeting, February 10, Young therefore issued what might be regarded as an ultimatum. If the Central board turned down his demand for the two seats, a proxy fight would begin the next morning. Promptly, at the close of the board meeting, their decision was announced to the public in a less than conciliatory tone.

It would be inimical to the best interests of the company to grant Mr. Young's request. . . .

. . . The company contracted some eighteen months ago with William White to be its president and chief executive officer, and the board is not willing that Mr. White relinquish his position as chief executive officer, nor that the responsibility of management be divided.

The board expressed its confidence in Mr. White and his administration and believes it to be in the best interest of the New York Central property and its stockholders that the programs and policies which he has instituted should be permitted to continue. The board considers that these programs and policies are proceeding satisfactorily to the benefit of the property.

The board further took note of the adverse effect that would result upon the morale of employees and officers of Central's vast system should the suggested change of management take place.[3]

In spelling out the denial of Young's request, the board made public for the first time the fact that Young had asked for more than merely two seats. White revealed that Young had requested that he be made chairman of the board and chief executive officer. Normally the Central board's position was to give recognition to large holders of stock, as in fact they did in 1947 when they invited Young and Bowman to become members of the board if they could get I.C.C. approval. But to offer the position of chairman of the board and chief executive officer to Robert R. Young, in face of what he had been saying about the Central and what he represented generally, was something the board could not do and still retain their self-respect. And for the moment, at least, the I.C.C. ruling of 1945 was binding and the Chase National Bank still was trustee of the 800,000 shares. Neither Young nor his good friend Cyrus Eaton, the new chairman of the C & O, could lay his hands on them.

White, aware of Young's threats when he distributed the prepared statement of the board, remarked, "If anyone should start a proxy fight, the New York Central board and management would also start soliciting proxies."

Young accepted the challenge and announced that a proxy contest was a practical certainty. The New York Central must be returned to its rightful owners, the stockholders.

His formal statement in reply to the Central board's rejection set a harsh tone.

This Morgan board now seeks to confuse the issues by asserting that I, the largest known individual stockholder, desire to substitute myself

[3] New York Central release of February 10, 1954. Published in the *Wall Street Journal,* February 11, 1954, p. 3.

for Mr. White as chief *operating*[4] executive. Nothing is further from the fact. This is attested to by my long and highly satisfactory relationship with Walter J. Tuohy, chief *operating* executive of the Chesapeake & Ohio Railway. He served subject to his stockholders and his board through me as their chairman.

The real issue is whether the owners of the properties are going to be made to continue to submit to a Morgan non-ownership board with its countless conflicting interests or whether they are to enjoy what every honest business under our American system must have if shareholders and the public are to be served instead of to be damned. That is an ownership board with a strong ownership voice in its chair.

The New York Central owners, I am sure, on May 26 will give the right answer.[5]

Young told reporters that he was going to New York for the "duration," and White in turn pledged a "bare-fisted" fight. The stage was being set for the biggest proxy fight in the nation's history.

Young arrived in New York from Palm Beach on February 15, this time officially and with proper fanfare, to assume charge of the proxy contest. When his train eased into Pennsylvania Station, he was met by a horde of representatives of the newspapers, radio, and television, as well as observers from Central's management. The scene had the electric atmosphere of a major political event; the stationmaster said he had never seen anything to compare with it. Young confidently predicted victory, placing the odds at a comfortable three-to-one in his favor. He did, however, issue a plea for all Central stockholders to vote for him. He damned the bankers' control of the Central and charged the management with inefficiency and failure to modernize. He was silent on questions relating to the 800,000 shares and whether or not his group was responsible for the purchase of large blocks of Central stock, now among the most active on the New York Stock Exchange.

The next day a small but eye-catching ad appeared in the *Wall*

---

[4] Italics supplied. The reader is cautioned to observe the distinction which Young was trying to make between chief executive officer and chief *operating* executive officer.

[5] New York *Herald Tribune*, February 11, 1954, p. 1.

Street Journal, the *New York Times,* and several other leading papers.
The advertisement provoked interest among many New York Central stockholders. One response was indeed dramatic. It was an offer of support from the owner of 41,800 shares of Central stock, Dr. R. Walter Graham, a physician well known in Baltimore politics. Though Young had not known Dr. Graham before, he immediately invited him to become a member of the Young-Kirby slate of nominees for the Central board of directors. Dr. Graham accepted Young's offer.

MEMO to:
NEW YORK CENTRAL STOCKHOLDERS
If you have any nominations for your new
OWNERSHIP BOARD OF DIRECTORS
to be elected May 26, 1954
please advise
ROBERT R. YOUNG and ALLAN P. KIRBY
ALLEGHANY CORPORATION
Chrysler Building, New York City

Both parties swung into action like armies mobilizing for a major war. Intelligence and counterintelligence measures were taken. Telephone and mail security was checked and rechecked. So were personnel. Headquarters were swept constantly for hidden microphones. Security experts were hired for twenty-four-hour service.

The New York Central halted its scheduled advertising and allocated everything for use in the proxy fight. White announced that the Central intended to use the press, magazines, radio, and television to get its story to the public.

To determine in which cities to advertise, the Central made an analysis of the distribution of the 44,000 shareholders and the approximately 6,500,000 shares of stock. The stockholders list was broken down by the states in which the stockholders lived and the number of shares they held. It turned out that New York State had by far the largest number, 14,000, followed by Ohio and Pennsylvania with 3000 each, Illinois, Massachusetts, and New Jersey with over 2000 each, California, Connecticut, and Michigan with over 1000 each, and Indiana, Maryland, and Virginia and the District of Columbia with over 900 each. In the District of Columbia, seat of the I.C.C., the S.E.C., the Department of Justice, Congress, and the White House, the message would have to be directed toward more than stockholders. As a result of the analysis, it was decided to concentrate Central advertising on the influential newspapers in eleven key cities: New York, Washington, Boston, Albany, Buffalo, Rochester, Syracuse, Chicago, Detroit, Cleveland, and Philadelphia.

The public relations approach was of special importance because of the fact that over 40 percent of the shares were held in "street names." This large percentage of stock was held anonymously in the names of Wall Street brokerage houses. There was no legitimate way that the principals could learn the identity of these stockholders, and neither was there any guarantee that the brokers would pass along the proxy material. The only effective way to reach these stockholders was through the mass media.

The Central engaged the services of Robinson-Hannagan Associates, Inc., one of New York's largest public relations firms, at a fee of fifty thousand dollars plus expenses. In addition, Central used the services of its regular advertising agency, Foote, Cone & Belding, in what turned out to be an extensive advertising program. Central's public relations director, Raymond F. Blosser, worked with the head of Robinson-Hannagan, William E. Robinson, and Robinson-Hannagan staffer Malcolm Johnson, whose credentials included a Pulitzer prize for his book *On the Waterfront*. The Central also employed Georgeson & Company as professional proxy solicitors, at a fee of ten thousand dollars plus expenses.

Assigned to the battle were members of Central's legal staff, Robert Brooks, James B. Gray, and Samuel H. Hellenbrand, among the most talented lawyers in the industry. In addition, Central retained as special counsel to cope with the fight the law firm Dorr, Hand & Dawson. Enlisted to help were some of the most respected law firms in New York: Cravath, Swaine & Moore; Rosenman, Goldmark, Colin & Kaye; Cleary, Gottlieb, Friendly & Hamilton.

The most formidable source of management strength was its board of directors and the financial and industrial institutions which they represented. There were four representatives of powerful banking firms with which the Central did business: George Whitney, chairman of the board of J. P. Morgan & Company; Alexander C. Nagle, president of the First National Bank of the City of New York; Percy J. Ebbott, president of the Chase National Bank of the City of New York; and Lawrence N. Murray, president of the Mellon National Bank and Trust Company. On the board were such industrialists as William E. Levis, director and former chairman of the board of Owens-Illinois Glass Company; Albert B. Dick, Jr., chairman of the board of A. B. Dick Company; Earle J. Machold, president of Niagara Mohawk Power Corporation; James A. Farley, chairman of

Photo taken just after the historic meeting on January 19, 1954, at which Young (*left*) resigned as C & O Chairman. Cyrus S. Eaton (*right*), a C & O director for many years, succeeded him. At center is Walter J. Tuohy.

(Courtesy of C & O Railroad)

the board of the Coca-Cola Export Corporation and the architect of President Franklin D. Roosevelt's campaigns in 1932 and 1936, and regarded as the pre-eminent strategist in handling political elections. The other members of the board also represented powerful interests: Robert F. Loree, chairman of the executive committee of the Emigrant Industrial Savings Bank, chairman of the National Foreign Trade Council, and a former vice president of Guaranty Trust Company; Malcolm P. Aldrich, president of the Commonwealth Fund, a nonprofit charitable organization which owned 32,522 shares of Central stock; Carl P. Dennett, president of Capital Managers, Inc., an investment fund management company; and Elton Hoyt II, senior partner of Pickands, Mather & Company, distributor of iron ore, coke, and coal. President William White was on the board, of course, and there were two Vanderbilts, Harold S., a third-generation Vanderbilt who had been on the board for forty years (and who was world-famous as the inventor of contract bridge), and William H., a fourth-generation Vanderbilt who had been elected to the board in 1947. A large majority of the board had many years of service.

This, then, was the board that entered the fray against Young. It was indeed a formidable combination.

The other side, the Young-Kirby-Alleghany team, had as its most important weapon Robert R. Young himself. Backing him up was Allan Kirby with his immense wealth, as well as the powerful Alleghany Corporation. Moreover there could be little doubt that Young came into the fray with the good will of the C & O and its officers and directors, particularly the chairman, Cyrus Eaton.

One key official of the C & O, Thomas J. Deegan, Jr., vice president of public relations and advertising, a director, and a member of the executive committee, resigned these positions, giving up retirement benefits and other emoluments, to become Young's chief of staff. All advertising and public relations in the fight came within his orbit; Young did not feel it necessary to hire an outside public relations or advertising firm.

Other youthful men immediately around Young were Charles T.

Ireland, Jr., Clifford H. Ramsdell, and William C. MacMillen, Jr.[6] Young's law firm, Lord, Day & Lord, assigned two of its senior partners, Garrard W. Glenn and Thomas F. Daly, to the proxy operation. Young planned at first not to hire a professional proxy-soliciting firm but changed this decision and employed Kissel & Company.

Young's strategy staff met at eight o'clock every morning, so that they had an extra hour before the start of business. Each day they reviewed the proxy returns, the publicity, and the other relevant matters. They also organized a telephone campaign to the forty-four thousand Central stockholders. Every nominee on the Young slate was given a selected list based on the amount of stock owned. As new nominees to the slate were added, they were included in the telephone brigade. Young not only personally made calls but followed up among his nominees to see that they were calling.

White held strategy meetings of his staff and advisers twice a week, every Monday and Thursday, with Willard Place second in command. White felt that meeting every day might prove a distraction from the fight itself and, what is more, he and other members of his staff had a railroad to run in the meantime.

Young began a calculated campaign to provoke White. He repeated an earlier charge that White was hired to run the railroad, not a proxy fight, and demanded that White get back to operating the property, which was in enough fiscal and equipment trouble already.

Young's acid words found their mark and drew a stinging retort from White.

The directors of the New York Central have decided it is inimical to the railroad's best interests for Mr. Young to take over. It is part of my job to keep this from happening. That means winning the proxy fight. It is just as much a part of my job as to run the railroad.

I have been running the railroad, will continue to run it, both from

[6] Ireland later became president of the Alleghany Corporation and then vice president of International Telephone & Telegraph. Ramsdell became vice president of Alleghany. MacMillen became president of Tower International, Inc.

Charles T. Ireland, Jr.
(Photo by Tommy Weber)

Clifford H. Ramsdell
(Photo by Tommy Weber)

Thomas F. Daly

the New York office and from all points along the New York Central's lines.[7]

Then, taking aim at Young personally, he fired, "But I will never run the railroad from Palm Beach or Newport."

Rising to Young's charge of banker control, White continued, "All dictators like to set up straw men. These are the *tactics of little Caesars.*

"The New York Central board isn't Morgan controlled nor is it controlled by Wall Street. It is controlled by all stockholders for the benefit of all, including employees, who are doing such a magnificent job of bringing the quality of service up to where we want it."

Helping White to refute Young's charges were the officials of J. P. Morgan & Company. Henry Alexander, the bank's president, particularly ridiculed Young's charge of Morgan control, pointing to the fact that the bank itself could not own stock and that the officers hardly owned enough stock to be in a dominating position.

A little later Henry S. Sturgis, vice president of the First National Bank, a director and chairman of the executive committee of the Erie Railroad, a former Pullman director, and an admitted foe of Young's, announced that he would aid White in the role of a "proxy coordinator."

My purpose in volunteering to aid in the fight against Young is that I think it would be a national calamity if Young were able to substitute his promoter type management for the present experienced management which is making such substantial progress in the affairs of the Central.[8]

White's success in lining up the vocal support of the banks became more obvious as their executives pushed to issue statements in his support.

The entrance of Sturgis, whom Young had battled in the Pullman case, provided Young with a chance to raise the issue of the anti-trust laws and incidentally to get some newspaper space .

Henry Sturgis is a director of the Erie, one of the Central's chief competitors. Mr. White has requested the I.C.C. to look into the enforce-

[7] *New York Times,* February 16, 1954, p. 35.
[8] *New York Times,* March 16, 1954, p. 37.

ment of the Clayton Act. I would suggest that he now request the I.C.C. to include Mr. Sturgis on the agenda.[9]

And so the verbal exchanges continued, colorful and barbed, but hardly decisive.

On the other hand, a potentially decisive element in the contest was the question of the 800,000 shares of Central stock owned by the C & O and trusteed to the Chase National Bank. If the Chase Bank voted the stock in accordance with the owners' wishes, it would probably have to vote for Young. But there was more than a mere suspicion that, if it followed its own inclination, it would vote for White. After all, its own president, Percy J. Ebbott, was a director of Central, had voted against offering Young a seat on the board, and was himself a contestant as a nominee on management's slate in the proxy fight. Young was particularly rankled by Ebbott's vote against him.

On February 24 there appeared in a number of papers the column of the respected financial writer J. A. Livingston, written for syndication several days earlier. Some of Young's supporters were deeply concerned, for its implications could be disastrous.

Livingston was the first newspaperman to spell out in public a major area of concern to the contestants: who would vote the block of 800,000 shares. "It's a good bet," Livingston wrote, "that as it goes, so goes the Central."

Livingston described the delicateness of Ebbott's position as a member of both the Central board and president of the Chase Bank. If the Chase voted for Young, it would have to repudiate its own president.

Moreover, as Livingston pointed out, there were cold, legal issues to consider as well as the emotional complications. The language of the trust agreement—"The trustee shall be entitled and it shall be its duty in respect to all shares of stock deposited hereunder . . . independently to vote upon the election of directors at meetings of stockholders"—could be interpreted differently by different lawyers.

[9] *Ibid.*

If the Chase decided it was its duty to vote the stock independently, it would have to ignore the preferences of the legal owner of the stock—Young's ally, Cyrus Eaton—and decide the issues on its merits.

Young and Eaton could try to enjoin the Chase from voting the stock, but the courts might consider this as interfering with the trustee's independence.

The big question, Livingston concluded, was whether the Chase would vote at all. "If it doesn't vote, what a commentary! The Chase has the investment staff resources to make a critical and intelligent judgment on the merits of Young versus White. It can really help investors in Central stock. If a five-billion-dollar bank won't take a stand, how can the small investor?"

Young and his friends on the C & O did not intend to let the Chase remain in such an ambiguous position for very long. Young was about to relieve the Chase of its perplexing obligation. In a manner resembling the sequence of challenge and response in a chess match between grand masters, he was calculating a series of moves to free the stock from the trap of the Chase trusteeship and instead make it one of his own pieces. Buying the stock directly from the C & O seemed on its face the most direct and also the least complicated approach.

After all, the combined resources of the Alleghany Corporation, Young, and Kirby were easily sufficient to buy the 800,000 shares from the C & O. But who could be sure that such a sale would be regarded by the I.C.C. or the courts as an arm's-length deal sufficiently bona fide in appearance and substance to escape the grip of the Chase trusteeship? Young's experience with voting trusts, moreover, warned him to move with extreme caution.

David Baird, a prominent securities broker and investment counselor who had been involved with Young in a number of deals, recommended that the block be purchased by an independent syndicate of unquestioned financial reliability, whose arm's-length stance would be unchallengeable. Baird then drew up a plan designed to interest such a syndicate. He had difficulty in pulling together such a group, mainly because no one with such credentials cared to invest in a donnybrook. Young, therefore, undertook to solve the problem himself.

His aim was to find a purchaser sufficiently independent to satisfy the requirement of an arm's-length deal, sufficiently friendly to vote the stock for Young, sufficiently wealthy to satisfy any credit arrangements, and sufficiently tough to stand the heat that would follow, both legal and personal. If Young could arrange it, he would try to induce such potential buyers with a guarantee against loss, as well as provide credit arrangements which would make the deal possible without a substantial investment of cash.

After determining in his own mind the kind of arrangement he could manage and who would be the most likely investors. Young went to work on the telephone—there was no time for personal visits. With Charles Ireland, who had already worked out the legal complexities, at his elbow, he called Cyrus Eaton, Allan Kirby, and the prospective investors in rapid-fire order. In an extraordinary tour de force, he secured the agreement of all the parties, pending formal arrangements to be worked out by the lawyers.

On February 23 C & O sold the entire block of 800,000 shares. But curiously enough, the first public statement about the transfer of this huge block of stock came neither from Young, the C & O, nor the purchasers. Instead, the first intimations that a deal had been completed came from William White of the Central. White issued his statement at 7 P.M. on February 24. He did not identify the purchasers but merely described them as "certain wealthy individuals who must have paid about $20,000,000." White continued:

> There seems to be some conniving going on. Exactly six years ago this very day Chesapeake & Ohio published a pamphlet stating the advantages to the Chesapeake & Ohio stockholders of Chesapeake & Ohio holding New York Central stock, but now that Mr. Young has other ambitions the interest of the Chesapeake & Ohio stockholders is apparently ignored.
>
> Notwithstanding all the public statements which have been made, there would seem to be continuance of a close relationship between Mr. Young and Chesapeake & Ohio. In any event, C & O has been very cooperative.

We understand that the C & O board of directors is going to have a special meeting tomorrow, presumably to ratify the sale which has already been made.

We consider this sale a favorable development for us. It explodes Mr. Young's claim that 90 percent of the New York Central stockholders are behind him.[10]

The rationale of this conclusion was hard to follow since it was highly unlikely that the C & O and its new dominating figure, Cyrus Eaton, would do anything with these shares to hurt Young or to help White.

The *New York Times* was expressing the general perplexity with White's statement when it included in the story the following paragraph:

The significance of the sale was not immediately apparent and Mr. White did not fully explain why he considered the transaction favorable for the railroad.

Some sophisticated observers regarded the sale as part of Young's general war plan, carefully thought out even before he resigned from the C & O. If the 800,000 shares were moved from Chase's trusteeship into Young's orbit, the result could be mortal to management's cause.

The 800,000 shares now became the vortex of the contest. To whom had they been sold?

The facts began to emerge. The C & O directors, at a special meeting on February 25, approved the sale of C & O's Central holdings. In the public announcement, it was revealed for the first time that the purchasers were two Texans, Sid W. Richardson and Clint W. Murchison. Their reputation for wealth[11] and financial acumen underscored the brilliance of Young's choice. Moreover, Young had already had a number of satisfactory business dealings with Murchison Brothers; Alleghany had been involved in a dozen joint ventures with them, including, amusingly enough, the Lionel Corporation, the largest manufacturer of toy trains.

10 *New York Times*, February 25, 1954, p. 1.
11 A story pointing up Richardson's enormous wealth started making the rounds. Richardson is supposed to have called Murchison and asked, "Clint, what was the name of that railroad we just bought?"

Not only was the sale of the stock a blow to the aspirations of the White team, but the appearance of Richardson and Murchison as active allies of Young was a financial and public relations coup. The fact that Richardson was an early and important backer of President Eisenhower found its way into almost every news story about the stock sale and served to emphasize Young's general sagacity in such matters.

Besieged by newsmen, Sid Richardson, whose trademark was "You ain't learning nothing when you're talking," remained silent, except to say it was "nobody's damn business."

Murchison, however, issued a statement of confirmation.

We did purchase some New York Central. We bought it for investment purposes. It made good earnings last year and we put our slide rule to it. It looks as if it should make much better in 1956. Our conclusion was that it was a good investment. We bought the stock based on the firm conviction that Eisenhower was not going to allow a depression to happen to this country.[12]

White, who had obviously received a severe setback, still made an effective point.

We are highly complimented by Mr. Murchison's statement that he and Mr. Richardson consider Central a good investment.

Just a couple of weeks ago, Mr. Cyrus Eaton, new chairman of C & O, was quoted as having said that the ownership of New York Central by C & O was a good investment for C & O stockholders. Today Mr. Clint Murchison, one of the purchasers of the same stock from C & O, says the New York Central stock was a good investment for him. It looks like the C & O stockholders have been pawns in this situation.

Sale of C & O's 800,000 shares of Central stock to interests friendly to Mr. Young shows up as a fallacy his statement that he had the support of 90 percent of Central stockholders. Obviously he doesn't think so today. This won't make any difference with respect to our fight.[13]

With the appearance of Richardson and Murchison on the scene, Young was now ready to present his slate of directors for the consideration of the Central stockholders. On March 2 he began to announce the names of those who would stand for election as general directors on his slate. In order to achieve maximum

[12] *New York Times*, February 26, 1954, p. 1.
[13] *Ibid.*

newspaper coverage, Young served up a portion of the names at a time. The first seven names proposed were indeed impressive: Dr. R. Walter Graham, Jr., the Baltimore physician who owned 41,800 Central shares; Daniel E. Taylor of Norfolk, Virginia, president of West India Fruit and Steamship Company; Earl E. T. Smith, a stockbroker (later to become famous as ambassador to Cuba under President Dwight Eisenhower); Young and Kirby, of course; and last but not least Murchison and Richardson. For the first time Young and Kirby's personal holdings in Central of 100,200 shares and 100,000 shares respectively were made public. Among these seven board nominees, the Young-Kirby slate controlled over 1,000,000 shares, or 18 percent of all New York Central stock. Young asserted that this accumulation of stock was enough to ensure victory

To this claim, according to the *New York Times*, White responded, "Young doesn't add very well."

The legal front now erupted. The next day, March 3, the Central petitioned the I.C.C. to make a sweeping investigation of Robert Young's campaign to take over control of the railroad. The attack on the sale of the New York Central stock by the C & O to Murchison and Richardson was now in full blast.

The Central wanted the I.C.C. to investigate a number of matters:

1. Was the C & O still controlled directly or indirectly by the Alleghany Corporation?

2. Was the "purported" sale of the 800,000 shares by the C & O made in such a way and to such persons as to fail to comply with the trust agreement under which the Chase National Bank held the Central stock?

3. Was the sale made for cash, or for notes, either in part or in whole, and was any of the purchase price borrowed from Alleghany?

4. Did Young or any of his associates advance any of the purchase money?

5. Was Eaton involved in any understanding to use the 800,000 shares in such a way as to benefit Young?

6. Did Alleghany hold or own any voting stocks of carrier corporations that it should have placed in trust?

The Central's attack was mounted from a prepared position on a familiar battleground, one upon which it had defeated Young six years earlier. The Central's gathering of intelligence about the enemy, a vital factor in any proxy contest, had provided enough reliable information so that it knew most, if not all, of the answers. Control of the 800,000 shares might very well hinge on the kind of information the I.C.C. was able to elicit on the deal.

Young lost no time in responding in kind. It was his turn to attack on a legal front. On the very next day, March 4, on behalf of himself, Kirby, and all other stockholders similarly situated, he filed suit against the Central and its fifteen directors asking for an injunction to prevent them from spending any funds of the New York Central Railroad Company for the purpose of continuing themselves in office.

The complaint demanded that the defendants be required to account for their acts as directors with respect to having "contrived a plan and scheme for a campaign involving unlimited expenditures of the funds of the corporation, but no funds of their own, for the sole purpose of securing their own re-election as directors of the company and defeating any effort by the plaintiffs or other similar large stockholders to obtain representation on the board of the corporation at the next annual meeting of stockholders to be held on May 26, 1954."

The attack by Young as to who should bear the burden of management's proxy costs was two-pronged. Not only did it have a public relations value by leaving the impression that a non-owning management was using corporate funds to entrench itself further, but it confronted management with the distinct possibility that they might be compelled individually to reimburse the corporation out of their own pockets. And such a reimbursement would not be unsubstantial the way the costs were mounting. The question of reimbursement also raised a problem for Young and his slate. How were *they* financing their assault? Apparently Alleghany was advancing the funds necessary. The question raised by both management and the Securities and Exchange Commission was whether Alleghany would reimburse itself out of Central funds in the event it won. At first Young refused to commit himself. As a result of the proddings by the Securities and Exchange Commission staff, Young backed up somewhat, and a compromise was reached. He agreed that the Alleghany proxy material would carry the statement that reimbursement of the cost of the Alleghany proxy expenses would hinge on the outcome of the lawsuit against the Central directors.[14] A somewhat vague statement was processed by the S.E.C. for inclusion in Alleghany's proxy material:

> Whether Alleghany and the nominees will seek any reimbursement from the Central of all or any part of their solicitation expenses will be determined in the light of the results of the litigation instituted by Messrs. Young and Kirby against your present directors. . . .

Whether by design or not, Young's lawsuit against the management had a Young twist. The action was titled *Young* v. *Ebbott, et al.* Percy Ebbott, president of the Chase National Bank, was only one of the Central directors sued; but specifying his name as the first defendant[15] emphasized the ambiguous position of the Chase Bank as the trustee for the 800,000 shares. It was a point Young hoped would not be lost on the court, the I.C.C., and most important, the press. The Chase Bank was discovering that its appointment as trustee in 1945 by the I.C.C. was not an unmixed blessing but was in fact a source of bitter embarrassment.

Young continued his attack on the Chase Bank and Percy Ebbott. In a presumably off-the-cuff speech before the National Press Club in Washington, D.C., on March 11 before an audience of 530— the largest crowd ever to have attended a Press Club luncheon— Young did nothing to ameliorate the Chase's discomfort as trustee for the 800,000 shares.

Taking aim at the Chase president, Young said:

> . . . Mr. Ebbott, who really . . . had a hundred shares of stock, but . . . swaggered around with this 800,000 shares that belonged to the C & O . . . said to me, "Why of course, the most I can be in this

---

[14] After 1956, as a result of this proxy fight, it would be a mandatory requirement under the revised S.E.C. proxy rules to make a specific statement about reimbursement of expenses.

[15] If the traditional form of listing the defendants alphabetically had been followed, Ebbott would not have been first and, hence, not in the title of the action.

situation is to be neutral and, Lord . . . I don't want to get in a fight . . . if there is ever a fight here, I am going to resign. I want to keep my pass on the New York Central; I want to keep the C & O's deposits . . . I don't want a fight, Bob."

Young then said that, in view of Ebbott's promise of neutrality, he was shocked to learn that Ebbott voted against seating Young on the board of the Central.

The *New York Times*, as part of its coverage of the Press Club speech, reported: "Mr. Young advised his Central opponents to hurry if they wanted to make a deal because 'there won't be room for six more directors after Monday.' "

Two days earlier, on March 9, John J. McCloy, chairman of the Chase National Bank, acutely sensitive to the problem presented by the trusteeship and Ebbott's uncomfortable position, agreed to arrange a meeting between White, Murchison, and Richardson. While there was some vagueness later as to who first broached the idea—Young claimed it was White who wanted to talk compromise, and McCloy insisted it was Murchison—the meeting did take place on the eleventh, the same day as Young's appearance before the National Press Club.

After the meeting between White, Murchison, and Richardson, rumors flooded Wall Street that a compromise was in prospect, particularly in the light of some of Young's remarks in Washington. So persistent were these reports that White felt compelled to call a press conference to deny them. He added, "I told them [Murchison and Richardson] that we would under no circumstances talk compromise with them unless Mr. Young backed completely out of the picture and that we were just as much convinced today as we were on February 10 that Mr. Young's association with the New York Central property would be harmful.

"I want to make it perfectly clear," said White, "that when Mr. Young and Mr. Deegan either say or intimate that we want to make a deal, that is a plain lie and the usual distortion which Young practices."[16]

16 *New York Times,* March 12, 1954, p. 1.

Other battlefronts in the meantime were erupting and other volunteers were enlisting.

Harry Hagerty, financial vice president of the Metropolitan Life Insurance Company, Young's target for over 15 years as a tool of the "money trust," dived in personally. Together with Lee P. Stack, vice president of John Hancock Mutual Life Insurance Company, he urged the I.C.C. to support the Central's request for an investigation of Alleghany, Young, Kirby, Eaton, the C & O, and the sale of the 800,000 shares to Murchison and Richardson. Metropolitan Life Insurance Company owned $134,000,000 of Central's bonds, and had lent the Central $60,000,000 between 1952 and 1954 to buy new equipment. John Hancock also was an important creditor of Central, owning $10,839,000 in bonds and guaranteeing an additional $3,975,000.

Hagerty and Stack were men with enormous standing in the financial community, as their positions attested. Like Morgan Stanley, they must have had their reasons for undertaking an action which appeared to confirm Young's repeated charge that the Central was dominated by the Wall Street bankers and large insurance companies who were only interested in protecting their creditor position and not the rights of the stockholders. Almost immediately after the Hagerty-Stack request to the I.C.C., Senator William Langer, Republican of North Dakota, chairman of the Senate Judiciary Committee and an admirer of Young's Populist-oriented pronouncements about "dambankers," Wall Street, and insurance companies, wrote to the I.C.C. to investigate interrelationships involved in the Central proxy fight. He was also a close friend and colleague of former Senator Burton K. Wheeler, one of Young's lawyers. Langer wanted an inquiry into the "interlocking relationships between the New York Central, the Pennsylvania Railroad, the Erie, and the Baltimore & Ohio Railroad, on one hand and the First National Bank of the City of New York, J. P. Morgan, the Chase National Bank, and the Mellon Bank of Pittsburgh, on the other hand."

With the annual meeting little more than two months away, the time had come to step up the campaign for the votes of the stockholders. In this department Young had a wide edge. The newspapers found his style more newsworthy.

Young continued his public relations gambit of announcing from time to time dramatic appointments to his slate. The name of his candidate Frederick Lewisohn, a respected member of the New York Stock Exchange, whose name would undoubtedly appeal to Jewish stockholders, was announced during his speech to the National Press Club. With Lewisohn's nomination came a number of "hate" letters. One, sent anonymously but in a distinctive hand-writing, charged Young with a plot to turn over the Central to "non-American" elements.

The appointment on March 21 of the ninth member was truly dramatic—a woman. She was none other than Lila Bell Acheson Wallace, co-editor and co-owner with her husband of the *Reader's Digest*, whose circulation was a good deal over ten million.

Young's selection of Mrs. Wallace evoked an enthusiastic response from Wilma Soss, president of the Federation of Women Share-holders in American Business, Inc. "We are delighted. . . . It is a wonderful opportunity for a woman to do a terrific job."

Young did nothing to reduce her enthusiasm when he gave as his reason, "We need a woman's touch on the railroads." And Mrs. Wallace agreed, "I think everything needs a woman's touch."

When Mrs. Wilma Soss asked White if he planned to nominate a woman on management's slate, White replied archly (to use one writer's description), "there are no vacancies on the board." He softened the refusal by adding that there was no board member who would object to a qualified woman director.

In planning his slate, Young even tried for a Vanderbilt. "It is unthinkable that the Central board should not have a single Vander-bilt." But no Vanderbilt accepted his invitation. Some of the wittier warriors on both sides of the contest claimed that Earl Smith, the stockbroker, was a Vanderbilt by proxy; after all, he was the divorced husband of Muriel Vanderbilt.

Young's choice for the tenth nominee was William H. Landers, a seventy-two-year-old retired Central engineer drawing a $170-a-month pension and owner of 80 shares of Central stock which he

Allan P. Kirby (*left*), Lila Bell Acheson Wallace, and Young

had purchased in 1931 and 1932 as part of an employees' stock purchase plan. As a result of this plan, the employees of the Central were a sought-after group in the proxy fight. Landers, a member of the Brotherhood of Locomotive Firemen and Enginemen, was typical of the employee stockholder. The board of a railroad needs a working man, said Young's press statement.

Young was most anxious to add an educator to his slate. He had met the president of the University of Notre Dame, Father Theodore M. Hesburgh, at an educational conference at the Greenbrier Hotel at White Sulphur Springs, West Virginia, some years before and was impressed by both his personality and keen intellect. Young had also kept in mind that Notre Dame was situated on the New York Central line in South Bend. He asked Tom Deegan if he would explore the possibility of Father Hesburgh's joining Young's slate. The clergyman-educator replied that he was flattered by the offer and intrigued by the opportunities for public service in the private sector but felt he must decline. However, if Mr. Young was interested in a nominee who shared Father Hesburgh's general outlook, he would be glad to offer a suggestion. Why not check with William P. Feeley of Chicago, a Notre Dame graduate and president of the Great Lakes Dredge and Dock Company? Young immediately called Feeley, who agreed to join Young's slate.

Young then announced the rest of his nominees—all men of solid public and financial credentials: Richard M. Moss of New York, a 10,000-share Central stockholder and chairman and president of Clinton Foods, Inc.; Eugene C. Pulliam of Indianapolis, also a 10,000-share stockholder, and publisher of a string of newspapers, of which the Indianapolis *Star* and Indianapolis *News* were the best known; Orville Taylor of Chicago, partner in the law firm Taylor, Miller, Busch & Magner; and Andrew Van Pelt, director of Alleghany Corporation, as well as a valued and trusted associate of Young and Kirby.

With the completion of his slate, Young began to circulate a comparison of the stock holdings of the nominees:

Alleghany slate		Management slate	
400,000	Murchison	60,000	Vanderbilt, H.
400,000	Richardson	4,200	Dennett
100,200	Young	2,000	Vanderbilt, W.
100,000	Kirby	1,100	Whitney
41,800	Graham	1,000	White
12,000	Smith	1,000	Dick
10,000	Moss	1,000	Hoyt
10,000	Pulliam	1,000	Levis
9,600	Lewisohn	500	Ebbott
3,000	Taylor, D.	500	Nagle
2,000	Van Pelt	500	Murray
1,000	Taylor, O.	500	Aldrich
100	Wallace	100	Loree
100	Feeley	100	Machold
80	Landers	100	Farley
1,089,880		73,600	

Back in 1946–1947, when Young was accumulating his first 400,000 shares, he was aware that the major forces in the Central had the financial power to mount a stock-purchasing campaign of their own. But no such thing happened. Harold S. Vanderbilt, who owned 65,000 shares in the spring of 1946, within a few months sold 25,000 shares. He further reduced his holdings, according to New York Central proxy statements, to 30,000 by April 1951, to 20,000 shares by 1952, to 10,000 shares by April 1953—or an investment worth less than $200,000 in a railroad known as the "Vanderbilt Line." The other representative of the Vanderbilt family on the board, William H., followed suit. He owned 8158 shares in 1949 and reduced his holdings to 1000 by 1953. Only after a proxy fight became a certainty in 1954 did the Vanderbilts demonstrate their support of White; Harold S. brought his holdings up to 60,000 shares and William H. increased his to 2000. (Upon reviewing the stock ownership of the Vanderbilts, Young remarked that their yachts cost more to maintain than the value of their holdings.) Young was sure that this state of affairs could not last. The huge financial interests in the Central would sooner or later make their influence felt in a stock-buying campaign.

In 1953 the entire Central board owned a mere 13,750 shares, with a market value of little more than $275,000. Alexander C. Nagle, president of the First National Bank, who owned 150 shares between 1946 and 1954, bought another 350 shares to help stop Young. George Whitney, chairman of the board of J. P. Morgan & Company, who owned 100 shares of Central stock between 1946 and 1954, bought an additional 1000 shares for the fight.

Young's suit against the directors to prevent them from using Central funds in the proxy fight continued actively both in the courts and in the newspapers. White entered a formal objection to testifying in the suit and further requested the New York State Supreme Court to limit the questions asked of him at the pretrial hearings.

In a speech on March 29 before the Association of Customers Brokers at Schwartz's Restaurant, then at 54 Broad Street, a few doors south of the New York Stock Exchange, Young made some graphic comparisons of what he described as well-managed and poorly managed railroads, using a series of charts. Quite naturally the Central was among those listed as poorly operated, and the C & O, as well-run. Also included among the well-managed railroads was the Denver & Rio Grande Western Railroad. As Young pointed to the figures on the Denver & Rio Grande chart, someone in the rear called out the question, "Isn't Al Perlman the Executive Vice President of that road?" Young thought for a moment and then responded, "Yes, Perlman represents the progressive kind of railroad man that I would like to put into the New York Central as President." By the time the story appeared in print, it had been garbled into a direct statement that Young would appoint Perlman as president of the Central in the event he won.[17] Perlman, when asked about this, answered, "I've never met Mr. Young and I've never considered holding the position of Central President."[18]

Henry S. Sturgis, who had known Perlman for some time, called him to ask if the story was true. Perlman repeated what he had told reporters, that he had never met or talked to Young, let alone been offered the presidency of the Central. Sturgis then asked Perlman if he would issue a statement to the effect that he would refuse the position if offered. Perlman told Sturgis politely but firmly that Young's remarks about him were very complimentary and that he had no intention of being ungracious.

After reporting Young's plans to invite Perlman, the *New York Times*, in the next paragraph, typified the way the public relations end of the struggle was going. The grim facts had a way of overwhelming management's attempts to achieve good public relations.

Meanwhile Mr. White said in Pittsburgh that freight business of the Central which began declining last October has been "holding steady" for eight weeks. He said that while the system's freight business is off 13 percent so far this year, compared with a year ago, the decline has been steady.[19]

[17] *New York Times*, March 30, 1954, p. 36.
[18] *New York Times*, March 31, 1954, p. 40.
[19] *New York Times*, March 12, 1954, p. 1.

And immediately below this story, in the same column, the *Times* reported that the New England Mutual Life Insurance Company, which "owns no stock in Central and hence has no voting power in that company but is the owner of nearly $12 million worth of Central bonds," joined Metropolitan and John Hancock in requesting an investigation of Robert Young. Vice President Sherwin C. Badger of New England Mutual wrote that his organization had "a vital interest in the successful operation of the company."

As a measure of the increasing tension of the contest, the three tellers who for years had tallied the stockholders' votes at Central annual meetings—G. William McEwan, Lyman C. Poole, and Walter S. Stedman—asked to withdraw. The position, in the past a mere ritual function, was now "too hot." The three did not care for either the abuse or the weeks of delay that might be involved.

The battle had assumed such heat that the *Wall Street Journal* noted that it was "similar to a political campaign, with charges and counter charges hurled in the public press, and with proxies solicited as solicitously as votes in a national election."

Young himself thought of the proxy fight in these terms: "Basically the purpose of the corporate election is to preserve the rights of ownership just as the popular election is to preserve the rights of citizenship." Nowhere was this approach more dramatically demonstrated than in his appeal to special ethnic groups for their votes. An example is his use of advertisements in Yiddish in the *Jewish Daily Forward.* Advertisements headed "Mr. Murphy Didn't Intend Any Harm," "Jim Farley vs. the Facts," and "Whom Do You Believe?" were translated into Yiddish. These advertisements also appeared in English in the major newspapers of the country.

The Murphy ad underscored the problems that politicians face in estranging one group while attracting another. In this particular matter, Young risked his relationships with the railroad industry generally—in fact, made permanent, irreconcilable enemies—in order to make a point to the small stockholder. Walter P. Murphy was the president of the Standard Railway Equipment Manufacturing Company, one of the large railway equipment concerns in the

Jim Farley vs. The Facts

JAMES A. FARLEY SAYS:

"We chose Bill White to be the new President of the New York Central on the basis of performances, not promises. He had already done a most outstanding job for the Lackawanna."

BUT FIGURES DON'T LIE:

דזשים פֿאַרלי געגען די פֿאַקטען

"Mr. Murphy Didn't Intend Any Harm'

‏,,מר. מוירפֿי האָט ניט געהאַט קיין בייזע אַבזיכטן"

United States. He died on December 16, 1942, and when his will was probated, it turned out that he left large tax-free bequests to forty-six railroad executives of companies which were his major customers. Principal among these were F. E. Williamson, then president of the New York Central, who received $100,000; Martin W. Clement, then president of the Pennsylvania, $100,000; Ralph Budd, then president of the Burlington, $50,000; W. M. Jeffers, then president of the Union Pacific, $100,000; Fred G. Gurley, then vice president of the Santa Fe, $50,000; John J. Pelley, formerly president of the Association of American Railroads, $50,000.

Young's disclosure of these bequests in his speech at the National Press Club on March 11, 1954, was a minor sensation. After listing the railway executives involved, Young asked, "Do you think for one minute that the chief executives of Chrysler or General Motors or DuPont or any other company would dare be remembered in the wills of the principal supplier? You know they'd be fired tomorrow. Why weren't these men fired? Because the people who were their bosses were doing exactly the same thing. The bankers, the investment bankers, who control these very railroads that I have mentioned were running their own rackets. . . ." That Young translated Murphy's gratitude and generosity into a posthumous kickback resulted in silent outrage in many areas of the industry. Eight days later, in a speech before the Association of Customers Brokers, White—who was not involved in any way—decided to speak for all of them when he belittled Young's charges, adding, "Fortunately, I was not remembered in Mr. Murphy's will, but I am sure *Mr. Murphy didn't intend any harm* to those he did remember in his will, and I am equally sure that Mr. Murphy thought that what he was leaving to those gentlemen were small amounts of money. . . ."

Young seized upon this remark, and the result was the "Mr. Murphy Didn't Intend Any Harm" ad which he ran in papers throughout the United States.

Young did his best not to alienate other blocks of voters. He met several times with Lewis and John Gilbert, whose appearances on behalf of small stockholders gained them the title of "the corporate conscience," as well as with Mrs. Wilma Soss, another representative of small stockholders. He even gave Mrs. Soss a certain amount of credit for the appointment of a woman on his slate. He also agreed to support the Gilberts in their campaign for cumulative voting, a method of proportional representation by which minority interests would be recognized by places on the board. Young learned early what many executives were to find out later on, that these were not crackpots but serious, if sometimes abrasive, participants in the questioning of corporate policy. What is more, Young recognized that they had an astute understanding of press relations and that they had a meaningful even though small following.

As the contest gained in intensity, the press came more and more to treat it as a public event rather than a private corporate contest. The Associated Press ran a lengthy interview with each of the two candidates, setting forth their views in detail, as if they were major contenders in a national election. A set of questions was presented each of them, and their answers were carried in full on April 2 and April 3 in almost every major paper in the country. Only a campaign for the presidency of the United States could command such involvement by the A.P. or consume such space in the American newspapers.

Some of the questions and answers are revealing.

Q. You have said you are going to win this fight. As of now what are your reasons for so believing?

Mr. White: We shall win this fight for the simple reason that Mr. Young cannot get enough backers to buy control of the New York Central. . . . The majority of the stockholders will want to be sure that their company is managed by experienced railroaders and not one who is a promoter and speculator and who admits he is not a railroad man.

Mr. Young: . . . The most compelling one is to ask the simple question of shareholders: Would you rather have large owners on your board whose interests parallel yours or bankers with nominal ownership, many of whose interests conflict with yours?

Q. In the showdown, what specific points do you think will win stockholders to your side?

Mr. White: . . . the record of the current management of the New York Central. . . . On the Young record they will have no assurance that he can bring competent and experienced management to the road. The stockholders will realize that his promise that he can pay $7 to $10 dividends is the worst kind of blue-sky demagoguery. . . . They will know from the record that Mr. Young's ideas failed miserably. . . .

Mr Young: White has said the Central is not likely to pay more than a $2 dividend within five years. . . . We, on the other hand, would not have paid as high as $25 for Central stock unless we believed it could pay much more. . . .

Q. *Actually how many shares do you consider on your side? Why?'*

Mr. White: The answer to this question is something that our adversary would like to know and I don't propose to disclose our full strength.

Mr. Young: Our board will actually own around 1,100,000 shares as against the 13,750 shares all the present directors were reported as owning in last year's proxy statement. No poll that we have taken gives us less than 60 percent of the independent vote. When we decontrolled C & O to take control of Central, we were convinced we could win even though the 800,000 shares owned by the C & O and trusteed with the Chase Bank were voted against us. . . .

Q. *Do you see any chance that either side will assume such a dominant position in advance of the annual stockholders' meeting May 26, that there will be no contest at the meeting?*

Mr. White: It is possible, but not for the Young group.

Mr. Young: I have been astounded from the beginning that they chose to fight rather than accept my reasonable offer of settlement for two directors, with the chairmanship. I had thought the fight they lost to me on the issues of competitive bidding had taught them caution. . . . I still do not believe they can afford the humiliation of a vote, but their judgment again seems to be influenced by their emotions.

Q. *Do you think Central's dividends can be increased? By how much and when?*

Mr. White: Certainly we believe Central's dividends can be increased. The whole effort of management is being directed toward that goal. However, we deal in performance and not in promises.

Mr. Young: If Central operated at C & O's rate of return on capital, it would earn $11 a share. If it operated at C & O's expense ratio, it would earn $12. In 1929, Central paid dividends of $8 a share. Other railroads are earning more than they did in 1929. Given last year's level of traffic, I would be disappointed if we could not bring the Central up to C & O's level of efficiency in five years. It should be conservative by that time to pay out 60 percent of these earnings in dividends.

Q. *Do you consider that arrangements could be made with other railroads to assure transcontinental through service without a Chicago layover? Specifically, what railroads?*

Mr. Young: I am sure that under new leadership arrangements can be made with other railroads to give better through service at Chicago. The New York Central presently operates through cars over four Western routes but with layovers in Chicago inexcusably averaging more than five hours.

Mr. White: Yes, it is physically possible to provide transcontinental service without a Chicago layover, but many considerations not known to Mr. Young are involved. The demand for such transcontinental passenger through service is not sufficiently apparent to warrant the costs and losses involved. We cannot disclose these now, but they are such that, no matter who controls New York Central, they cannot be ignored.

Q. *What is your last word in regard to this present struggle for control of the Central?*

Mr. Young: "Whom the gods would destroy they first make mad." By ganging up on behalf of Central's present board in this fight will the insurance company–banking–railroad monopoly group bring down new legislation on their heads just as they did by their excesses in 1929?

Mr. White: Not only New York Central stockholders but the American public will be made aware of the fact that Mr. Young's grandiloquent promises cannot be fulfilled; that the innovations of which he speaks so fluently failed of accomplishment on the Chesapeake & Ohio, and if attempted on the New York Central with its extensive passenger service would subject the railroad to the risk of bankruptcy; that Mr. Young has demonstrated a lack of knowledge of the basic nature of the railroad business; and that the programs and policies instituted by the new management now in control for 20 months are proving beneficial to the property. These things can and will be disclosed to stockholders and thus we will win. The danger of the threat of Mr. Young's device is beginning to be apparent to all. If a campaign of distortion, vilification, misrepresentation and pressure on newspapers and government can displace a sound and progressive management, the stability of every good enterprise can be threatened. Demagogues are dangerous in our political life. Demagogues in business or industry could, if successful, ruin important sections of our economy.

While acrimony and vilification flared at every point of battle, both sides kept their eyes on the status of the 800,000 shares. Gradually, as the various lawsuits plodded along, the details of the stock purchase by Murchison and Richardson unfolded. In both Alleghany's annual report and in the Central's action before the I.C.C. against Young, Kirby, and Alleghany, it was disclosed that Murchison and Richardson were not required to put up a cent of their own money. Alleghany lent them $7,500,000 cash toward the purchase price and, in addition, gave them a "put." Stated simply, this meant that, even if the price of Central stock fell below $25, Murchison and Richardson could pay the loan back with Central stock with a per share value of $25 despite the lower price. If the stock rose above $25, the borrowers could either keep the stock or sell it and pocket the profit. Thus the borrowers, while protected against loss, could keep any profits for themselves. Kirby lent them $5,000,000, and the Central National Bank of Cleveland, $7,500,000, with Alleghany giving the Texans a "put" for this $12,500,000. Murchison and Richardson made a fine deal; if they chose to exercise the "put," their only risk was the solvency of Alleghany. Young, for his part, felt he made a fine deal by placing the 800,000 shares in his corner.

The details of the Murchison-Richardson purchase brought a quick response from White.

"It is interesting to note," said White in a press release, "the $7,500,000 loan to Clint W. Murchison and Sid Richardson in connection with the purported sale to them by Chesapeake and Ohio of New York Central stock. Especially is it interesting to note that, in addition to the loan, Murchison and Richardson are guaranteed against loss in the transaction and that other documents not disclosed are involved." He added that the disclosure supported Central's contention that the sale of the 800,000 shares held by the Chase National Bank had been in violation of the trust agreement.

"We believe that other loans from sources close to Young [Allan P. Kirby and the Central Bank of Cleveland] are involved and that these two purported buyers have not put up any of their own money and are guaranteed against loss in connection with the commitments which they may have made."[20]

---

[20] *New York Times*, April 5, 1954, p. 34.

White did more than merely issue statements, as chief executive officer of the Central; he held up the transfer of the 800,000 shares. Until the shares were transferred, Murchison and Richardson would be unable to vote them. "We have not transferred the stock into the names of Murchison and Richardson because the papers presented to us are defective, our outside counsel advises." The New York Central, unlike most other corporations, acted as its own transfer agent. For this reason, it was in a position to prevent the transfer. Young claimed that Central's acting as its own transfer agent was merely another proof of its outmoded method of operation. But in this case the arrangement seemed to be serving Central's purpose.

On April 6 the I.C.C. refused the petition of the Central to investigate Robert Young and the C & O sale of Central stock to the Texans, stating that the Central's allegations did not provide sufficient grounds for an investigation.

White reacted sharply: "In the light of what is now public knowledge, it is difficult to understand how the Interstate Commerce Commission can afford to have its authority impugned and its prestige impaired." He attacked the "Murchison-Richardson-Alleghany transactions," adding that in spite of this the Commission had made its own decision and would have to bear the consequences.

That same day, Central made another effort to get the I.C.C. involved in the proxy fight. This time it petitioned the I.C.C. for a declaratory order ruling that if Alleghany, Young, and Kirby won control, such control would be unlawful. Central's lawyers claimed that acquisition of control of the Central by Alleghany would automatically carry with it acquisition of control of two other roads, the Pittsburgh & Lake Erie and the Indiana Harbor Belt, Central subsidiaries. According to this reasoning, the Central System was not one railroad but at least three and acquisition of control would therefore require formal merger proceedings under Section 5. If Central's viewpoint prevailed, the whole proxy fight would be in vain for Young and Alleghany; even if they won, they would not be in lawful control. The Central said it was filing its petition in order to be advised before the annual meeting as to whether "any vote for the election of Young or Kirby or for the proposed Alleghany-Young-Kirby board of directors can, consistently with Section 5, lawfully be cast at the meeting or, if cast, can lawfully be counted, and if the candidates should receive a plurality . . . whether such directors can lawfully be seated."

At the same time on April 7, a 500-share stockholder of Alleghany, Mrs. Sadie Zenn, filed a stockholder's suit against Chairman Young, President Kirby, the six other directors of Alleghany, and Murchison and Richardson. She alleged that the $7,500,000 loan to Murchison and Richardson was detrimental to the best interests of Alleghany and demanded an accounting for damages and profits. She petitioned that the loan be rescinded and that Murchison and Richardson be required to repay the loans in cash.

In the next few days more facts surrounding the transaction for the 800,000 shares were unfolded. Again, J. A. Livingston's syndicated column was the first to disclose many of them.

Livingston asked some penetrating questions, such as whether the two Texans were paying for the valuable "puts" they had obtained from Alleghany, and where Alleghany had dug up the cash to lend the Texans. From a detailed study of Alleghany's finances, Livingston concluded that the corporation had not had $7,500,000 available. If not, had the corporation borrowed the money, and was it paying interest?

Livingston wanted to know whether, in order to save the Central's Aunt Janes from the banking clique, Young was "forgetting his own relatives, the Alleghany Aunt Janes?"[21]

According to Livingston, White had implied that Young and Kirby had once before personally profited at the expense of Alleghany Aunt Janes. He quoted White as saying:

I wonder if you heard the little story of how Mr. Young and Mr. Kirby each acquired 24,062 shares of Investors Diversified Services at $8.14, which a month later was quoted at $16, and is now bid at

[21] "Aunt Jane" was Young's reference to the small stockholders, many of them middle-aged women, who looked on their stock as part of a modest retirement. Young regarded himself as the champion of the Aunt Janes.

$144. A neat little profit of 6½ million dollars for Mr. Young and Mr. Kirby and not for Alleghany.

That stock was in Alleghany's portfolio, all right, but it was released from Alleghany's portfolio in exchange for their [Young's and Kirby's] Alleghany preferred.[22]

Filling out the story on the 800,000 Central shares transaction, Livingston said that, according to White, the two Texans had not put up a cent of their own money to buy the shares. White said that in a deal negotiated by C & O officers (who owed their positions to Young), Cleveland banks had supplemented the Alleghany loan with another $7,500,000.

The pressures to examine the C & O sale to Murchison and Richardson mounted. Shortly after the I.C.C. refused the request of the Central to look further into this sale, the annual appropriation for the I.C.C. was being considered by the Senate Appropriations Committee. The petition of the Central to the I.C.C. charging Young with attempting illegal control of the Central in violation of Section 5 (4) was still pending. Under questioning by Senator Dirksen, Chairman J. Monroe Johnson of the I.C.C. gave a clue to future Commission action when he made it quite explicit that he not only believed that the purchase by Murchison and Richardson was legal and proper but that Young himself could have bought the 800,000 shares from the C & O without interference from the Commission. As far as Johnson was concerned, the I.C.C. had looked into the transaction and reached its conclusion. There was no need for further investigation or action.

Senator Dirksen, politically powerful even then, was by no means satisfied with Johnson's testimony. To Dirksen the whole deal for the 800,000 shares was "all very bewildering." Johnson offered the Commission's report to Dirksen. Dirksen, unconvinced, did not consider such submission necessary and suggested instead that the Senate Judiciary Subcommittee on Antitrust and Monopoly, of which he was a member, might find the matter "a fruitful field" of investigation.

The battle over the 800,000 shares continued with undiminished

22 Washington *Post & Times Herald*, April 9, 1954, p. 57.

vigor. While Johnson was submitting to the Senate the views of the I.C.C., Murchison and Richardson were filing suit in the New York Supreme Court to compel the Central to transfer the stock to them. They charged that the Central's procrastination, based on defective transfer papers, was frivolous.

To keep the litigating pot at a sufficient boil, two weeks later the Central, through the chairman of its executive committee, Harold S. Vanderbilt, filed for an injunction in the New York Supreme Court to restrain the Chase Bank from turning over the proxies for the 800,000 shares to Murchison and Richardson. Vanderbilt charged that the "purported" sale by the C & O was "a sham and a device" to circumvent the 1945 I.C.C. order trusteeing stock held by C & O or Alleghany in any carrier outside the C & O system. The Texans were not really purchasers but were acting only as nominees, Vanderbilt argued, implying that in time Young and Alleghany would recapture the stock.

During the hearing, Vanderbilt's attorney, Samuel I. Rosenman, petitioned Supreme Court Justice James B. McNally to delay the annual meeting until all the complicated legal issues could be disposed of. Since it was unreasonable that such a request could stem from strength, a pall descended on those whose interests were associated with management. Thomas F. Daly, counsel for Young, was quick to exploit this feeling. He charged that the move to delay the meeting was nothing more than an effort to "postpone the inevitable."

The parade of litigants appeared endless. A 3000-share Alleghany stockholder, Harry C. King, entered the fray by intervening in the Murchison-Richardson suit to compel the Central to transfer the big block of stock. King demanded, however, that at least 300,000 of the shares be transferred not to Murchison and Richardson but to Alleghany. It was on Alleghany's behalf, after all, that Murchison and Richardson purchased the stock in the first place, King alleged.

In the meantime, interesting material concerning the expenses of the proxy fight was revealed. White, testifying at a pretrial examination in Young's suit to prevent Central's management from spending company money to conduct their end of the proxy contest, totaled some of the expenses up to the time of the testimony: newspaper advertising to combat Young's "raid," $141,857; publications sent to stockholders over the past two and one-half months, $13,046; public relations fee to Robinson-Hannagan Associates, $50,000 basic fee, plus expenses, so far totaling $7312; proxy solicitor Georgeson & Company, $10,000 fee, plus expenses totaling $13,487 (but expected to reach $40,000 before the fight was over). White was sad to say that the original $350,000 approved by the Central directors would be insufficient. (In the final tally it was estimated that $876,596 was spent by management on the fight. Young spent even more—the total was to exceed $1,300,000.)

On the I.C.C. front, there was increasing activity. Harold S. Vanderbilt on April 22 formally joined the Central in its petition for a declaratory order. On May 7 a protective committee composed of some of Central's leased lines operators and their bondholders intervened and also filed a complaint alleging that Alleghany and C & O, along with Young, Kirby, Richardson, Murchison, and C & O's Cyrus Eaton were undertaking control of the Central and C & O in a common interest, in violation of Section 5 (4).

Oral argument on Central's and Vanderbilt's petition took place at the I.C.C. on May 14. The crucial question was whether Young's group would have to secure Commission approval before they could be given legal control of the Central. C. H. Hand, representing Central and Vanderbilt, told the Commission that "the plain meaning of the words in the law" require such advance approval; thus, even if Young were to win the proxy battle, his attempt to exercise control would be illegal. Young's attorney replied that if that were the law, then the Central management had been violating it right along. "They are grasping at straws. They know they are beaten."

With only a week remaining before the annual meeting, a series of legal victories for Young's cause began to take shape. On May 15, New York Supreme Court Judge McNally denied Central's request for the preliminary injunction. However, he granted Central three days to appeal the case to the Appellate Division. On May

18 the I.C.C., refusing to become involved in the Central contest, denied the petition of Vanderbilt and the Central. Without further explanation, it held that "the interests of justice would not be advanced" by granting them.

On the same day another deep wound was administered to Central's management. Associate Justice Edward Dore of the Appellate Division, in support of Judge McNally's ruling, directed the Chase Bank to deliver the proxies of the 800,000 shares to Murchison and Richardson. But Dore did grant the Central a hearing to argue the preliminary injunction before the Appellate Division. In the tradition of a cliff-hanger, this hearing was set for May 25, the day before the annual meeting. Counsel for the Central, Samuel I. Rosenman, indicated that he would repeat the request at the Appellate Division hearing on May 25 for a postponement of the annual meeting. Rosenman pointed out that if the Young group won at the annual meeting, then "it would be necessary to oust them if plaintiffs were successful at the trial." A merry-go-round of managements was no way to run a railroad.

This last-ditch attempt failed. The court took no action to delay the meeting or to enjoin the voting of the 800,000 shares. Although technically the court could act at any time before the meeting started, Presiding Justice David W. Peck said, "You can assume we are not going to adjourn the meeting." But the Central lawyers assumed nothing of the sort. They would be in court the next day— and, if necessary, while the annual stockholders' meeting was taking place.

* * *

During the entire period while the storm over the 800,000 shares was raging in the New York courts and in the Interstate Commerce Commission, another area of turbulence was generating in the Securities and Exchange Commission. As early as January 1954, the S.E.C., alerted that a major proxy contest was gathering force, began a watch on Young's activities.

The S.E.C. by law was the referee of proxy contests involving any corporation listed on a national stock exchange. The proxy rules formulated by the S.E.C. and administered by its Division of Corporation Finance had evolved over the score of years before the Central contest.

The proxy rules in effect in 1954, according to the S.E.C., were "designed primarily for the conventional solicitation of proxies by management." The rules did not contemplate the kind of proxy contest involving the scope, size, and character of the Central battle, with its vast number of shareholders, its array of law and public relations firms, its army of employees, its lawsuits and Commission hearings, its press, radio, and television conferences, its extensive newspaper and magazine advertising, and, above all, its dramatic and flamboyant personalities. These rules generally were directed to the typical solicitation of votes for directors and resolutions and motions upon which stockholders' approval was sought by management. The problem of the insurgent stockholder group, though relatively minor, was considered to be encompassed by the general terms of the rules. The Commission's statutory role as a referee in cases of dispute was based on a philosophy of disclosure, intended to ensure that stockholders be fully and fairly informed concerning the persons seeking election, so that they could act on an informed basis when their votes were sought. That is what the proxy rules sought to provide, by requiring that stockholders be given certain specific information concerning the solicitors and their nominees, and by prohibiting the dissemination of misleading statements in connection with solicitations. This statutory scheme was considered necessary to protect the private investors, the brokers, the stockholders, managements, and above all, the public. Not only did there have to be a measure of fullness to the truth, but false, misleading, and fraudulent information had to be guarded against. The aim of these rules was, in a phrase, "truth in securities"—a phrase, incidentally, which was part of Young's arsenal in his various corporate battles.

In the normal course of a corporation's operation, the S.E.C. proxy rules directed that information essential to an understanding of actions to be taken at a stockholders' meeting was to be supplied in a proxy statement. This statement had to be filed with the S.E.C.

prior to distribution. But the Commission did not clear, approve, or disapprove. Instead the Commission staff examined or "processed" the material. The word "process" was not jargon but was a pragmatic term meaning that the Commission staff could prevent violations of the Securities Exchange Act by giving solicitors an opportunity to revise their material instead of waiting until the damage was done and then having to seek corrective action in the courts. In this sense the staff action was preventive and prophylactic. The Commission staff thus checked in advance to see that the statement did not conceal basic facts about the finances and operation of the company and that it did not contain fraudulent and misleading information. Information was to be submitted about nominees for directors, including their business experience, dealings with the company, salaries, options, bonuses, and all other material facts. In time a series of standards evolved, based on common sense and experience as to typical matters considered by the Commission to be materially misleading, including such things as:

1. distortion of business or financial facts for the purpose of creating inferences or impressions favorable to the contestants which were unwarranted by the underlying facts;

2. expressions of opinions or conclusions concerning the operations of the company not supported by or contrary to the known facts;

3. the use of out-of-context statements made by courts, congressional committees, and administrative agencies, and similar bodies or reference to indictments or unproven charges or similar matters under circumstances which implied conviction or guilt which had not in fact been established;

4. the expression as fact of that which should be clearly identified as opinion;

5. personal attack charging association with criminals or Communists; references to illegal acts or events regarded generally as contrary to the public interests; or the use of reprints or extracts from newspapers and periodicals of a generally derogatory nature;

6. the use of libelous, defamatory, or scurrilous material;

7. claims, promises, or projections as to future earnings, dividends,

sales, and increases in value of assets or stock based on mere conjecture or distortion or reconstruction of past operating results of the company without regard to generally accepted accounting, statistical, or financial principles.

In the event the submitted material appeared to the Commission staff to be incomplete, misleading, or inadequate, it could urge changes, usually by way of a letter of comment. But the Commission had no statutory power to compel corrections or changes or to prevent or require a stockholders' meeting. Its power merely was to ask a federal court for an injunction to prevent the issuance of the material in question, or to prevent use of proxies obtained through such improper soliciting material, or to request postponement of a stockholders' meeting. However, the Commission's role should not be underestimated. Where there was no heated war among shareholders, a tap on the shoulder of management suggesting a reappraisal was generally sufficient to convince the erring party to make the indicated changes. Only on rare occasions was court action necessary. The Commission, moreover, took the position that its staff's examination did not guarantee the propriety or accuracy of the material but that the ultimate responsibility for the information furnished stockholders rested on those who prepared and distributed it.

In a sense the solicitation of proxies by management, especially when no contest was in the offing, developed in a relatively stereotyped manner. The original proxy material was sent to the Commission at least ten days in advance of the mailing or other distribution, including by advertisement. Usually the Commission staff made certain suggestions or comments, the company revised its material, and the matter was resolved swiftly and efficiently.

This was in effect the position of the S.E.C. and its rules on proxy fights in 1954, at the opening of the proxy contest for control of the New York Central Railroad. But even before the dust of that proxy battle cleared, it was plain that some new proxy rules were required.

The S.E.C. became aware that a proxy contest might be under way for control of the Central when the newspaper stories appeared in the middle of January 1954 regarding Young's and Kirby's resignations from the C & O. Since the announcement included the phrase "free to take over another railroad," the Commission suspected, at least, a coming solicitation for proxies. But it no longer had any doubt on February 16, with the appearance of Young's ad requesting nominations for the Central "Ownership Board of Directors."

The Commission reacted promptly. Harry Heller, assistant director of the Division of Corporation Finance, wrote Young and Kirby on February 18:

> Our attention has been called to an advertisement appearing over your names on page 16 of the *Wall Street Journal* for Tuesday, February 16, 1954, addressed to New York Central stockholders. The advertisement requests these stockholders to advise you if they have any nominations for their "new Ownership Board of Directors" to be elected May 26, 1954. News stories in this and other newspapers quote statements attributed to Mr. Young that he plans to organize the New York Central stockholders in a proxy contest against the present management of the Corporation and in favor of an opposition slate of directors to be supported by him.
>
> Section 14 (a) of the Securities Exchange Act of 1934 prohibits the solicitation of proxies in respect of any security registered on a national securities exchange in contravention of such rules and regulations as the Securities and Exchange Commission may prescribe as necessary or appropriate in the public interest or for the protection of investors. Pursuant to this statutory authority, the Commission has issued Regulation X–14, governing, with certain exceptions, all solicitations of proxies with respect to securities registered on a national securities exchange.
>
> The regulation defines solicitation to include any request not to execute a proxy as well as any request for a proxy. Furthermore, the power of the Commission over proxy solicitations extends not only to the regulation of a proxy strictly as such, but also "to any other writings which are part of a continuous plan ending in solicitation and which prepare the way for its success." (SEC v. Okin, 132 F. 2d 784, C.A., 2d, 1943; SEC v. Topping, 85 F. Supp. 63, S.D.N.Y. 1949)
>
> The Commission takes the position, in the light of the above decisions and the language of its rules, that preliminary letters, advertising and announcements in respect of the election of directors of the New York Central Railroad are proxy soliciting material. Accordingly, all such material should be filed with this Commission in preliminary form pursuant to the provisions of Regulation X–14 before it is released to the public.
>
> There are enclosed for your convenient reference copies of the Com-

mission's proxy rules as amended. It is requested that these proxy rules be complied with in connection with any future advertisements, letters or other soliciting material issued by you to New York Central stockholders.

For the next three and a half months, Heller was to have few tranquil moments. The sparring had now begun between Young and the S.E.C. regarding Commission powers and the form and character of proxy material and what constitutes "solicitation." The struggle for the Central placed an unprecedented strain on the S.E.C., for it quickly became apparent that this was no run-of-the-mill proxy fight.

Instead of remaining confined to its stockholders, who really are the electorate of a corporation, the New York Central contest took on the trappings of a national election for public office. No longer merely a mattter of narrow interest for the financial community, including stockholders and participants, the battle for the Central had become a national spectacle, stimulating widespread interest and

Drew Pearson and Young during one of Pearson's *Merry-Go-Round* television shows at the time of the second battle for the Central.

comment. Newspapers and news media assigned full-time reporters to cover every aspect as well as all the personalities. Radio and television crews tripped over each other as though they were following presidential candidates on a campaign tour. The participants appeared before almost every kind of club and organization. Television and radio discussion programs deluged them with offers to appear—and rarely did they refuse. They were stopped for street interviews, were called at home and at their office, and were for the moment among the nation's most sought-after celebrities. On their part they missed no opportunity for public comment. In this atmosphere a war erupted between the S.E.C. staff and the participants. While the contestants wrenched, twisted, and tore the rules to shreds, the staff of the S.E.C. had to stretch the rules to cover the new situations.

In the Commission's view, it was obvious that if no controls were imposed on campaign literature prior to a formal solicitation of a proxy, the stockholders could be "conditioned." It was obvious that every public pronouncement by Young on Central's management was made with the impending proxy contest in mind and was calculated to induce eventual success in that contest. While the exercise of Commission jurisdiction over such preliminary literature had received judicial support and was settled administrative practice, the attempt to monitor the barrage of oral statements, impromptu and otherwise, issued by both sides, and to see to it that they conformed to the rules, became a physical impossibility for the S.E.C.

The S.E.C. faced an almost unsolvable problem with respect to the solicitation of stockholders' votes in unrehearsed radio and television programs. In such a program, how could an ad lib answer which resulted in a solicitation for stockholder votes be submitted to the S.E.C. for processing? Between February 19 and May 26, the day of the annual stockholders' meeting, Young and White appeared on over a dozen national network programs. Since the purpose of these performances was to impress the electorate of the Central, the S.E.C. was officially concerned. Programs with large audience ratings and network hookups, such as "Meet the Press," the "Today" show, interviews with Eric Sevareid and Dave Garroway, Igor Cassini, Tex and Jinx McCrary, and Drew Pearson, made Young and White into

William White (*left*), Lawrence Spivak and Young just before the coin toss to see who would go first **on** *Meet the Press.*

television and radio celebrities. The two men delivered numerous speeches—for example, before the New York Society of Security Analysts, the Association of Customers' Brokers, the Sales Executive Club of New York, the Federation of Women Shareholders. When there was a prepared text, the processing procedure before the S.E.C. went relatively smoothly, but the question and answer period gave the S.E.C. staff nightmares.

The Commission recognized that as a practical matter it appeared both undesirable and impossible to require prior filing of all answers to spontaneous and unsolicited inquiries from the press, radio, and TV, even though the replies generally were of a soliciting character. The Commission sought to distinguish between prepared oral statements and spontaneous responses to unsolicited inquiries. It considered that the former constituted soliciting material which had to be filed prior to use while the latter did not. Of course, the lines of distinction were most difficult to draw, especially with an unorthodox personality like Young. Young generally complied with the proxy rules to the extent of filing copies of proposed advertisements and of letters proposed to be distributed or published, but he never did file a copy of a press release or of a speech.

The speech to the National Press Club, on March 11,[23] apparently was composed from notes which Young placed on the lectern. He announced that because of the S.E.C.'s rules he could not have copies for distribution. The result, of course, was to increase the demand for them. Several hours later, however, mimeographed copies of the speech were made available, obviously from stenographic notes, since on-the-spot questions and answers were included.

Young's attitude with respect to the necessity of filing prepared releases is again indicated by an article in *Financial World,* April 28, 1954, which stated that Young in a press conference in his office read his statement from a typewritten document prepared in advance. When asked by reporters if copies would be available, Young was reported as saying that his statements had not been "cleared" by the Commission under the proxy rules and therefore could not be handed out. Some commissioners began to mumble that Young was satirizing their rules. The Commission was in a difficult position; it was seeking on the one hand to keep some control over solicitation of stockholders, in the interest of full disclosure, and, on the other hand, to avoid any impression of infringing on constitutional guarantees of freedom of the press and freedom of speech. The Commission was hard-pressed to determine whether an oral statement given to the press or on radio or television was prepared in advance or not, and in effect was relegated to asserting jurisdiction only when written copies or summaries were prepared for distribution. Moreover, the Commission sought to emphasize that its proxy rules applied only to persons taking part in a solicitation; it did not intend to control or regulate newspaper stories. But the Commission could not escape the

[23] See p. 159.

charge that its proxy rules as applied in the processing of prepared speeches, press releases, and scripts, was contrary to the First Amendment.[24]

Few elements in the Central proxy fight troubled the S.E.C. more than did the lack of disclosure about the Murchison-Richardson purchase of the 800,000 shares. But at the time there was no definitive requirement that participants in a proxy fight identify their interests, whether they were principals or mere "fronts." All kinds of interests got into the New York Central proxy fight, signing advertisements, writing letters, making public statements, and, above all, soliciting proxies. While in most cases the interest of the parties was obvious and well known, in others it was somewhat ambiguous. The essential facts in the Murchison-Richardson purchase were always confusing.[25]

[24] A year later, in 1955, the S.E.C. received adverse comments from the American Society of Newspaper Editors and others on this point. This problem was not resolved until the proxy rules were revised in January 1956, mainly as a result of the Central proxy fight. The annual report of the S.E.C. for 1056 stated, ". . . in its revised rules the Commission has expressly provided that press releases, prepared radio and television broadcasts and speeches need not be filed with the Commission prior to their use, although they remain subject to the cardinal requirement of our rule that they must not be misleading. They must also be filed promptly with the Commission after their use. Such material, of course, may be submitted to the Commission prior to its use, if the contestant so desires. A practical reason for this change in our rules, in addition to the importance of safeguarding freedom of speech and freedom of the press, is that time limitations and the pressures of a proxy contest frequently necessitate the use of these documents as quickly as possible. The Commission is gratified to report to the Congress on this aspect of the thrust of its rules that responsible elements of the press are now completely satisfied that our rules do not impinge upon the freedom of the press or freedom of speech, particularly in view of the fact that they impose no prior restraints on press releases, press conferences and radio and television broadcasts and speeches."

[25] Disclosure of interest was one of the principal aims of the S.E.C.'s proxy rule amendments of 1956. As the annual report for 1956 stated, one purpose of the new rules was to "bring all of the participants in a proxy contest out on the stage to be gazed upon by the shareholders; no participants may be left lurking in the wings. . . . These provisions should make available to the security holders information about the background and the financial and other interests not only of all persons who are nominees for election as directors, but also of all persons who may represent the real interest behind

The vagueness of the proxy rules at that time resulted in a running battle between Young's representatives and the S.E.C. over the content of proxy material. Telegrams were sent almost every night demanding S.E.C. action against management for violation of the proxy rules and defending Robert Young's material. In the view of the S.E.C. staff, Young was reacting like a "wet paint toucher," unable to keep from smudging the S.E.C. rules. They were convinced that when Young wanted to touch on a prohibited area, he would answer what seemed to be a bona fide question from a newspaperman but what the staff suspected was a planted question. The Commission took the position that failure to file copies of prearranged questions would be considered an infraction of the proxy rules. It kept constant pressure on Young.

Young more than reciprocated. He lashed back at the Commission, with a unique disdain for its official power. He made no secret of the fact that he regarded certain members of the S.E.C., including the chairman, as partial to the banking interests.

Without realizing the door it was opening, the S.E.C. gave Young an opportunity to make this impeachment public. During the fall of 1953, when there was not even the intimation of a proxy fight, the S.E.C. announced hearings on a proposed relaxation of Rule U–50, the competitive bidding requirement which Young always proclaimed was his brainchild. The S.E.C. proposed to permit negotiation to replace compulsory bidding in certain areas where the issuance and sale of the securities involved were subject to state regulatory bodies.

The hearing was scheduled for February 18, 1954, by coincidence the same week Young officially opened his battle for control of the Central. He seized the opportunity to use the Commission's proposed amendment of U–50 as an indication of the pervasiveness of the banking community; more than anything else this was the theme of his proxy fight.

---

the formal nominees, and should reduce substantially the difficulty the Commission has had in the past with undisclosed principals, or 'fronts.'" From that time on, all participants in a proxy fight were required to file a statement concerning their interests. This is entitled Schedule 14–B of the S.E.C. proxy rules, a monument in part to the New York Central proxy contest.

The major figures to appear at the hearing in opposition to the amendment, in addition to Young, were Otis & Co., Halsey, Stuart & Co., and the Congress of Industrial Organizations. Appearing in support of the amendment were the representatives of the leading underwriters and banking firms of Wall Street, including John S. Wright, a partner of Morgan Stanley & Company. Extra chairs had to be brought into the hearing room to accommodate the large audience, and the newspapers noted the unusual number of S.E.C. employees present, an index of Young's celebrity status.

Young's appearance generated a measure of excitement. As the *New York Times* reported:

> During his fifty-five minutes before the Commission, Mr. Young said that he still believed in states' rights but that there should be no "breakdown" in Federal regulation of the sale of securities to the public.
> Such a development, he declared, would serve to benefit only such large concerns as Morgan Stanley and Kuhn, Loeb & Company and "those who prosper or suffer with them." He described the effort to change the U–50 rule, and other moves to "thwart necessary public regulations" of some segments of the economy, as "treason in the canyons of Wall Street," which "can be almost as harmful as treason in the laboratories of Fort Monmouth."
> "The concentration of wealth in New York is unfair to investors," Mr. Young told the Commission at one point in a discussion that covered his early years of gaining control of the Van Sweringen industrial empire including the Chesapeake and Ohio Railway, which is the largest single stockholder in New York Central.[26]

Outside the hearing room, Young continued his attack during an impromptu press conference. He charged that the New York Central was "Morgan-dominated." But his most dramatic statement and the one that gained the headlines charged that big-business interests in the Eisenhower administration were trying to undercut the President's stand against monopoly. In this context, he charged that the idea to change Rule U–50 "did not originate in the staff of the Commission" but that "word came down" to change the rule. When asked from whom word came down, Young refused to elaborate. When asked if

[26] *New York Times,* February 19, 1954, p. 35.

MEMO NO. 1 ON COMPETITIVE BIDDING:

A Three Billion Dollar Success Story

How the Alleghany Corporation Smashed the Private Negotiation System for Selling Bonds to The House of Morgan and Kuhn, Loeb & Company, and Helped to Gain Competitive Bidding for the Entire Railroad Industry

MEMO NO. 2 ON COMPETITIVE BIDDING:

Congratulations to A.T.&T.!

From Alleghany Corporation on saving $58,000,000 in bankers' fees by breaking the private system of selling bonds to the House of Morgan.

With sidelights on the use of a "dummy Director" in the secret fight
for control of the world's largest industrial corporation.

it was a cabinet officer, he still refused to answer, explaining "I've got enough enemies now."

Young's charge did provoke an official response from Ralph H. Demmler, S.E.C. Chairman: "I want to state on behalf of myself and my fellow Commissioners that the proposal was developed wholly within the Commission and in consultation with its staff without any suggestion from anyone outside the Commission and without the prior knowledge of anyone outside the Commission."[27]

Young continued to level his guns at Morgan Stanley & Company, Kuhn, Loeb, and the S.E.C. itself. Convinced that he had fastened in the public mind the image that the Central management and the big bankers were hand in glove, he followed his testimony with an ad in the major newspapers of the United States entitled "A THREE BILLION DOLLAR SUCCESS STORY—How the Alleghany Corporation Smashed the Private Negotiation System for Selling Bonds to The House of Morgan and Kuhn, Loeb & Company, and Helped to Gain Competitive Bidding for the Entire Railroad Industry."

Young had touched an open nerve. In an uncharacteristic move, Morgan Stanley answered in the style established by Young himself.

In any event, Morgan Stanley stood up to be counted as an enemy of Young. It ran a full-page advertisement with these headlines:

MORGAN STANLEY SAYS . . . "LET'S LOOK AT THE RECORD"
WHAT DID JUDGE MEDINA SAY ABOUT MR. YOUNG?
FREEDOM OR COMPULSION, MR. YOUNG?
WE DO NOT BELIEVE IN *compulsory* COMPETITIVE
BIDDING FOR CORPORATE SECURITIES

The competitive bidding advertisements should have alerted the S.E.C. to the nature of the proxy battle to come.[28] The assault upon the stockholders for their votes was being mounted. The hurricane of solicitations had an intensity probably never even approached in previous proxy contests over which the S.E.C. had jurisdiction. Until the very day of the annual meeting, appeals to stockholders continued with unparalleled heat and volume. Both sides used every means possible to reach the stockholders.

The solicitation battle for stockholders' votes took a dramatic turn at the close of April. *Fortune* magazine in its May issue ran a devastating portrait of Young under the title "The Sound and Fury of Robert R. Young."

---

[27]*Wall Street Journal,* February 19, 1954, p. 18.
[28] The S.E.C. gave up its attempt to amend Rule U-50 when on July 2, 1956, it put the whole matter to rest with the announcement that "after thorough consideration of the entire record it had decided not to adopt the proposed amendment to the rule."

To New York Central Shareowners:

New May ▮Fortune▮ magazine sizes up New York Central—

and cuts Robert Young down to size!

Every shareowner of the New York Central System is urged to study the May, 1954, issue of FORTUNE Magazine. It contains both an Editorial and an article on the New York Central System. This completely objective report by the magazine of business management should help you greatly in deciding how to vote your proxy May 26. For the benefit of those who may not be able to obtain a complete copy of the publication, key excerpts are published below.

Following are highlights from the Editorial on page 79 of the May, 1954, issue of FORTUNE titled:

The Sound and Fury of Robert R. Young

director of the Central, 'had the crust to vote against a man chosen as one of America's twelve foremost business leaders'—i.e., Mr. Young himself. He specifically names half a dozen top railroaders, including a deceased president of the Central, and charges them with 'committing a fraud on their shareholders' through improper purchase of equipment. He blasts railroad executives in general for coloring to the 'ice and grease dealers.'

Nineteenth Century Limited

"So much for Mr. Young's estimate of the industry that he presumably aspires to lead. Having vilified it, he now proposes to reform it. What does he offer? First of all, he proposes a number of flamboyant railroading ideas for the Central. These include the adoption of the light

Fortune gave emphasis to the article by setting it up in the magazine as their lead editorial. With this expression of opinion, it ran a story entitled "The Central Rolls Again," which delighted White even more and brought cheer and comfort to the management slate. At first management tried to buy reprints from *Fortune* but were refused, since the magazine did not want to be in the position of appearing as an active advocate for the Central against Young. But management, unwilling to give up the enormous value of *Fortune*'s prestige in the financial community, particularly among owners of stock, chose to press forward. It made its own reprints without *Fortune*'s permission, which was required under copyright, and mailed them to all its stockholders and anyone else they thought could affect the proxy vote. In addition, it planned full-page advertisements in the major newspapers of the United States with a bold-faced headline "To New York Central Shareowners: New May *Fortune* Magazine Sizes Up New York Central—and Cuts Robert Young Down to Size!" So important did management consider the *Fortune* article that it spent $85,000 on reprints and advertising quoting from it.

At one point management had even tried to buy up copies of the magazine itself. When Young learned of this, he fired off a telegram to the Central directors:

I have been informed that you are buying up all available issues of the May FORTUNE in order to use the volumes and misleading material contained therein as solicitation material for your proxy solicitors. The purpose of this telegram is to warn you that if we should find evidence of the fact of such use unauthorized by the S.E.C., we will hold you and the directors legally liable and attack the validity of the proxies so procured.

Young's lawyers also called on Time Inc., which owned *Fortune*. The publishing executives were less concerned with the validity of Young's legal position than they were with the fact that the prestige of their organization had been placed on the line for one combatant against another in a private fight. And the timing of the article could not help *Fortune*'s reputation for objectivity; the attack, appearing in their magazine the same month as the annual meeting, gave no chance in their publication for replies and rebuttals.

Roy Larsen, President of Time Inc., issued the following statement:

Although approaches were made to us requesting permission for the New York Central to use copies of the magazine or reprints of the editorial and article on the New York Central System, we refused all such requests for use of the *Fortune* editorial material. The newspaper page on Monday and the reprints of the editorial material which were sent to Central stockholders were without our knowledge or consent. This use is a violation of our copyright and our trademark and is also a violation of *Fortune*'s established policy.

Henry Luce, whose wife was an admirer of Young's philosophy and pluck and in fact was a member of the Public Advisory Committee of Young's Federation for Railway Progress, was not about to get deeply involved in the Central fight. On May 4 *Time* filed suit in the U.S. District Court for the Southern District of New York against the New York Central, requesting an injunction to bar further use of the editorial and article. A week later on May 12, the court granted the injunction and awarded *Time* $2000 counsel fees and $5000 damages. White said it was the best $7000 the Central spent in the entire proxy fight.

Young did nothing to ease *Time's* discomfort. He formulated a reply in the form of an advertisement and had a draft made up in anticipation of its appearance in every important paper in the country. The advertisement's lead was an eye-catching headline, "Fortune's Lowest Ebb, What Makes Luce Talk When New York Central's Lawyers and Morgan Find Their Grip on a Railroad Slipping?" When the ad was filed in preliminary form with the Commission staff, it created a minor commotion.

Among other things, the Securities and Exchange Commission staff, in its examination of the proposed ad, commented that it dragged extraneous material into the proxy fight and attempted to establish guilt by association. Part of the proposed ad included the information that a partner in a law firm representing Time Inc. had been indicted for bribing a federal judge but was not convicted, having pleaded successfully the statute of limitations.[29] The S.E.C.'s major opposition stemmed from the fact that the case had nothing to do with *Time* or the New York Central.

A revised version of Young's ad on *Time* and *Fortune* did appear, headed "Time Inc. Sues N. Y. Central. . . . At Issue: Illegal Use by Present Central Management of a Biased *Fortune* Article Attacking Robert R. Young. . . . Time Inc. Seeks Injunction and Damages."

Another ad submitted by Young to the Commission but turned down for processing contained information about antitrust violations of four of Central's directors. (The antitrust cases in question had nothing to do with the New York Central.) The S.E.C. maintained that it was unfair and carried an implication of guilt by association.

The restraining influence of the S.E.C. was always present. Both parties had difficulty obeying the S.E.C. warning about misleading promises of dividends. Dividends are the aphrodisiac of corporate love. Nothing captivates the little stockholder more than the promise

[29] In its 1956 annual report, the S.E.C. referred to this advertisement in the following terms: ". . . other misleading devices have been attempted. One is that of imputing guilt by association—often the most remote type of association. . . . For example, a magazine which had published articles favorable to the management was sought to be disparaged by the opposition group, not on the ground of any illegal or immoral act which the magazine had committed but on the ground that it employed a law firm one of the partners of which had been accused, although never convicted, of bribery of a Federal court."

TIME, INC. SUES N. Y. CENTRAL

At Issue: Illegal Use by Present Central Management of a Biased Fortune Article Attacking Robert R. Young ... Time, Inc. Seeks Injunction and Damages

Roy Larsen, President of Time, Inc., has this to say about the Central management's unlawful use of the material appearing in Fortune's May issue:

"Although approaches were made to us requesting permission for the New York Central to use copies of the magazine or reprints of the editorial and article on the New York Central System, we refused all such requests for use of the Fortune editorial material. The newspaper page on Monday and the reprints of the editorial material which were sent to Central stockholders was without our knowledge or consent. This use is a violation of our copyright and our trade mark and is also a violation of Fortune's established policy."

FORTUNE vs. THE FACTS

of higher payments. It is a thralldom of which no management can afford to be unaware. The S.E.C. thus demands that the promise of dividends be dispensed by prescription only.

Robert R. Young knew full well the effect on stockholders of the promise of dividends. In his first public statement after arriving in New York, he expressed the opinion that the New York Central "should be on a $7 to $10 a year dividend basis and would be if it had the right kind of management." This was an arresting tune to stockholders, who had received no dividends from 1932 to 1942 and only sporadically thereafter.

White reacted, "That's a lot of hokum. I consider it a very unfair thing to do to stockholders to hang before them bait like a big increase in dividends when we know it can't be produced, at least to the amounts that Young talks about, and certainly not in his lifetime or mine. But he's the one who'll have to answer for that. I will make no false promises. The basic problems of the Central are its heavy terminal costs in the East and big passenger deficits. Meanwhile passenger revenue is off 5 per cent and freight revenue off 11 per cent while the railroads' fixed burdens remain. These are just basic ideas and don't respond to any magic touch."[30]

When Young tried to process soliciting material suggesting Central should be able to pay an $8 dividend, the S.E.C. staff raised questions as to the misleading nature of specific projections regarding future dividends. Comments such as this did not cause the relations between the S.E.C. and Young to become less strained.[31] To meet the staff objections, Young revised the material to state generally the opinion that under his sound management the Central stock could pay far in excess of its present dividends.

The door was again opened to Young on his specific future dividends claims, when management circulated the *Fortune* editorial referring to Young's prediction of $7 to $10 dividends as a "pie-in-sky promise." In seeking to defend himself on this point, Young submitted proposed soliciting material in which he presented his views as to why he thought it possible to forecast $7 to $10, and this time the Commission staff did not question his right to state his position.

---

[30] *New York Times*, February 17, 1954, p. 41.

[31] Several years later, in its 1956 annual report, the S.E.C. referred to this entire episode, without mentioning Young by name:

> In another case, misleading comparisons were sought to be made by an opposing group in a contest for control of a railroad that the company's stock had sold in 1929 at $250 per share. This statement was coupled with the assertion that if the opposition group succeeded in its efforts the stock would go to $100 and pay an $8 dividend. In view of the pronounced changes that have occurred in our economy since 1929, particularly in the growth of strongly competitive forces in the transportation industry such as automobiles and trucks, plus the fact that the company had earned $8 a share only three times in its history, the Commission insisted upon the deletion from the solicitation material of these comparisons.

Failure to be precise may have led the S.E.C. itself into a "misleading comparison." While it was technically accurate to say the Central paid $8 a share only three times in its history, the figures would have been less misleading if the Commission had indicated that these three times covered seventeen years (1870 to 1874, 1876 to 1884, and 1928 to 1930). In addition, the Central paid $10 one year, 1875.

A Dismal Dividend Record

I invested over three thousand hard-earned dollars in New York Central— earned shovelling coal from the deck of a locomotive.

Destination–Dividends!

William White outlines a realistic program of potential savings and earnings for New York Central

---

Bold New Passenger Plan
Can Provide Finer Rail Travel...
and Save Millions for New York Central

Why New Top Direction of the
New York Central Is So Urgently Needed

To New York Central Shareholders:

What manner of man
is Robert R. Young?...

...who asks you to give him power over your money in New York Central?

LITTLE WHITE LIES

An Answer to the Smear Attack on Robert R. Young, Showing How

10 Half Truths Equal 10 Wholly Misleading Statements

––––––

Big Black-and-White
TRUTHS
about Robert R. Young

––––––

Mr. White's
SLICK PAPER BOOKLET

––––––

A Contrast in

MORALS and METHODS

TOO GOOD
FOR STOCKHOLDERS?

*...How does Mr. Young
make this inside deal jibe with*

"MORALS AND METHODS?"

A Morgan "Myth"

Or How New York Central Shareholders Failed to Get $247,000 Due Them

A Letter to Mr. George Whitney, Chairman of J. P. Morgan & Co.

Neither did the S.E.C. staff question an advertisement containing statements about past dividends made by William H. Landers, the retired railroad engineer who was on Young's slate. Under the heading "A DISMAL DIVIDEND RECORD," he said:

I invested over three thousand hard-earned dollars in New York Central—earned shovelling coal from the deck of a locomotive. . . .

When I bought this stock I thought that I was laying up something to help me out when I retired. But I have received dividends from this great New York Central property, in only ten out of the last 23 years. . . . In 23 years I have received a total of $13 per share in dividends. That comes to just a shade more than 1% per year on my investment. I could have done much better by leaving my money in a savings bank. Even if I'd tucked the cash in my mattress I'd have been better off because I would have saved my principal, since the stock which cost me $40 is now worth only $20, thanks to the way the road has been run.

White hit back with an ad headed "Destination Dividends! William White outlines a realistic program of potential savings and earnings for New York Central."

Ordinarily I prefer to talk about progress *after* it is made and profits *after* they are earned. But these are not ordinary times.

Within the next few weeks, New York Central stockholders must decide whether they will continue the progress present new management has made and is making . . . or whether they will throw all that out of the window in favor of some will-of-the-wisp promises.

The attacks in the proxy material were often personal. In an Alleghany proxy letter sent to Central stockholders and reproduced as an advertisement, Young attacked Central's contract with White:

Ask yourself for what reason Mr. White, when he was promoted from the related Lackawanna, got a contract at $120,000 a year until at age 65 he retires, $75,000 a year until age 70, and $40,000 a year thereafter. Certainly, such a contract can remove much of the incentive for hard work, and in our opinion is inimical to your interests.

White almost immediately announced that he would sever all connections with the Central in the "unlikely event that Robert R. Young and his associates should prevail" and that he would forgo all future payments under the contract. White said he had insisted upon the option of dissociating himself from the company and giving up "very valuable rights."

I am not a wealthy man and I have to continue to work for a living. However, the interest of the New York Central property is paramount, and sacrificing the security of myself and family in a situation like this is of secondary importance, even though I would give up a position that would pay me $120,000 a year for the next nine years, then $75,000 a year for five years and from the time I am 70 years of age $40,000 a year until the end of my life.[32]

Young, on hearing of this announcement, remarked that White's contract "obviously was embarrassing to the board," and it was "too bad the bankers on the board do not also relieve the company of their own embarrassing connections."[33]

One New York Central advertisement resulted from Harold Vanderbilt's apparent failure to do his share in the contest. When the president of a leading bank volunteered to help secure proxies and organize a stock-buying campaign, he asked for a meeting with the two most important directors, George Whitney and Harold Vanderbilt. For a volunteer with such important credentials, it was not an unreasonable request. He was informed, however, that Vanderbilt was resting on his yacht off Palm Beach and that Whitney was on a vacation out West. Incredulous, the banker picked up his hat and left. At this point one of White's assistants decided to turn adversity into advantage. The result was an advertisement in the form of a letter from Vanderbilt to Central shareholders, explaining why Young should not run the Central:

> You do not learn railroading relaxing at Palm Beach, Newport and the other resorts at which Mr. Young spends the greater part of his time. I know, because in recent years, I have spent a good deal of my time engaged in more or less similar pursuits. But then, I do not aspire to be chief executive officer of the New York Central.

Young's knack for getting under the skin of his opposition was epitomized by the "warning" which appeared in small type as a footnote at the bottom of Alleghany's proxy letter to Central shareholders:

> WARNING—If any banker, lawyer, shipper, supplier or other person solicits your proxy for the present New York Central Board, ask him what his special interests are, or what your Company is paying for his services. Like the bankers now on your Board, he, too, may

[32] *New York Times*, April 15, 1954, p. 45.
[33] *Ibid.*

be hoping to receive special favors from your railroad or from the bankers.

If your stock is held in a broker's or other nominee's name, take special care to see that he follows your instructions and that we receive your proxy.

But some of those affected did not react as though it was a mere footnote. Alexander C. Nagle, president of the First National Bank of the City of New York, considered himself insulted. In an open letter to Young which was carried as an advertisement in many newspapers, he replied:

. . . It is difficult for us to believe that those associated with you can give support to the attempt on your part to revive the threadbare demagogic charges of banker domination and banker wickedness.

Especially is it difficult to believe that they subscribe to the "Warning" at the conclusion of your proxy material. You imply that any banker, lawyer, shipper, supplier or other person, who, in the proper exercise of his personal judgment, demonstrates his confidence in the recognized excellent management of the New York Central under President William White, by helping to obtain proxies for the present Board, is to be suspected of ulterior motives. Surely even you cannot believe that.

Young then raised the footnote to the dignity of a separate advertisement, emphasizing the word "WARNING" in large, block type, simulating a newspaper headline.

The advertisements continued to appear right up to May 26. The day before the stockholders' meeting, the "Alleghany-Young-Kirby Ownership Board" ran an advertisement:

Not once in a generation do we have an effective voice in determining the policies of a great corporation—tomorrow we do.

Only once in four years do we vote for a change in the President of the United States. Not once in a generation do we have effective voice in determining the policies of one of our great corporations as we do this year.

That is why the New York Central proxy fight is on every tongue and the Armory in Albany on Wednesday, May 26th, promises to be the center of the Nation's interest. . . .

. . . We hope you have kept your letters from both sides. Even though you do not desire to refer to them now, they constitute a unique record which schools, libraries and collectors may one day seek.

The letters and advertisements produced by the Young-Kirby side were principally the result of the joint efforts of Young and Clifford H. Ramsdell. After consultation with Young and Deegan, Ramsdell drafted, laid out, and arranged for the placement of the ads—all without the use of an advertising agency.

The battle of the advertisements was followed with intense interest, quite naturally, by the advertising fraternity. *Tide* magazine, a trade paper for that profession, polled twenty-two hundred top marketing executives. Their prediction, by a two-to-one majority, was that William White would defeat Robert R. Young; on the other hand, they voted five-to-three that Young had done the better public relations job. Representative reasons given for betting on White:

"White is a railroad man's railroad man," "Big blocks of conservatives as well as widows and orphans are afraid of Young," "The Street resents attempts to push it around."

Sentiments of those who bet on Young:

"He's rough, tough, used to winning—and he's pretty right on his ideas," "Young is a 'shot in the arm' guy. The New York Central, like so many sprawling giants, can use such therapy," "Young has been and is a terrific power in railroading," "Young has enough influential backers to unseat White."[34]

Despite the prediction of a White victory in *Tide's* poll, reports from the brokers indicated that the vote among the independent stockholders was going two to one for Young.

When May 26 arrived, two trains were waiting at Grand Central Station in New York City to transport to Albany stockholders, television crews, operating, legal, and public relations staffs, and the usual army of hangers-on and corporate annual meeting buffs.

The trains were packed with people from every level of society, many of them wearing buttons and waving banners emblazoned either "Young at Heart" or "We Want White." Never before had a proxy contest for control of a corporate entity looked so much like a political convention. The two principals, Young and White, walked through the train shaking hands with anybody who was willing. They

[34] *Tide,* May 22, 1954, p. 26.

On the way to the annual meeting of May 26, 1954, President White (*left*) greets two Central stockholders. At the other end of the train Young was also making the rounds.

(Courtesy of New York Central Railroad)

Part of the crowd of more than 2200 "delegates" and newsmen who packed the armory.

(Courtesy of New York Central Railroad)

did not meet mid-train, however. When they were only two cars apart, the train stopped at Poughkeepsie and White transferred to the other section.

From the train, the eight hundred "delegates" poured into the National Guard Armory, where some fourteen hundred others were already waiting. Although one of the smallest men present, Young, with his ruddy complexion and shock of white hair, the center of a milling group of followers, was the most easily identifiable figure in the hall. To the press he was the most newsworthy; to the assembled crowd he was the most charismatic. Both groups found it difficult to take their eyes off him. Like the celebrity he was, he had to be protected by his aides from the physical oppression of well-wishers, who insisted on asking for autographs and giving gratuitous advice. White, even in his key position on the platform, did not seem to be able to compete with Young for the crowd's attention.

Promptly at noon President White gaveled the meeting to order. Although it was difficult, he managed to keep the meeting moving. Since the two sides had agreed on the organization and agenda, the preliminaries took little time.

Management's candidates were placed in nomination by W. Wendell Reuss, vice-chairman of a committee of Central stockholders. Twelve of the fifteen candidates were present, including such celebrated ones as Jim Farley and Harold and William Vanderbilt.

Thomas J. Deegan, Jr., Young's chief of staff, nominated the insurgent slate, and the crowd was obviously disappointed that Texans Murchison and Richardson were not there. In fact, there was only one stereotype of a Texan with a Stetson hat, who periodically gave out with a piercing rebel yell. Upon investigation, it turned out he was from Indiana.

With the nominations now formally presented, there was a short recess, during which a box lunch was provided for everyone present. Two thousand people caught up in the excitement of the moment and eating chicken with their hands was an arresting sight.

After the luncheon recess, the meeting was reopened for questions and discussions, much of it dominated by Mrs. Wilma Soss, president of the Federation of Women Shareholders in American Business.

Mrs. Soss spoke in favor of the election of Mrs. Wallace, cumulative voting, a change in the date of the annual meeting, and most important, the election of Robert R. Young. At one point Mrs. Soss climbed onto the speaker's platform and held the floor briefly before being physically escorted off.

During the voting, rumors ran through the armory which raised the pitch of the buzzing sound generally associated at conventions with impending important developments. There were many rumors: the 800,000 shares would be voted for management; they would not be voted at all; the New York Central directors would not permit

(*From left to right*) Garrard Glenn, Young, Thomas J. Deegan, Jr., and William C. MacMillen, Jr., watch as the matter of the 800,000 crucial shares is brought up.

(*Courtesy of New York Central Railroad*)

the 800,000 shares to be counted; the Chase had recaptured the proxies; the court had just enjoined Murchison and Richardson from voting the 800,000 shares. Even when Don Carter, who represented Murchison and Richardson, formally cast their 800,000 proxies for the Young-Kirby slate, the rumors were not stilled.

Actually what happened was that the Appellate Division had just denied a last-minute request by the Central management for a reconsideration of the court's ruling on the 800,000 shares. The court also dismissed as "academic" a Central motion to postpone the meeting.

It was shortly after this vital piece of information reached the armory that Young jumped to his feet and interrupted the meeting to claim victory by as much as a million shares. White, still on the platform, vehemently questioned Young's authority to make such a statement. Nothing would be final until the proxies were counted. White had earlier made it clear to intimates that, if Young's victory hinged on the 800,000 shares, the matter would be in the courts for years. Young knew this was true. He must win with a margin of more than 800,000 votes.

It was nearly three weeks before any determination was official. The tabulation of the proxies was a monumental job, carried on behind barred, guarded doors by three law professors—Robert W. Miller of Syracuse University, John Hanna of Columbia University, and Covington Hardee of Harvard Law School.[35]

Complicating their task was the large number of duplications of that more than 90 percent of the stockholders responded. But a signed proxies. Both slates had sent proxies to Central's more than 40,000 shareholders on seven different occasions. It was estimated stockholder could change his vote as many times as he wished before the closing of the polls, and many signed several proxies; some signed all fourteen. The proxy with the latest-dated signature counted, so the election inspectors first had to weed out prior-dated proxies and then certify the validity of the remaining ones. Each side had the right to challenge.

Besides this tedious but vital bookkeeping chore, the inspectors found themselves saddled with the decision on those crucial 800,000 shares: should they be included in the official tally?

[35] Later general counsel of Union Pacific.

Two days after the annual meeting, the inspectors held a closed-door hearing on this issue and listened to an hour and a half of argument by opposing sides.

On June 2 the word was out. Young had won a total victory.

The inspectors had accepted Murchison's and Richardson's proxies, but Young would have won without them. A Young spokesman claimed that for all practical purposes the election was over and done with. Contesting the 800,000 shares in court would serve no practical purpose. White capitulated. The very next day the Central confirmed this and dropped its February suit involving the 800,000 shares.

With White's concession Young had fulfilled his ambition. The Central was now a Robert R. Young road.

The rest was mere formality. By Friday, June 11, the exact count was finished. It was official the following Monday, June 14, when the final session of the 1954 annual meeting in Albany was convened. Young had won by 1,067,273 proxies—a clear-cut victory even without the proxies for the 800,000 shares owned by Murchison and Richardson. At the final meeting, William White handed over to Young's representative, Charles T. Ireland, Jr., secretary and legal counsel of Alleghany, the formal papers confirming the election of the new board.

Within minutes after the official announcement in Albany, Young, surrounded by news photographers and accompanied by Lila Bell Acheson Wallace, Tom Deegan, Garrard Glenn, and the man chosen to be the new Central president, Alfred E. Perlman, walked triumphantly from Alleghany headquarters at the Chrysler Building to Central headquarters at 230 Park Avenue. (Originally it had been planned that the entire board would make this march, but at the last moment Young decided it might not be in good taste.)

Then the new board met for the first time. Young was elected chairman of the board, at an annual salary of one dollar. Alfred E. Perlman was elected president and Charles T. Ireland, Jr., secretary. The board waived all directors' fees for attending board meetings and also all executive committee fees until a $2 dividend rate could be achieved.

Young had reached the zenith of his career.

On the walk from the Chrysler Building to 230 Park Avenue (*above*) Young (*second from right*) was flanked by Glenn (*far left*), Perlman, Mrs. Wallace, and Deegan. At the door of the New York Central Building (*below*), Young gave a victory salute.

(*Photos by Tommy Weber*)

7

The View from the Thirty-second Floor

TWO NIGHTS before the annual meeting, William White had given a dinner at the Biltmore Hotel for some three dozen newspapermen covering the Central contest. Looking worn and almost sick, he spoke briefly. "If we should get licked in this fight—" and then, noticing the horror-stricken faces of his public relations staff, "I mean in the unlikely event that we should get licked—I want to see Mr. Young up there on the thirty-second floor meeting our day-to-day problems. I'd just like to see him sit down, by God, and stick it out five years."[1]

White was in possession of a terrifying fact, one not known to Young. The Central was bankrupt.

Amidst the turmoil of the proxy fight, Willard Place, vice president, finance, had informed White that by the end of May Central's losses would be $9,000,000. He had reported further the threat of an even more immediate disaster—there would be only $6,000,000 on hand to meet a $35,000,000 payroll. The legal department was book-deep in the study of the bankruptcy laws. James B. Gray, who was later to become vice president, law, of the railroad, had already drawn the necessary papers and was in the process of selecting a jurisdiction in which to file them. The implications, both legal and financial, made this project the most closely held secret of the proxy fight.

Unaware of the Central's insolvency but with the knowledge that he had an excellent chance to win his fight for control, Young

[1] As reported by John Brooks in *The New Yorker* of July 3, 1954.

realized that he had better be ready with a man to replace White. As the odds of his winning became more favorable, the problem became more pressing.

The search had begun in earnest at the end of March 1954. It was at that time that Young suggested the name of Alfred E. Perlman. As far back as 1946 Young had read reports of the Denver & Rio Grande Western starting a railroad laboratory, which to Young represented railway progress; Young had never heard of a railroad with a lab before, at least not one as modern or with as much imagination in scope and leadership as the one at the Denver & Rio Grande. Two of Young's most trusted aides—William C. MacMillen, Jr., then president of the Federation for Railway Progress, and Thomas J. Deegan, Jr., at the time vice president of the C & O—had made a trip around the United States to learn firsthand on behalf of the Federation about the state of the railroad industry. Young had suggested that they look in on the Denver & Rio Grande.

Among the things they reported about the Denver & Rio Grande was the unusual laboratory set up by Perlman, where technicians in white smocks analyzed lubricating oils by spectrograph, submitted pistons and bearings to a magnaflux test under ultraviolet rays, inspected rail welds with gamma-ray tests, and in general introduced the latest advanced scientific developments of the time to railroading. MacMillen and Deegan, at least, had noticed nothing comparable anywhere else.

In 1948 it was decided to run a series of articles about railway men of progress in the journal of the Federation for Railway Progress. David Hill, a member of the advisory board, suggested that Perlman would be a good subject. As a result, "Perlman of the Rio Grande" by Pasquale L. Marranzino, ran in the August issue. The article further convinced Young that Perlman indeed belonged to a new breed of railroad men.

Sometime at the end of March 1954, when the scent of victory in the proxy fight had become sharper to Young, he began an investigation into Perlman's background and reputation. He often made these inquiries by telephone from Room H of the Cloud Club, with a check list in front of him. One of these calls was made to Jerry Hart,

Young's outside counsel in charge of the battle to get the Missouri Pacific out of reorganization. Hart lived in Denver and was familiar with Perlman's work and personality. Young kept Hart on the phone for over an hour questioning him about Perlman's family life, his philosophical attitude, his politics, his drinking and smoking habits (was it cigarettes, a pipe?) his relations with friends, and—since it was Young asking the questions—his relations with his enemies. That Young was interested in knowing about Perlman's enemies probably gave a better insight into Young than Perlman. Unlike Young, Perlman had few personal enemies. Typical of Young, the investigation was designed mainly to confirm what he had already decided to do; he was determined to have Perlman as his Central president. The answers Young received supported his decision.

Young, a college dropout in an industry whose operating leaders were often men of little formal education, gave great weight to what he learned about Perlman's educational background. Perlman had graduated from M.I.T. with a B.S. in engineering at the age of twenty and had studied railroading at the Harvard Graduate School of Business. Men like Norbert Wiener, famous in the field of cybernetics, and William Z. Ripley, the renowned authority on transportation, had been early influences on him.

There was hardly a facet of the modern railroad industry with which Perlman had not had some experience, from operations to regulation. From 1920 on, the government had been involved in railroad management more than ever before—in such programs as the I.C.C. consolidation planning in the 1920s, the government investigation into various railroad consolidation plans, the Reconstruction Finance Corporation rescue operation in the 1930s. Perlman was not only familiar with them all but in one way or another had been involved personally. Ripley's influence on him had gone back to his student days at M.I.T., when he had attended classes on railroad consolidation. Later, while with Northern Pacific, he was assigned to work on consolidation plans as they applied to the Northwest. He was involved thereafter with the R.F.C. in the Railway Division. While with the R.F.C., he had done studies on bankrupt railroads, including the New Haven. Anyone who studied the New Haven had to be the better for it—like a young intern studying at a big city hospital ward, through which passes every known disease.

Perlman's long suit was railroad operations. His practical railroading started with summer jobs when he was a teen-ager, sweeping out coaches, wiping down engines. In his first regular job with a railroad, the Northern Pacific, after he graduated from M.I.T., he had worked on the construction of line extension into the Rosebud coal fields of eastern Montana. The day he went to work for the Chicago, Burlington & Quincy in the early summer of 1935, a main line in Nebraska washed out, and he spent five months rebuilding it. His performance is still talked about at the Burlington. He is said to have averaged about three hours' sleep a night and lost thirty-two pounds. Although obviously an exaggeration, these reports reflect accurately the spirit with which Perlman attacked the job. At the big celebration when the road was reopened, Burlington's President Ralph Budd disclaimed all credit and said, "If you want to know who was responsible for this quick job of reconstruction, it was a spark plug named Al Perlman."

In 1936, after the Denver and Rio Grande Western went into bankruptcy for the fourth time, Perlman was borrowed from the Burlington to work out a program of rehabilitation. He was then invited to carry out his own recommendations and took what he thought would be a two-year leave of absence. He stayed on eighteen years, and as the *New York Times* later said, "transformed two streaks of rust with high mountains and low traffic into the money-making Denver and Rio Grande."[2] He introduced diesels and spent over $75,000,000 in improvement, on the theory that "if you want to make money, you have to spend money."[3] He switched from steam-powered on-track work equipment to off-track maintenance, with trouble-shooting task forces hauled by truck to trouble sites. He set

---

[2] *New York Times,* April 28, 1966, p. 58.
[3] *Railway Progress,* "Perlman of the Rio Grande," by Pasquale L. Marranzino, August 1948, p. 25.

up a modern communications system; in 1946 the F.C.C. granted the Rio Grande the first regular license in the United States permitting installation and operation of end-to-end and train-to-wayside radio communication. He established his unique research program, with the lab paying for itself through outside research.

For stockholders he achieved the finest measure of success; the Rio Grande started paying dividends, the first in its existence. By 1953 the road ranked among the first ten systems in revenue growth. Perlman had earned his decorations as a physician for sick railroads.

This was really what Young wanted to know. The New York Central was sick, very sick.

Young did hear dissenting voices regarding Perlman. Perlman's measure of a railroad success was freight, and this might interfere with Young's preoccupation with passenger service. Both Young and Perlman were strong, opinionated, and sure of themselves. This would be fine when they agreed. But could Young sit still while Perlman placed the emphasis on freight?

The Central was in a sorry financial plight, much worse than Young realized during his campaign oratory about the desperate circumstances of the Central. The Central would need every bit of help that the established financial and railroad powers could provide. It was no secret that in these quarters Young was looked upon as a spoiler, a demagogue and promoter. The ugly fact had to be faced that among the big banks and railroad presidents, Young was a pariah. If the established powers in the railroad industry and financial institutions were to provide any succor at all, their hands would at best be grudgingly offered to Young. The traditional attitudes of this compact group suggested the possibility that Perlman would fare no better. It was argued that instead of another innovator, Young really needed someone who could be an ambassador to the establishment, one of its own.

Young was not the only one hearing voices of dissent. Among Perlman's friends in the railroad business, some feared for his future with Young, dreading to see such a "good man" get tied up with a man of such an unpredictable nature and such unstable relationships—a man with such a short fuse. To prove their point, they totaled up the number of broken friendships and the number of lawsuits between Young and his former associates. Perlman's friends pointed out that Young had the reputation of being a little Caesar, who crushed all those about him. They predicted that Young's close associates would try to stand between him and Young and even sabotage his efforts.

The most telling point made by those who tried to dissuade Perlman was the strong possibility of New York Central's bankruptcy. It would be disastrous for Perlman to be tied up with such a debacle, especially since it was not of his own making. As one prominent banker friend said to Perlman, "Al, you're very foolish to come here because all you're going to do is arrive just in time to sign the sheriff's papers to enter bankruptcy." As it turned out, this did not detract very much from Young's offer. The challenge was more than Perlman could turn down.

The two men met for the first time on May 25. Young had asked Perlman if he could meet with him the night before the annual meeting. Perlman accepted the invitation.

The two men took an instant liking to each other. Their conversation ranged over every area of the railroad business and its history. Perlman was a little surprised to learn how much he agreed with Young on the majority of railroad issues. He did tell Young, however, that, whatever ailed the Central, emphasis on passenger traffic was not its salvation. The answer was to be found in freight traffic, as well as the introduction of twentieth-century technology and methods.

Perlman believed that a glamorous passenger road with futuristic trains would not be the solution in Central's struggle for economic survival. Instead he would rely on automation and expanded basic research, particularly as applied to more efficient freight service.

Young, of course, did not retreat from his passenger bias. It was too much for him to abandon the principle implicit in the "hog ad," Train X, his fight for better Pullman service, no tipping, more efficient ways of handling reservations.

On one point there was utter agreement. Perlman, like Young, was absolutely wedded to the concept of consolidation as a means of preserving the railroads. In fact, Perlman's background on the subject of consolidation antedated Young's by a decade and a half. Young's espousal of consolidation went back to 1937, when he acquired Alleghany, but Perlman's went back to the early 1920s, when he studied under Ripley.

They parted with the understanding that Perlman would use the next few days to review and weigh the offer of the presidency of the Central which Young had now extended. It was May 25, after all, and Young's victory was not yet a certainty. It did not come, in fact, for three more weeks. Perlman had made it plain, however, that if he did accept he would have to be made a member of Central's board of directors. Young said that would be no problem. He would get one of his own slate to resign to make room. Also if Perlman were to be president it had to be in fact as well as in title. His relations with Young would be direct, not through intermediaries, no matter how loyal or how long they had been with Young. Young agreed.

On the first day after change of command of the Central, Young and Perlman learned with a cold chill of the insolvency of the Central. After reviewing Central's disastrous financial condition, Young looked at Perlman with a face of concern and asked, "Al, aren't you frightened?" Perlman said, "No, but we'd better go to work."

Rescue of the Central from bankruptcy was first on the list of priorities. On his first tour, Perlman was dismayed at the state of disrepair and lack of innovation in the physical plant. One of the first things he would have to tackle would be a complete change-over of the tracks so that they could accommodate the modern freight trains he had been working with on the Denver & Rio Grande.

Under the new management, the Central appeared to start out with a surge. The net income in 1955 of $52,000,000 was Central's highest for any year since 1943. But both Young and Perlman expressed caution along with their optimism, pointing out that these earnings reflected nonrecurring federal income-tax benefits because of past losses and accelerated amortization of certain equipment and facilities. Moreover, the Central was embarking on a costly five-year program of physical improvement.

Young still had great expectations for the Central. The price of Central stock on the stock exchange had shot up to 49½; Young

The newly elected Central board (*from left, clockwise*): Richard M. Moss, Frederick Lewisohn, William H. Landers, Allan P. Kirby, R. Walter Graham, Jr., William P. Feeley, Alfred E. Perlman, Young, Garrard W. Glenn (Vice-President, law, acting as counsel to the board), Mrs. Wallace, Andrew Van Pelt, Orville Taylor, Daniel E. Taylor, Earl E. T. Smith, and Eugene C. Pulliam. Clint W. Murchison and Sid W. Richardson were not present.

(*Photo by Tommy Weber*)

confided to friends that he expected that the stock would go up to $100, and he urged them to buy. Many did.

Alleghany was also prospering. Not only were its holdings in the Central worth about twice its original investment, but the successful resolution of the Missouri Pacific bankruptcy meant that Alleghany's common stock holdings had appreciated many millions of dollars.[4]

However, in 1957 the entire railroad industry began to falter, and with it the New York Central. There was an economic recession in heavy industry which was quickly reflected in a sharp decline in freight car loadings. The Central, moreover, had its special prob-

[4] In July 1954 the I.C.C. approved a Missouri Pacific reorganization plan which included the common stock. The plan finally went into effect in March 1956. MoPac, the first railroad to go into reorganization under Section 77, was the last one out.

Young, Deegan and Perlman beneath a portrait of Commodore Vanderbilt in
the New York Central board room, thirty-second floor, 230 Park Avenue.

(Photo by Tommy Weber)

lems: it faced damaging competition from the newly completed New York State Thruway (which paralleled the Central's main route almost mile for mile) and would soon have to compete with the nearly finished St. Lawrence Seaway.

Young himself had been distracted by a series of derivative stockholders' suits growing out of the proxy fight. The first was filed even before the proxy fight was won, and finally so many suits had been filed that the court ordered a consolidation of the pending suits into a single action[5] and, "to prevent further harassment of the defendants and to permit the court to make a final disposition of the consolidated actions," a halt to the filing of any more related suits. In the suit Young and Kirby were charged with manipulating the Alleghany Corporation for their personal profit and to the detriment of the stockholders, particularly in connection with the Central proxy fight.

Attempts at a compromise settlement resulted in seemingly endless and fruitless proceedings before a court-appointed referee and special master. By the end of 1957, the case was still not settled and was a distracting irritation.

Another lawsuit troublesome to Young involved the recapitalization plan for Alleghany. In order to wipe out the huge dividend arrearage which had accrued under the Van Sweringens on the 5.5 percent cumulative preferred stock, Alleghany had issued new 6 percent convertible preferred stock. But the day the new stock was being issued, in the summer of 1955, the stock was suddenly frozen by court action[6] as the result of a legal challenge by dissident stockholders. Because of the freeze, owners of the new preferred stock could not sell it; they could not receive dividends; they could not use it for collateral. At the end of 1957, two and a half years later, the stock was still in this terrible limbo, while the problem was being fought out in the courts. Young owned a great deal of this stock and was placed personally in a momentary financial bind.

Rumors began to circulate that Young was in deep financial trouble. The price of Central common stock had dropped from a high of 49½ in 1955 to a low of 13½ in late 1957. This meant a

---

[5] *Zenn, et al.,* v. *Anzalone, et al.*
[6] *Breswick & Company, et al.,* v. *United States of America, et al.*

large paper loss to Alleghany and Allan Kirby. Between 1954 and 1956 Alleghany acquired approximately 600,000 shares of Central and Kirby 200,000 at a price of $25 a share under the "put" agreement with Murchison and Richardson. Young was particularly upset about the friends and associates who had bought stock at his urgings while it was in the forties. He felt personally liable, and to some of them he made the offer to repurchase at their cost. None availed themselves of the offer, but the situation preyed on Young's mind, and one associate at least believes that Young felt this was a binding obligation.

The papers carried stories that Young had been forced to reduce his holdings in the Central from 100,200 to 21,700 shares. However, a Young spokesman explained that Young had merely sold most of it to Mrs. Young, and had bought a block of stock from her, in "an adjustment of collateral and because [of] the present low prices and the freezing of Alleghany securities by court order."

In the fall of 1957, the general railroading situation had become desperate. Young and Perlman concluded that consolidation was the only salvation of the railroads, particularly the New York Central, and with this in mind, they made overtures to the Pennsylvania Railroad executives. The apparent logic of the situation brought the parties to a very quick preliminary agreement. On November 1 Perlman and Pennsylvania's President James M. Symes jointly announced that they were considering a merger of their two roads "to halt deficits." They cited the big decline in earnings. Pennsylvania's earnings had dropped from $31,291,000 for the first nine months in 1956 to $19,581,000 for the same months in 1957. Central's drop was even more drastic—from $28,172,000 in the first nine months of 1956 to $8,700,000 for the same period in 1957. Perlman and Symes had concluded that the only way for railroads to meet the competition from other forms of transportation was railroad consolidation. But even if they were able to get beyond the hurdles of the I.C.C., the Antitrust Division, Senator Kefauver's antimonopoly committee, and the courts, it was obvious that a merger would have a long and rocky road to travel before it could be consummated. In the meantime, there was the problem of survival.

By January 1958, the precarious state of the railroads had become so critical that the Surface Transportation Subcommittee of the U.S. Senate Interstate and Foreign Commerce Committee began an investigation into what Chairman Smathers called the "sick and declining railroad industry." Two dozen rail heads testified as to the looming disaster. Perlman appeared before the hearing on January 14 and said that the passenger deficit problem was the gravest threat to the financial stability of the New York Central and that in the preceding eight years the Central had lost over half a billion dollars on passenger service. State regulatory commissions, Perlman pointed out, were no help.

. . . We can be nibbled to death in 49 places at once, and no one is responsible when the patient dies. The nibbling away of our great interstate railroad systems can go on for a little while longer. The railroads can stagnate and deteriorate and continue to die slowly. But unless you take steps now, don't expect to wave a magic wand when emergency or catastrophe is upon the country and expect to have up-to-date, modern and efficient railroads to do your bidding. Then it will be too late.[7]

Observers of the railroad scene were moderately surprised that Young was nowhere to be seen or heard. Not a word appeared in the press from the usually assertive Young. His closest associates became vaguely aware of a languid remoteness, but none gave it more than a passing thought. On the surface he seemed tired and disinterested but clearly in touch with reality.

On January 20, 1958, the Central directors held a special meeting in Palm Beach with Young to review Central's finances. The road's earnings had plunged from $39,104,259 in 1956 to $8,423,078 in 1957. Reluctantly the directors voted not to pay a dividend for the next quarter, the first time this had happened since Young came to power. It was shattering to Young's pride. He would find it a problem to face his close friends and associates who at his urging had invested heavily.

---

[7] Hearings before the Subcommittee on Surface Transportation, Committee on Interstate and Foreign Commerce, U.S. Senate, on S. 3778, "Railroad Problems," January 15, 1958.

During the board meeting Young was so quiet that some of the directors, knowing of his immersion in the problem of the frozen Alleghany stock, thought he might be worried about personal finances and offered to help. Young thanked them for their offer but declined, indicating his finances were in good order. He assured them that the Alleghany 6 percent preferred stock case which tied up so much of his own assets would very soon be decided favorably by the Supreme Court. His confidence was not misplaced, for on Monday, January 27, the Court decided in Alleghany's favor.[8]

Young was not to know this victory. Two days earlier, alone in the billiard room of his Palm Beach mansion, he ended his life with a blast from a shotgun. He had been chairman of the Central barely three years and eight months.

A mythology has grown up around Young's suicide. The explanations have extended from business difficulties to personal problems. The most persistent concerned a letter Young was supposed to have read shortly before his death. When Young's body was found, the newspapers reported that on his desk was a letter from a widowed Aunt Jane who had now lost everything because of Young's betrayal of the small stockholder. Actually there was such a letter, purportedly from the sister of a widowed Aunt Jane but in the handwriting of the anonymous hate letter written to Young during the proxy fight, complaining of the appointment of Frederick Lewisohn to the Young slate. No one now will ever know if Young ever read the letter or was affected by it.

To exaggerate Young's business troubles would be misleading. Past history demonstrated graphically his capacity to deal with such problems. While the lawsuits filed against him contained aggravating charges with more serious consequences than he, at first, thought possible, nevertheless lawsuits were nothing new to a man often called "litigious" himself. Despite the difficulties of the Central and the complications that developed in their wake, Young was a wealthy man with a net worth in the millions. His personal checking account had over a million dollars on deposit. Then there was

[8] *Alleghany Corporation* v. *Breswick & Co., et al.* 353 U.S. 151.

always his steadfast friend Allan Kirby ready to back him. Young's position in the Central and Alleghany was absolutely secure. Alleghany had prospered dramatically—common stock that was worth minus $100,000,000 in 1937 when Young purchased it had an equity of $75,000,000 twenty years later—an enormous source of personal gratification to Young. He had few doubts that the Central's merger with the Pennsylvania would show the way to renewed prosperity.

Why then did Young end his life? Futility confronts all who search for answers. Only vague and contradictory clues remain and time has done nothing to give them meaning.

> And he was rich—yes, richer than a king,
>   And admirably schooled in every grace;
> In fine, we thought that he was everything
>   To make us wish that we were in his place.
> So on we worked, and waited for the light,
>   And went without the meat, and cursed the bread;
> And Richard Cory, one calm summer night,
>   Went home and put a bullet through his head.[9]

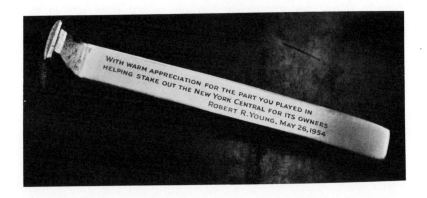

To commemorate participation in his battle for the Central, Young presented to each close comrade a golden spike.

[9] From "Richard Cory," by Edwin Arlington Robinson.

On February 1, 1968, the New York Central Railroad and the Pennsylvania Railroad merged to form the Penn Central Transportation Company. Two months later, an equivalent share of Central stock in the new company was selling for $105 a share. The Central had come a long way since that fateful day in January 1958 when its stock was selling for $15 a share.

These ten years contained a century of drama. Not one but two major proxy fights thundered across the scene. One was the tug of war between the New York Central and the C & O for control of the B & O, the other the great contest between the Murchison Brothers and Allan P. Kirby for control of the Alleghany Corporation. For scope and excitement these were worthy rivals for the "Battle of the Century." Then there was the ten-year struggle for the Penn Central merger itself, full of the vicissitudes and uncertainties implicit in a corporate marriage of this magnitude. Not only was the merger opposed by a half-dozen major and minor railroads, but the opposition was spiced by the intense hostility of old friends appearing as new enemies. Other hurdles were the Department of Justice, a Senate committee, and several municipalities—to say nothing of the requirements of the bankrupt New Haven. The bitterly fought and protracted hearings moved from city to city like a carnival troupe. The contest ricocheted between the I.C.C. and the courts until the issue was finally settled in early 1968 by the Supreme Court, and Penn Central became a reality.

When the New York Central finally became part of Penn Central, Perlman, sitting on the thirty-second floor of 230 Park Avenue, had served longer than any other president of the New York Central, eleven years longer than William White, and even a year longer than Chauncey Depew himself.

Index

(Numbers in *italics* refer to illustrations)

About the Author

JOSEPH BORKIN has had a distinguished career as an economist, lawyer, educator, and writer. He began his professional life during the New Deal of President Franklin D. Roosevelt, serving on the staffs of several Congressional committees, the Federal Communications Commission, and the Antitrust Division of the Department of Justice. In 1946 he entered private practice to represent Robert R. Young and his interests. He became one of Young's closest associates. He continues to include among his clients the Alleghany Corporation and the New York Central Railroad's successor corporation, the Penn-Central Transportation Company.

Borkin is Chairman of the Federal Bar Association's Committee on Railroad Law, Chairman of the National Press Club's Town Meetings Series, and Professional Lecturer at the American University School of Business Administration, conducting seminars on the "Problems of Fiduciary Obligations and Conflicts of Interest in the Modern Corporation."

His other books are *The Corrupt Judge,* 1962; *Germany's Master Plan* (with Charles A. Welsh), 1943; and *Television: A Struggle for Power* (with Frank C. Waldrop), 1938. His articles have appeared in the *Chicago Law Review,* the *Columbia Law Review* and *Law and Contemporary Problems* of the Duke University School of Law. He has contributed to the Twentieth Century Fund's *Stock Market Control* and *The Security Markets;* and is the author of the article on "Impeachment" in the *Encyclopaedia Britannica.*